The Diocesan Clergy

*St. John
Vianney, the
patron of all
parish priests*

Maurice Rocher
étude, 1959

Msgr. A. M. CHARUE

BISHOP OF NAMUR

THE DIOCESAN CLERGY

HISTORY AND SPIRITUALITY

Translated by REV. MICHAEL J. WRENN

DESCLEE COMPANY

NEW YORK — TOURNAI — PARIS — ROME

1963

NIHIL OBSTAT
JOHN A. GOODWINE, J.C.D.
Censor Librorum

IMPRIMATUR
✠ FRANCIS CARDINAL SPELLMAN
Archbishop of New York
July 13, 1963

The nihil obstat and imprimatur are official declarations that a book or pamphlet is free of doctrinal or moral error. No implication is contained therein that those who have granted the nihil obstat and imprimatur agree with the contents, opinions or statements expressed.

Library of Congress Catalog Card Number : 63-20669

Printed and bound in Belgium by Desclée & Cie, S.A., Tournai

Sit amoris officium pascere Dominicum gregem. [1]
(Saint Augustine)

Si diligis, ... pasce.
(Pius XII)

---

[1] Cited by Pope Paul VI in his first public address as Supreme Pontiff, June 22, 1963.

Table of Contents

Preface of His Eminence
Cardinal Van Roey,
Archbishop of Malines

When "His hour" had come, "hora mea," as He referred to it, [1] the hour for which the Father had sent Him into this world, Jesus instituted the Eucharist and the priesthood at the Last Supper, which He chose to celebrate with His disciples in order to perpetuate "His hour" until the end of time.

On this solemn occasion, He prayed for His first priests and through them for all priests to come. "Holy Father, sanctify them in truth. As you have sent Me into the world, I also send them into the world. For them do I sanctify Myself, that they also may be sanctified in truth." [2]

He prayed still again that "they may be one, as You, Father, in Me, and I in You, that they may be made perfect in unity." [3] These final words of Jesus, which exalt the priesthood almost to the point of joining it, so to speak, to the inmost life of the Holy Trinity, constitute an unfathomable mystery of faith and love.

Thus the Catholic Church, conscious of the divine gift with which it has been entrusted, has always considered her priests as the animators and vivifiers of the "Mystical Body of which Christ is the Head." [4] From the beginning, the Church has set about investigating the inexpressible mystery of the priesthood in order to bring to light its priceless value and to safeguard its sublime dignity by preserving the purity and holiness of her priests as "the ministers and dispensers of the mysteries of God." [5]

[1] Jn 2, 4; 13, 1.　　[2] Jn 17, 18-19.　　[3] Jn 17, 21.　　[4] Col 1, 18.　　[5] 1 Cor 4, 1.

For the last nineteen centuries, every phase of clerical literature, theological, canonical and liturgical, spiritual and pastoral, ascetical and mystical has taken, as the prime object of its studies, the divine gift of the priesthood. This subject has been considered by the Fathers and Doctors of the Church, beginning with St. John Chrysostom and by the great Bishops, such as St. Ignatius of Antioch, as well as by the most zealous shepherds of souls in all ages. The Popes of modern times, and particularly those of our own century, have given eloquent testimony of their great concern for the priesthood.

What doctrinal riches, what treasures of spirituality this literary current continuously has supplied over the centuries to the life of the Mystical Body of Christ!

I have just finished reading, thanks to the kindness of the author, a new work which will rank, I believe, among the most excellent works of spirituality of our time. It was written by the zealous Bishop of the Diocese of Namur and has as its title, *The Diocesan Clergy*. From his earlier writings we are aware of the great devotion and understanding that this author exhibits in treating questions relative to the diocesan clergy.

For my part, I wish to state that my reading of this new and important work was one of sustained interest and complete satisfaction.

It is not my place to extol the great merits of this work, thus depriving astute readers of an opportunity to discover them for themselves. However, I do wish to point out a few of them.

First of all, one is immediately struck by the exceptionally abundant information which the author has at his disposal, and which indicates, on his part, a long and painstaking amount of research. The historical documentation is truly impressive. This is particularly apparent both in the historical introduction, which comprises the first part of the book, and also in the fifth part, in which the author considers the models and patrons of the secular clergy. No less remarkable is the theological,

canonical and ascetical material of the author which shows
how well acquainted he is with all of the literature relative
to the questions that he considers.

There is, in my opinion, another merit in this work. The
spirituality of the diocesan clergy, which is the subject under
consideration in this book, requires examination and, if possible,
the solution to several delicate questions, which were and still
are the object of some lively controversies. The author avoids
none of these. He is not afraid to come to grips with any
problems that may arise. After having faithfully presented
the question, he seeks, with perfect objectivity, to present
the best solution to it — one which seems to him to agree with
recognized and authorized writings and to be based on the
soundest arguments. This observation applies especially to
the problems which are raised in regard to the nature of the
episcopacy and the states of perfection.

Finally, I am pleased to draw the attention of the reader to
the valuable pastoral directives and practical recommendations
for the diocesan clergy which are to be found in the final section
of the book.

Clerical literature certainly abounds in excellent books
on the priesthood and particularly on the diocesan clergy.
Nevertheless, I do not hesitate to say that the present work
of Bishop Charue will certainly constitute a spiritual enrichment
of this field since it sheds a new and perhaps decisive light
upon several important questions.

I confidently recommend the reading of this work to
priests and to all those who are interested in works of sound
spirituality. *Tolle et lege.*

✠ J. E. Cardinal van Roey,

Archbishop of Malines.

Foreword

At the decisive high point of His earthly life, Jesus, on leaving the cenacle for His approaching Passion, besought His Father to consecrate and sanctify, through the merits of His own priesthood, immolation and holiness, the apostles and those who would continue their work. [1]

Since that time the Hierarchy has always endeavored to protect this gift which God gave to His priests and to impress upon them an awareness of the obligation that they have to be worthy ministers of the Altar. We find St. Paul, for example, exhorting Timothy to rekindle the divine charism that he received through the imposition of hands on the day of his ordination. [2] Recent Popes have made similar appeals to the clergy since they are firmly convinced that priests must lead a pious, virtuous and exemplary way of life if they expect their priestly apostolate to bear fruit. Our Holy Father declared his hope of seeing the present Ecumenical Council promote " a greater sanctification of the clergy. " [3]

Since I have been concerned, like every other bishop, with this particular task, I have over the years attempted to determine the nature of the spirituality of the diocesan clergy.

An awareness of the distinct originality and purpose of this clergy and the providential role that they play in the Church is necessary if secular priests are to be successfully guided and encouraged in the fulfillment of their mission.

Gradually, as the work of synthesizing the spirituality of the clergy began to take shape, the area of our reflection was enlarged to such a point that it encompassed large areas of Theology, History, Canon Law and Ascetics. This type

[1] Jn 17, 11-19.

[2] 2 Tm 1, 6.

[3] Pope JOHN XXIII, *Homily for Pentecost*, *L'Osservatore Romano* (May 18-19, 1959).

of synthesis, which we have just outlined and which we are presenting in this volume, quite possibly never existed before in the vast literature devoted to priestly spirituality. At any rate, this is what we have been told. May this publication aid our priests to advance confidently toward the lofty ideal which their vocation offers them!

* *
*

The nature of the times demands that we focus our attention upon another important consideration. We all realize that the trend of the world today is presenting the Church with many problems of adaptation especially in the area of the parochial ministry.

Consequently it is very important that seculars and regulars join ranks for the purpose of harmonizing their apostolic activities. Pope John recently stated that the Second Vatican Council must strive to effect " the generous collaboration of the two clergies, under the direction of the bishop, who is the shepherd of the entire flock. " [1]

Since the bishop is chiefly responsible for the diocesan clergy entrusted to his care, he should fully appreciate and be able to explain to others the status that his priests enjoy in the Church and the obligations which result both for him and for them.

* *
*

The table of contents fully describes the approach and purpose of this work. We are endeavoring to discover not only if sanctity is possible in the secular clergy, but also if there

---

[1] Pope JOHN XXIII, *Message to the Clergy of Venice* (April 23, 1959), *L'Osservatore Romano* (April 24, 1959). Several studies on this question have already appeared, especially in regard to religious. Note in particular, J. HAMER, " Place des religieux dans l'apostolat de l'Eglise, " *La Nouvelle Revue théologique*, Vol. LXXXI (1959), pp. 271-81.

is any one way in which it can best be attained. It will become quite apparent, in the course of this work, that the Church can rely upon her secular priests to respond in the best possible way to the calls of the Hierarchy and the Christian community.

Into the hands of Our Lord Jesus Christ we commend this work. Our one aim is to cause Him to increase in the Church a sentiment expressed in the motto of our episcopate : *Christum oportet crescere.* [1] We likewise commend it to the assistance of Our Lady, the Queen of the clergy. Finally we commend it to the goodwill and, at times, the indulgence of our readers.

* *

The story is told that on one occasion when the Curé of Ars heard the confession of a bishop, he merely gave this counsel : " Your Excellency, love your priests. " [2] This love for our priests, which we pray Christ to continue to increase in our heart, spurred us on in the preparation of this book, which was completed during the centenary year of St. John Vianney. Paternally, we dedicate it to our priests.

Namur, August 9, 1959.

---

[1] Jn 3, 30.

[2] Msgr. M. LALLIER, " Etude sur ' Le projet de l'établissement d'un séminaire dans un diocèse,' présenté par M. Olier à l'Assemblée du Clergé en 1651," *La Tradition sacerdotale, Etudes sur le sacerdoce* (Le Puy, 1959), p. 207.

I

Historical

Introduction

The reform brought about by the Council of Trent, sometimes unfortunately referred to as the Catholic Counter-Reformation, dominates the entire modern and contemporary periods of the Church's history.

This should be especially borne in mind when examining the movement of sacerdotal spirituality during the last few centuries.

For this reason it seems opportune to present a general historical introduction before embarking upon a study of the specific questions regarding the spirituality of the diocesan clergy. We do not pretend to be presenting an exhaustive historical investigation. We are simply attempting to place in its proper historical perspective a study which is intended to be pastoral, and which, as we have already said, concerns every bishop, namely the sanctification of his priests.

Chapter 1

The Period
of the Council of Trent

The fourteenth and fifteenth centuries represent in the over-all view of the Church's history a period of moral decadence which led to the dangerous Renaissance period and ended in the great catastrophe of Protestantism. The Papal Court, bishoprics, monasteries and rectories did not escape corruption. Nevertheless, reactions to this were not lacking. By the fifteenth century local reforms can be noticed, particularly in Spain, where, as we shall see, great holiness flourished throughout the sixteenth century. However, this did not exclude the necessity of the Council of Trent's enacting a profound and lasting reform especially through the revitalization of the priesthood and the pastoral ministry. The reform was, therefore, the full blossoming of a spiritual revival which already pre-existed here and there in various areas of the Church.

The collective work of the Fathers of the Council of Trent can be best explained only in the light of the providential role played by a number of great men in the Church during this period. There were some, before the Council, who embodied in themselves and foreshadowed this great spiritual restoration. There were also some after the Council who carried out the reform according to the conciliar decrees, demonstrated it by their example and facilitated its success by the personal prestige which they gave to it. [1] Consequently, we will first

[1] Much could be written about the remarkable strides made by the Church in fulfilling the monumental work of Trent. We will mention only the names of a few who contributed in great measure to its success although there are many others equally deserving of recognition. Mention would necessarily have to be made of the new religious societies, particularly the Jesuits, the reform of the established orders such as the Capuchins as well as the influence of such pious associations as the Oratory of Divine Love in Rome. There are certainly many different factors which have to be taken into account by historians. On this subject see : H. JEDIN, *A History of the Council of Trent*, Vol. I, Eng. trans. Dom Ernest Graf (London Nelson, 1957), pp. 139-62. DANIEL-ROPS, *The Protestant Reformation* (New York : Dutton, 1961)·

present a brief synthesis of priestly spirituality according to the mind of the Council of Trent before considering some of the great names of the sixteenth century who figured as the precursors of the reform. After this we will discuss those who were the guides of the clergy after the Tridentine Reform.

* * *

The name of St. Charles Borromeo naturally comes to mind when the influence of the Council on the life of the clergy is discussed. However, there are two bishops in particular, an Italian and a Portuguese, who were regarded by the Archbishop of Milan as masters of doctrine and models of life. Each in his own way had a definite effect upon the deliberations and decisions of the Council.

At the time when the bishops were meeting in Trent in 1543, there lived at Verona a saintly prelate, Matthew Giberti, of whom it has been written: " The Fathers of the Council of Trent had always the Bishop of Verona in mind in their projects of reform and the decrees of the Council for the entire Church embody most of his recommendations. " The author of these words adds that the portrait of Giberti hung in the quarters of the young Archbishop of Milan. [1]

St. Charles had likewise met, in the beginning of his priestly life, another saintly bishop, Blessed Bartholomew of the Martyrs, who ruled the See of Braga in 1548 and who played an important role at Trent. Devoting himself with great fervor to the reform of his clergy, Bartholomew wrote the *Stimulus Pastorum*, the portrait of a model bishop, which he dedicated to his friend in Milan.

A number of other names from the Hierarchy of that period should also be mentioned, such as Cardinal Peter Caraffa, the future Paul IV, and Cardinal Reginald Pole, Archbishop of

---

[1] F. MOURRET, *The History of the Church. The Renaissance and The Reformation*, Eng trans. N. Thompson, Vol. VI (St. Louis : Herder, 1947), pp. 8-138.

Canterbury. We will now consider Spain whose influence was very great indeed. According to St. Charles Borromeo, the Spanish clergy of the sixteenth century were " the nerve center of all Christian activity. " [1] An attitude of healthy reform motivated a good number of the bishops there. In the beginning of that century the energetic, though sometimes debatable, but generally beneficial activity of Cardinal Ximenes restored diocesan and monastic circles. Under the influence of Francis de Vitoria, a brilliant professor at the University of Salamanca, the Spanish bishops became more and more concerned with the quality of their clergy. This was also the period in which holiness flourished in an exceptional way throughout the land. It was the time of St. Teresa, St. John of the Cross, St. Ignatius, St. Francis Xavier, St. Francis Borgia, St. Peter Alcantara and St. John of God. In order to appreciate the concern that was had for linking closely together personal holiness and the active ministry, we have only to peruse the writings of the contemplative Teresa of Avila. Priding herself on being a daughter of the Church, she aspired, as she said, to strengthen with all her might, by means of the prayers of Carmel, the apostolate of priests, especially those captains in the forefront of the battle who have need of great grace in order to fulfill their mission with the necessary amount of holiness. Her religious likewise knew that they must pray especially for the bishops of the Church and above all for the bishop of the diocese in which their convent was located. [2] Thus the contemplation of Carmel became a collaborator in the apostolate of the Hierarchy.

It is remarkable to observe the tremendous influence enjoyed by a humble secular priest of the Diocese of Cordova in sixteenth century Spain. This priest, John of Avila, who died almost at the age of seventy on the tenth of May 1569, was very soon after referred to as the " Apostle of Andalusia, '

---

[1] L. Von Pastor, *History of the Popes*, Vol. XVII (St. Louis : B. Herder, 1929), p. 236.

[2] St. Teresa of Jesus, *The Way of Perfection*, Eng. trans. E. Allison Peers, *The Complete Works of St. Teresa of Jesus*, Vol. II (London : Sheed and Ward, 1946), p. 15.

and in 1946 he was proclaimed by Pius XII the heavenly patron
of the secular clergy of Spain. [1] Throughout his life he was
regarded as an exceptional spokesman on the things of God.
Master John of Avila, *El Maestro Juan de Avila*, as he was
commonly known, had been the spiritual director of Francis
Borgia, John of God and Louis of Granada, his biographer.
On occasion he served as the spiritual director of St. Teresa,
St. Ignatius and St. Peter Alcantara. It is only proper then
that the role of this man should be more greatly emphasized.
The Acts of his beatification in 1894 extol his virtues, apostolic
activity and the wisdom of his writings as well as his direction
of souls. [2] Like the founder of the Society of Jesus, whom
he inspired, he " saw the establishment of a lasting renewal
of the Church through the instruction of youth and the common
people and through the formation of good priests. " [3] He did
not take part in the Council of Trent, but " his spokesman,
Peter de Guerrero, Archbishop of Granada, as well as his model,
Venerable Bartholomew of the Martyrs, Archbishop of Braga,
were present there. " [4] If the conciliar decrees concerning
the organization of seminaries were inspired by the experiments
made in England by Cardinal Pole and those made at the German
College by the Jesuits, [5] it seems that similar Spanish experiments,
particularly those of John of Avila, [6] have not been sufficiently
considered by historians.

[1] *Decretum reassumptionis causae canonizationis* (March 14, 1952), *Acta Apostolicae Sedis,*
Vol. XLIV (1952), p. 795. This decree is similar to the brief of Pope Pius XII (dated July, 1946)
which is reproduced in the book *El Beato Maestro P. Juan de Avila : Conferencias pronunciadas
en la Semana Nacional Avilistica en Madrid* (Madrid 1952), pp. 7-8.

[2] Decree of the Sacred Congregation of Rites *De Tuto* (February 15, 1894) for the
Beatification of John of Avila, *Acta Sanctae Sedis,* Vol. XXVI (1894), pp. 629-30; Brief of Pope
Leo XIII (April 6, 1894) proclaiming John of Avila Blessed, *ASS,* Vol. XXVII (1895), pp. 75-76.

[3] L. Von Pastor, *op. cit.,* pp. 236-37.

[4] P. Broutin, " Le Pasteur d'Eglise au cours de l'histoire, " *Le Courrier de Mondaye*
No. 51 (1957), p. 1.

[5] J. A. O'Donohoe, *Tridentine Seminary Legislation, Its Sources and Its Formation* (Louvain,
1957); Msgr. H. Jedin, " Domschule und Kolleg : zum Ursprung der Idee der Trienter
Priesterseminars, " *Trierer Theologische Zeitschrift,* Vol. XLVII (1938), pp. 209-23.

[6] A. de la Fuente, " El Beato Maestro Juan de Avila, alma de la verdadera reforma
de la Iglesia española, " *Conferencias de la Semana Avilistica, op. cit.,* pp. 231-50.

* * *

The importance placed by the council on the question of seminaries shows how greatly the Fathers preoccupied themselves with the formation of the secular clergy. Their deliberations on this matter demonstrate conclusively that the quality of pastors determines, to a great extent, the success of every reform in the Church. Such a conviction had been in 1523 the basis for the formation of the first institute of *Clerics Regular*. The idea for this new foundation came from St. Cajetan of Thien. In order to achieve success in this undertaking, he enlisted the valuable assistance of Peter Caraffa, Bishop of Chieti and the future Paul IV. The Theatines, named after the city of Theate, which was later called Chieti, wished to join themselves with other clerics and to exercise with them, and in the same manner as they, the sacred ministry in the world. They were to wear the same habit and in spirit to distinguish themselves from other clerics as little as possible, while at the same time remaining a religious society with common life and the profession of religious vows. They hoped thereby to be able to act in the same way as leaven acts in dough, to win over by their good example a great number of secular priests and to guarantee for the general reform of the Church a virtuous and more apostolic clergy. As noble as their purpose was, their results were unfortunately quite disappointing. Their zeal was found to be excessive and often misdirected, and their influence suffered because of this.

The dynamic and very popular institute of St. Philip Neri differed in many ways from that of the Theatines. Philip Neri had no idea of the great work that he was going to accomplish. When he sought papal approval, he stated that the real founder of his institute was God alone and that, unknown to him, Providence had actually directed his undertakings. If there was one plan that he had from the very beginning and which he would never abandon, it was to go to the humble and lowly, to mingle with the people and to put the spiritual life within the reach of all by speaking, as he said to his disciple Talpa,

con familiarita e domestichezza, convincingly and simply.   When,
soon after, his disciples and helpers began to increase, he
assembled them together to pray and to be instructed in the
things of God, and thus from these pious gatherings or *Oratorios*
the institute was born.   Philip finally organized more closely
around him a group of the priests, who worked with him.
In this way they would be able to enjoy the advantages derived
from life in common and from fraternal cooperation.   On this
very point Philip Neri many times stated that he never envisioned
the institution of a congregation of priests, but that his plan
was originally only to group more closely around him some
of his spiritual sons.   It is certainly impossible to live and to
work together without a minimum of organization, but this
type of organization is so flexible in the Oratory of St. Philip
Neri that its members can leave at any time and have returned
to them the original possessions with which they entered.
The Rule of the Oratory was written towards the end of Philip's
life.   It was inspired by the successful experiment of priests
fraternally linked together by bonds deriving from the
priesthood, a common mission and filial devotion to the founder.

One of the great qualities of St. Philip Neri was his childlike
submissiveness to Providence.   Because of this he had great
ease in complying with the advice given to him by his colleagues.
It is still more remarkable that he never compromised the
secular character of his institute.   Despite constant pressure,
some of which was exerted by his own followers, he never was
partial to the idea of religious vows for his disciples.   Nor did
he have disdain for religious orders as is proved by the great
number of recruits that he secured from various religious communities.   But he did wish that the priests of the Oratory would
never be anything but secular priests.   After his death there
was written into the constitutions a provision whereby the
institute would never be able to oblige its members to take
vows, and those, who might in the future attempt this, were
at this time excluded from membership in the institute.   Popes
increased their recognition and esteem of the Oratory by elevating

two of Philip's first followers, Baronius and Tarugi, to the College of Cardinals, and Clement VIII declared that this completely new idea of a thoroughly secular congregation was to be accorded full recognition by the Church. In fact, the institute had been approved by Gregory XIII during the lifetime of the founder. The Oratorian Talpa, who had for a long time campaigned for the taking of vows, finally admitted that Philip's apostolate owed its great effectiveness to the secular state of its priests. In the kingdom of God there are many mansions and varied vocations as is evident from the fact that Philip Neri was canonized in 1622, at the same time as Ignatius Loyola, Francis Xavier and Teresa of Avila. [1] Many Oratories of Philip Neri were founded in various countries. It was in imitation of them that Newman organized his English Oratory in 1847. These institutes have no central organization and are directly dependent upon the local ordinary.

* * *

In the meantime, the Council of Trent had finished its task. It put the parochial clergy back again into their proper place in the Church in order to revitalize them, says Father Broutin, who adds : " The Tridentine conception of a priest-pastor still influences our present day Code of Canon Law. On some points it has progressed, on others, it leaves, I believe, much additional work still to be done. " [2] The following is an example of how this author explains Trent's reform in this area :

> The chief cause of all the clerical misfortunes, described in the writings of this period, is that the clergy, as Lamennais would later say, was a loosely knit group of priests without roots in any diocese. These wanderers, even as late as the

---

[1] See especially L. PONNELLE and L. BORDET, *St. Philip Neri and the Roman Society of His Time,* Eng. trans. Ralph F. Kerr (London : Sheed and Ward, 1932).

[2] P. BROUTIN, " Le Pasteur d'Eglise… " *loc. cit.,* No. 49, p. 8; on the profoundly pastoral and missionary orientation of the Tridentine Reform, see also H. JEDIN, *Reformation oder Gegenreformation?* (Lucerne 1946), pp. 59-60.

seventeenth century, spent their lives in constant moving about always in search of a more lucrative position. In order to remedy this situation completely, the Council tightened the bonds between the bishop and his clergy. Its first principle was that the clergy engaged in the pastoral ministry are a territorial and residential clergy, for whom incardination entails an obligation of stability. The Council's chief task, in this regard, was to settle parish priests in their parishes in the same way as it sought to settle bishops permanently in their dioceses. The Council realized full well that, in the eyes of the faithful, the parish embodies the Church, its traditions, authority and laws. The parish was understood to hold so great an attraction for the faithful and to include so many possibilities for sanctification that its deficiencies could in no way be compensated for either by the personal holiness of the bishop or by the energy and zeal of the regular clergy. This is why the Council strove at all costs to have pastors and parish priests resume their parochial duties by residing in the midst of their flock so that their preaching of the word of God and their administration of the sacraments would be the source of the Church's grace. The second principle of renewal was that the entire clericate is a charism with profound social implications. One is not a priest, a deacon, an acolyte or a lector for himself alone but for the sake of others who are members of a complex society and who are closely related to one another. The Council desired that the formation of clerics be done through and according to the spirit of the various clerical orders.

Thus the insistence that the interstices be followed. Father Broutin regrets that the rules regarding the interstices are nowadays too often neglected and he recalls that, according to the mind of the Council, seminaries were to lay equal stress both on the intellectual and moral formation of clerics as well as on their gradual introduction into the active ministry.

St. Charles realized this desire of the Council by arranging the curriculum of his seminaries in such a way that an actual period of residency in a rectory was included as part of the seminary course. To the decrees on the ministry the Council of Trent, in considering the qualities of a good pastor, added an urgent plea for holiness : " Clerics destined to have the Lord as their inheritance must regulate their lives and conduct in such a manner that in their attire, their speech and everything else, they do not allow anything to appear which is not sound, discreet and consistent with religion. Let them avoid the slightest faults, which in them would be considerable, in order that their actions may inspire in all a feeling of esteem. " [1]

The situation of the bishops received even greater attention at the Council. " In all its decrees it never ceased, " wrote Dom Gréa, " to restore the independence and sovereignty of the bishops as the heads of their churches. It sought to destroy, as far as possible, the various local customs and other obstacles to their authority which had arisen over the course of centuries. It continually affirmed its desire to see the episcopacy embody in itself, as in the early centuries, all the strength of the Church and to become once again the center of all its vital undertakings. " [2] This important concern was also expressed, as we shall observe, by the Popes of our own century.

---

[1] P. BROUTIN, *ibid.*, pp. 8-9.

[2] Dom GRÉA, *De l'Eglise et de sa divine constitution* (Paris 1885) p. 415. He gives numerous references to the sessions of the council. On the discussions and decisions of Trent concerning the residence of bishops and pastors see especially : H. JEDIN, *A History of the Council of Trent*, Vol. II.

Chapter 2

From the Council of Trent
to the French Revolution

It is not our intention to consider here all that was done to implement the decrees of the Council relating to the clergy. Later on in this work we will consider the organization of seminaries for the formation of the clergy, but at this time we feel that it is important to consider a few of the characteristic efforts used during this period to promote priestly spirituality and to aid secular priests in living it.

At the time that the Council of Trent ended its work of reform, Philip Neri, the protégé and friend of Popes, especially of St. Pius V, was on the best of terms with St. Charles Borromeo, who saw in him " one of the most enlightened and active agents of the Catholic reformation. " [1] In fact, the Archbishop of Milan consulted the founder of the Roman Oratory for the purpose of securing some helpers to assist him in effecting a reform of his diocese in keeping with the spirit of the Council of Trent. The proposed foundation of Philip Neri at Milan did not materialize, and very soon the differences of opinion between the two saints became apparent. However, this did not deter the great reformer of Milan from seeking the advice of Philip and from being inspired by the activities of the Oratory.

On the 16th of August, 1576, St. Charles canonically established the *Oblates of St. Ambrose,* an institute composed solely of secular priests who made an *oblation,* a vow of perfect obedience, to their archbishop. The Cardinal always denied having founded a congregation of clerics regular. Besides, he seems to have refrained for a long time from imposing on his Oblates the vow of obedience which was certainly not in keeping with the spirit of the Oratorians at Rome. It is difficult to say

---

[1] L. Von Pastor, *History of the Popes,* Vol. XV (London : Kagan Paul, 1928), p. 41.

exactly how he was led to this. It is quite certain that he had a very exalted and extremely demanding conception of the apostolic ministry. Is it necessary to maintain, as some have, that his own strong personality may have inclined him to strengthen his authority?[1] Perhaps, but what is certain is that he did have difficulties in dealing with religious societies. This probably resulted in his decision to organize a few priests who, by professing perfect obedience, would be subject only to him, would find their sanctification in their own ministry and would therefore be of great assistance to him in his plans for pastoral reform.

In the *Life of St. Charles*, which he wrote with the valuable help of Msgr. Ratti, the future Pope Pius XI, who was at one time an Oblate of St. Charles, Msgr. Orsenigo does not hesitate to say that the rule of the Oblates of Milan is the most authentic expression of the ideal of the secular clergy as conceived by the saintly Archbishop. It consists in obedience to the diocesan bishop, which stems from a share in his priestly fervor, and demands a spirit of perfect dedication to the pastoral ministry of the apostles and their successors. The Oblates were always numerous among the clergy of Milan, but only after the canonization of the founder in 1621 did the title *Oblates of St. Charles* prevail.[2]

* * *

The influence of St. Charles Borromeo was very great. " St. Charles, " wrote the late Pope John, " was aptly hailed as the master of bishops. In the light of his example and teaching there arose throughout Italy, especially during

---

[1] *Vie des Saints et des Bienheureux selon l'ordre du Calendrier, avec l'historique des fêtes*, by the Benedictines of Paris, Vol. XI (1954), p. 160.

[2] Cf. Cesare Orsenigo, *Life of St. Charles Borromeo*, Eng. trans. Rev. Rudolph Kraus (St. Louis : Herder, 1943). St. Charles also considered imposing the vow of poverty; he gave up the idea on the advice of Philip Neri who considered it inconsistent with the pastoral office.

the twenty years spanning the pontificates of Pius V and Gregory XIII (1566-1585), such a renewal of strength and vigor that nothing similar has ever been known in any period of the Church's history. " [1] In Spain, Blessed John of Ribera, Archbishop of Valencia, who died in 1611, actively concerned himself with the preparation of the secular clergy as well as with its spirituality and drew much of his inspiration from the teachings of the Archbishop of Milan. As for France, this is the judgment of Father Broutin :

> During the whole of the seventeenth century, St. Charles Borromeo cast over the Church of France the great light of his pastoral genius. Although in Italy he had followed Matthew Giberti in many points of clerical reform, he nevertheless appeared in France as the undisputed master in whom all confided. In the opinion of the best bishops and priests, he was the bishop of the Council of Trent, the pastor of souls par excellence. The Ambassador of Venice, Soroni, went as far as saying that the example of Borromeo had more meaning than all the conciliar decrees. The prophecy was fulfilled : through the Archbishop of Milan the ideal had become a reality; his life and methods had more effect on souls than the most carefully reasoned arguments.

Among the bishops who were more directly under the influence of St. Charles Borromeo, we should mention St. Francis de Sales, Venerable Allan de Solminnihac, Bishop of Cahors, Francis de la Rochefoucauld, Bishop of Clermont and later of Senlis. It must be stated, however, that along with many other influences, the influence of Milan was to be found wherever the Tridentine Reform was being implemented. [2]

In the Low Countries the example of St. Charles was also followed. On September 20, 1625, the Prince-Bishop of Liège approved the *Oblates of St. Lambert and St. Charles* on the request

---

[1] Card. A. G. RONCALLI, *Gli Atti della Visita Apostolica di S. Carlo Borromeo a Bergamo* 1575), Vol. I, part. I (Florence 1936), p. 34.

[2] P. BROUTIN, *La Réforme pastorale en France au XVIIe siècle*, Vol. I (Paris 1956), pp. 37-38. Cardinal Manning organized a society of priests in 1857 patterned after the Oblates of Milan.

of Jacques Marchant, Dean of Couvin, who was the founder
and the first superior of the group. These Oblates were not
bound to community life. For the most part, they were spread
throughout the very large diocese of Liège but were nevertheless
united by the same ideal, the same rule and the same spiritual
practices. The spirit of this institute was exactly the same
as its Milanese counterpart, but the Belgian Oblates could
choose between the vow of perfect obedience to the bishop
or simply a renewal of the promise of obedience made at
ordination. Under the evident influence of the Berullian School,
the spirituality of Jacques Marchant insisted upon the possibility
of priests attaining perfection in the world through devotion
to Christ particularly as a priest, through devotion to the Mother
of God and through the sanctification inherent in their ministry. [1]
In line with this he wrote :

> There is a common and widespread misconception that
> only those are bound to perfection who have consecrated
> themselves to God through religious vows and have cut
> themselves off from contact with the faithful in order to
> live by themselves for God alone. As a result they think
> that perfection can only be acquired in the cloistered life
> and that there is no obligation to seek perfection placed
> on those working in the world.

After defending the opposite of this thesis, Marchant considers
the case of secular priests who abandoned their ministry in
order to lead a cloistered life.

> Many are deserting the priestly state and the pastoral cares
> to which they are still bound. They are like soldiers

---

[1] Jacques Marchant was born in Couvin in 1587 and died there October 20, 1648.
He received the licentiate from the University of Louvain, taught theology in the abbeys of
Floreffe and Lobbes and then was named pastor and dean of Couvin in 1622. He is the author
of numerous works. One writer has said of them : " Many authors have treated the same
subjects; none of them, not even the most renowned, could even come close to equalling him.
What is striking is that he combines a great depth of thought with a simplicity of style. "
(*L'Univers*, 1876, cited by Dom Th. Réjalot, " Jacques Marchant, sa vie, ses œuvres, " *Annales
de la Société archéologique de Namur*, Vol. XXVII (1908), pp. 19-104; it also appeared in pamphlet
form (Namur 1908). His principal work, written for the Oblates is his *Virga Aaronis, hoc est,
Directio vitae sacerdotalis* (Mons 1630).

eserting their posts because of danger from the enemy, in order to provide more carefully for their own safety. We are not unaware that sometimes this can be done prudently on a call from God. However, whenever it is done due to weakness of spirit and without sufficient reflection, we can assert that the spirit and the teaching of the saints demand that the will of our Sovereign Commander, Jesus Christ, be followed, and therefore they should persevere and vigorously wage combat in the post in which they were placed. Just as God sees the many dangers existing in the life of priests and bishops working in the world, so He guards them against such dangers by helping them with His graces and special protection if they place their trust in the Lord, whose glory they pledged themselves to increase by their state of life. Otherwise, if He did not sustain it in its difficulties by means of His grace and special help, God could be said to be lacking in the necessary care for His Church; the Church, especially at this time, needs workers who will expose their own souls to dangers in behalf of others by exercising their ministry in the world. [1]

During the lifetime of Marchant there were Oblates to be found almost everywhere throughout the vast Diocese of Liège, " in Hesbaye, in Ardennes, in Fagnes, in Hainaut, and they were related to groups in other dioceses, particularly in the Diocese of Cambrai. " [2]

*   *
*

The influence of the Oratory of St. Philip Neri was particularly great in Italy and France. Not only did Oratories, in imitation of the Roman Oratory, spring up in different areas, but some very eminent men drew inspiration for their

---

[1] J. MARCHANT, *Virga Aaronis, op. cit.*, pp. 27, 45-46.

[2] J. MARCHANT, *ibid.*, p. 10. On pages 611-61 Marchant gives an historical survey of his Oblates, their statutes and some official documents relating to them.

own attempts at spiritual reform from its spirituality and system of organization.

As has been said, it is certain that St. Francis de Sales was a great admirer of St. Charles Borromeo. He even considered the possibility of organizing an association of priests similar to that of the Oblates of Milan. However, we do know that in the year 1599, during a visit to Rome, he frequently visited the Oratory of St. Philip Neri. When he experimented with a community of priests at *Sainte-Maison*, in Thonon, he gave them the rule of the Oratory and he secured as their protector Cardinal Baronius, the disciple and first successor of St. Philip Neri. [1]

In the formulation of his own spirtuality, the Bishop of Annecy underwent several influences, which he nevertheless carefully evaluated and adapted to his own way of thinking and which he expressed in a manner that was readily understandable. Among these influences, mention certainly must be made of John of Avila, St. Ignatius and St. Charles Borromeo, but apparently the influence of St. Philip Neri was the greatest.

So many parallels can be drawn between the maxims of St. Philip Neri and the *Introduction to the Devout Life* that one is inclined to agree with the opinion of one historian : " In plotting his spiritual course for Philothea, it would not have been unlikely for the Bishop of Geneva to have had in mind the teachings and approach of St. Philip. " [2]

Be that as it may, St. Francis de Sales had great esteem for the clergy and he believed that there were tremendous possibilities for their attaining a high degree of sanctity. In this regard an incident of his youth should be recalled. Following the ceremony at which he had been invested with the cassock, Monsieur Bouvart is said to have remarked to him : " It really seemed as though you had taken the habit of a Capuchin. "

---

[1] St. Francis De Sales, *Letter to Msgr. J. J. Ancina* (Nov. 23, 1606), Annecy edition, Vol. XIII, p. 235.

[2] L. Ponnelle and L. Bordet, *op. cit.*, pp. 526-28.

The young man quickly replied : " Ah, but I took the habit of St. Peter! " [1] This remark clearly indicates that nothing has greater claim to our esteem than the priesthood, with which Peter and the apostles were first favored. As one who often reminded the faithful that perfection could be achieved in many different ways, he must have realized even then that the priestly state, as the Berullians taught, demanded perfection and furnished the necessary means to guarantee its attainment. Towards the end of his life he ventured to say in all earnestness that there are some Carmelites who wear the mantle of Elias without possessing his spirit, just as there are some secular priests, who, without ever having worn the habit of the prophet, have nevertheless received his spirit, his zeal and his holiness. [2] Bishops are therefore correct in choosing St. Francis de Sales as the patron of their seminaries as are also priests who pattern their striving for priestly perfection on the Salesian method.

* * *

The experiment with the *Sainte-Maison* at Thonon did not succeed, but the Bishop of Geneva did not cease to be obsessed by the idea of a project for the sanctification of the clergy. He discussed this many times with the young Pierre de Bérulle who strongly urged him to devote himself to such a project. When Bérulle founded his own Oratory in 1611, Francis desired to spend the remaining years of his life there, and said on that occasion that " if he could have chosen to be someone, he would have wanted to be Monsieur de Bérulle. " [3]

Even though the founder of the French School drew much of his inspiration from the teachings of the Spanish spiritual

---

[1] F. TROCHU, *St. Francis de Sales*, Eng. trans. Ernest Graf (London : Burnes, Oates & Washbourne, 1949), p. 240. We find the same thought in Juan de Avila : I. ROMERO, *Fuego de cruzado : Estampa de sacerdocio del Maestro Juan de Avila* (Vitoria 1947), p. 54.

[2] St. FRANCIS DE SALES, *Lettre à la Sous-Prieure du Carmel d'Orléans* (1620 or 1621), Annecy edition, Vol. XIX, p. 409.

[3] F. TROCHU, *op. cit.*, pp. 627-28.

writers, especially from the Carthusian Anthony Molina, and from Master John of Avila, he nevertheless was, like Francis de Sales, an admirer and disciple of Philip Neri. [1] This dependence is particularly noticeable in the very name adopted by the foundation of Bérulle, *The Oratory of Our Lord Jesus Christ*. The chief purpose of both institutes was to bring together priests who were tending toward perfection without requiring them to take any religious vows. Both Oratories were also careful not to add any authority to that of the bishop, any law to that of the sacred canons, any form of piety to the piety of the Church. Although it is true that the French Oratory very soon devoted itself almost exclusively to teaching, this was not the intention of the founder whose primary concern was for the parish and the training of pastors and curates.

Even from the point of view of doctrine, the relationship between the two Oratories is apparent, although their spiritualities were soon to differ greatly from one another. As has been already mentioned, St. Philip, who was by no means an outstanding theologian, was totally imbued with devotion to the Christ of the Altar whom he lovingly encountered each morning at Mass. It was particularly this main point of the Berullian Oratory's spirituality which resulted in an impressive theological synthesis on the various states of Christ and the priesthood. What seemed to be only sentimentality among the early followers of Philip Neri developed into a well devised spiritual system among the Berullians as we shall later observe. [2]

The decree establishing the Oratory of France advised its members that their " first and most important purpose was to strive completely for the perfection of their priestly state, " and in order to do this, " to have a special and personal devotion to Jesus Christ, Our Lord, the Eternal Priest and source of the priesthood in the Church. " The thought of the founder in this regard is clear even in the first instruction that he gave to his disciples :

[1] P. POURRAT, *Le Sacerdoce : Doctrine de l'Ecole française* (Paris 1931), pp. 16-17.

[2] L. BOUYER, *L'Oratoire de France* (Paris 1950), pp. 23-29.

The same God, who in our time has restored, in many religious families, the spirit and fervor of their original foundation, seems to desire also to impart the same grace and fervor upon the priestly state, which is the most important, the most essential and necessary to His Church and to revive in it the status and perfection which belongs to it and which it enjoyed from the time of its institution. In order to reap this grace from heaven and to receive this spirit of our Lord Jesus Christ, our High Priest, and to live and act according to His promptings as well as to preserve it for posterity, we have assembled in this place and have begun this form of life.

Yet, Bérulle further states :

The priestly state requires in the first place a very great perfection and even sanctity, secondly a personal relation to Jesus Christ Our Lord, to whom we are joined in a very special way because of the ministry . . . God has been pleased to endow each religious family with the care and profession of some special virtue, in such a way that, while nevertheless possessing them all, each religious family appears conspicuous for the exercise and profession of some virtue in particular. Thus, the Capuchins can lay claim to poverty, the Carthusians to solitude, the Jesuits to obedience. The special task of loving and honoring deeply and personally Jesus Christ Our Lord ought to be the area in which this little congregation will distinguish itself. [1]

This contemplation and love of Christ should be directed especially to His priesthood. The Oratory endeavored to relive all the various states of the life of Our Lord, but most especially the state of His priesthood, in which He is, at the same time, both Priest and Victim. [2]

This then was the aim of the Berullian Oratory : to restore and revitalize the priestly state and to attain this exalted end by

---

[1] P. DE BÉRULLE, *Œuvres complètes* (Paris : Migne, 1856), pp. 1270-72.

[2] See particularly the doctrine of Charles de Condren, who succeeded the founder, in H. BREMOND, *Literary History of Religious Thought in France*, Eng. trans. (London : S.P.C.K., 1928-36), Vol. III, pp. 312-17.

living the priesthood to perfection.   This is done, as has already
been said, by living as priests and only as priests, while nevertheless drawing the necessary inspiration for this from solid
spiritual doctrine rooted in dogma and based on union with
Jesus Christ, the High Priest.   From this teaching, there was
soon elaborated by Bourdoise, Olier and St. Vincent de Paul
a complete plan for pastoral renewal which included the organization of seminaries, the winning over of souls by parish missions,
and the revitalization of parish life.   This tripartite plan of
action, *seminaries, missions* and *parishes,* was characteristic,
together with the spirituality of the Oratory, not only of
seventeenth century France, but it also left its mark on
subsequent centuries. [1]

" The foundation of the Oratory and similar groups such
as Saint Sulpice, the Congregation of the Missions and the Eudists,
which in imitation of, or under the direct aegis of Monsieur
de Bérulle, strove to restore the priestly state, " wrote Bremond,
" marks the high-point of the French Counter-Réformatisn, " [2]
Such then was the important part played by Bérulle.   The
presentation of his spiritual teachings was not always the clearest
nor the most popular, but the beauty of his doctrine was so
great that it shone forth in all its splendor.   His personal renown,
more than anything else, assured him of devoted and zealous
disciples from among the best priests in France.   St. Vincent
de Paul was under the spell of this man whom he once described
as " one of the holiest men that I have ever known. " [3]   As we
have already observed, St. Francis de Sales was of the same
opinion, and indeed many others could be mentioned who also
shared this view.   Even today he is still considered " The
Spiritual Master of the French School, " and recently it was
written, at least as far as the French scene is concerned : " The
foundation of the French Oratory was the primary reason behind
all of the attempts made by the parochial clergy during the

---

[1] P. BROUTIN, *Le Pasteur d'Eglise, loc. cit.,* No. 51, p. 5.

[2] H. BREMOND, *op. cit.,* p. 133.

[3] Cited by H. BREMOND, *op. cit.,* p. 216.

last three centuries to return once again to the perfection of their priestly state. Reviewing the history of this great movement without prejudice, one is surprised to see how the Tridentine ideal was realized by means of this system begun and constantly encouraged by Bérulle. " [1]

* * *

To guarantee to secular priests a truly exalted spirituality, to tighten the bonds uniting them to their bishops, and to instill in them zeal for the active ministry, such was and still is the purpose of the movement, aimed at pastoral renewal, which was begun by the Council of Trent. Notice must also be taken of the council's attempt to free the clergy from the dangers of isolation and individualism.

Under the old system many parishes were served either by chapters of Canons Regular or by monasteries. The Premonstratensian Order even made a rule by which the active ministry would be closely united to the duties of their canonical office. Since they had to live in country rectories, these religious were spread out at great distances from their abbey or were grouped together in priories. Nevertheless, they were required to return periodically to their abbey. Whatever the relative value of a community life for the parochial clergy may be, it is necessary to examine the facts and to see if such a life can be suitably adapted to the present historical situation, which is often irreversible. Very soon there were to be found priests widely scattered throughout villages and towns. For this reason the Council of Trent enacted a statute, dealing specifically with these rural priests. This statute obliged them to reside among their people and also pointed out the great value they could thereby derive for their pastoral ministry. It was particularly for the country priests that great pains were taken to devise practical means by which they would be able to achieve sanctification and properly fulfill their sacred ministry.

[1] P. BROUTIN, *La Réforme pastorale, op. cit.*, Vol. II, pp. 413, 23-24.

A number of attempts were made before the French Revolution to establish communities for secular priests, but these attempts generally did not meet with long range success. The Oratories of St. Philip Neri, as numerous as they were, encompassed only a few very select groups.

The foundations of Vincent de Paul, John Eudes, Louis Marie Grignion de Montfort and others did not remain within a diocesan framework. Some local communities had a longer life. The Community of Saint-Nicolas du Chardonnet, founded at Paris by Adrian Bourdoise in the beginning of the seventeenth century, is just one example.

The foundation of Venerable Bartholomew Holzhauser is especially important both because of its size and also because it has continued to a limited extent even up to the present. Holzhauser, a priest of the Diocese of Salzburg, founded in 1640 an institute of secular priests living in community, *Institutum clericorum saecularium in commune viventium*. The Bartholomites, as they were called, took no vows and remained completely under the authority of the local bishop. However, they held their goods in common and bound themselves by an oath to remain within the congregation. They had as their superiors, a local director, usually the rural dean, a diocesan director and a general director. The society spread rapidly, especially during the eighteenth century, in many European countries and even as far as South America. It was suppressed in 1804 and has never been restored despite the efforts of several bishops, such as Ketteler of Maintz, Dupanloup of Orleans and even despite repeated recommendations by Pius IX and Leo XIII. The Apostolic Union of Bishop Lebeurier, which is still functioning as a sacerdotal association, was patterned after Bartholomew Holzhauser's institute. We will treat of it again.

It was particularly during the last two centuries that associations for priests were organized. These associations were satisfied with a moral community between priests rather than with an actual life in common. This was not an entirely new idea. It seems that the oldest association of priests which made no provision for common life had been established at Münster in Westphalia by John Heidemeich Stodtbroek. It was known as the *Confraternitas sacerdotum bonae voluntatis*. At any rate, the way had already been opened by the Third Orders. The priests or lay tertiaries were associated with a religious order whose spirituality they adopted and whose special observances they followed. It is noteworthy that one of the very first tertiaries of St. Francis of Assisi was Blessed Davanazato († 1295), the pastor of a small parish near Florence. [1] There also existed, beginning in the sixteenth century, a number of more or less closed and secret groups whose purpose was to help their members protect themselves against the dangers of heresy and irreligion. The oldest group, probably founded in Padua, soon appeared in a number of dioceses in France and Italy. Such great names as Francis de Sales, Ignatius Loyola and Vincent de Paul are mentioned as having been members of these societies. Particularly important was the society of *Aa*, which was also engaged in preserving its members from the dangers described above, but which positively and clearly strove for the sanctification of souls as well. The founding of *Aa* dates from the seventeenth century when the Jesuit Bagot devised a more clearly defined and more stable set of rules for the various associations at La Flèche and Paris which were dedicated to Our Lady. The Jesuit influence remained very great up until the time of the French Revolution, and it is undeniable that this influence helped to preserve among the clergy of the Ancien Regime a spirit of zeal and priestly loyalty. The laity were not exluded from membership and the institute achieved great success especially in protecting vocations and guiding young people to seminaries and religious orders. Moreover, priests were soon recruited; and thus a sort of sacerdotal association was formed for the clergy. A number of branches of *Aa* existed in many cities in France as well as in Italy, Switzerland, Germany and Canada. From the *Aa* there arose a number of apostolic groups such as the *Paris Foreign Mission Society* found-

---

[1] The cause of Blessed Davanazato has recently been reintroduced in Rome.

ed in the seventeenth century. After the French Revolution a
branch of the *Aa* still survived in Toulouse under the direction
of the Servant of God, Canon Maurice Garrigou, and it exerted a
great influence there throughout the nineteenth century. This
influence was extolled not long ago by Cardinal Saliège. [1]
Still another survival of *Aa*, as we will see, was at Turin where
it was under the direction of another Servant of God, Pio
Brunone Lanteri.

What does this strange title *Aa* stand for? Both Father
Cavallera and Bishop Tournier hold that it " undoubtedly
stands for Assembly. " [2] Some have completed it thus :
" *Assembly of the Associates.* " [3] It should be remarked that the
biographers of Lanteri refer to the *Aa* at Turin as *Amicizia
Anonima*. Msgr. Frutaz believes that this is not the exact
meaning, and he bases this opinion on what is contained in the
dossier relating to the cause of the Servant of God, Pio Brunone
Lanteri. [4]

At any rate, the association of Turin is worth considering
because it was quite successful and also because Lanteri founded
an association strictly for priests, the *Amicizia sacerdotale*, which
soon spread throughout all of Piedmont, into Lombardy and
even as far as Tuscany. Each member lived in his own rectory,
entered into close relationships with other members of the
society, and in order to devote himself more completely to the glory
of God, renounced any claim to honors and ecclesiastical
preferment.

Absolute secrecy was compulsory. Recruiting was done
by means of recommendation and those so chosen were only
gradually initiated, and even in this many precautions were taken.
Although Lanteri's group may have added a few things to the

---

[1] Msgr. C. TOURNIER, *Le chanoine Maurice Garrigou* (Toulouse 1945); preface by Cardinal
J. G. Saliège, pp. XI-XII.

[2] F. CAVALLERA, " Aux origines de la Société des Missions étrangères, l'Aa de Paris, "
Bulletin de Littérature ecclésiastique, Vol. XXXIV (1933-34), pp. 173 ff. Msgr. C. TOURNIER, *op. cit.*,
passim.

[3] A. P. FRUTAZ, " Aa, " *Enciclopedia cattolica*, Vol. I (Città del Vaticano 1949), cols. 1-2.

[4] A. P. FRUTAZ, *ibid.*, col. 2.

requirements set down by the early *Aa* groups, it nevertheless retained the spirit and purpose of the original organization. [1]

There were also associations set up to give material assistance to secular priests. One of the most interesting of these was founded in 1619 by Don Jeronimo de Quintana. It was first known as the *Congregacion de San Pedro Apostol de Presbiteros seculares*. It was chiefly through the efforts of this highly successful association, now known as *Mutual del Clero*, that John of Avila was recently declared the patron of the Spanish clergy and that his cause for canonization was reopened. [2]

Finally, we must not fail to mention all that the bishops of the Ancien Regime did to implement the decisions and recommendations enacted by the Council of Trent. This included the erection and organization of seminaries, the improvement of some already existing institutions, parish visitations, a closer relationship between bishops and their clergy, as well as diocesan synods, provincial councils, parish missions, directives for the priestly ministry, retreats and conferences for priests, etc. All of these efforts were chiefly aimed at sanctifying the clergy and helping them to fulfill their pastoral ministry. For a more detailed treatment of the pastoral reform in France in the seventeenth century, readers are referred to the two-volume work published by Father Broutin on this subject. The reader will come to admire the great discernment and zeal of the French clergy. From the beginning of the religious reformation, the author says : " There were many priests who strove, each in his own way, to clear the air and to make the soil in France fertile once again. " [3]

In Belgium also, the bishops swiftly did their very best to implement the decrees of the Council of Trent; and the clergy there soon earned great praise for their exemplary way of life,

---

[1] P. T. PIATTI, *Il servo di Dio, Pio Brunone Lanteri, apostolo di Torino* (Turin 1934), pp. 44-73.

[2] *Reglamento de la R. V. et I. Congregacion de San Pedro Apostol de Presbiteros seculares naturales y oriundos de Madrid* (Madrid 1942), pp. 6-7.

[3] P. BROUTIN, *La Réforme pastorale, op. cit.*, Vol. I, pp. 27-28. Note that the information in this book, though copious, is judged incomplete by L. Cognet in a review. See *Revue d'histoire ecclésiastique*, Vol. LII (1957), p. 574. However, it is extensive enough for our treatment.

their great integrity and virtue. [1]   In practically every Catholic
country during the sixteenth, seventeenth and eighteenth
centuries there lived many saintly bishops and priests, several
of whom have been canonized, and many more whose causes
have been presented to the Congregation of Rites for eventual
beatification.   Italy, during the eighteenth century, produced
another St. Charles Borromeo in the person of St. Gregory
Barbarigo, a Venetian priest, who was in turn Bishop of Bergamo
and of Padua. [2]   Patterning his life entirely on that of the great
Archbishop of Milan, he was outstanding for the zeal that he
exhibited in all of his undertakings.   At Padua he established
a seminary whose reputation spread far and wide because of its
stress on the study of oriental languages and also because of the
emphasis placed on developing what we now refer to as an
ecumenical spirit.   He founded the *Oblates of SS. Prosdocimus
and Anthony* and gave them the rule of the Oblates of Milan.
However, he did make provision for a vow of poverty for
those members who desired it. [3]

This great bishop, who deserves to be better known, died
in 1697, was beatified in 1761 and canonized in 1960.

*   *
*

Undoubtedly, the general tone of the eighteenth century
leaves much to be desired, but this should not be over-
exaggerated.   What was said of the Middle Ages may also be
applied to this period : " History has for all time accurately
recorded the scandals of this age but has completely overlooked
the lives of those truly virtuous men who lived quietly without
leaving us any record of their accomplishments. " [4]

---

[1] E. DE MOREAU, *L'Eglise en Belgique* (Bruxelles 1945), p. 178.   For the diocese of Namur
see for example, L. JADIN, " Histoire du Séminaire de Namur, " *Revue diocésaine de Namur*,
Vol. XIII-XIV (1959-60).   We would like to see this series of articles in book form.

[2] G. ALESSI, *Vita del Beato Gregorio Card. Barbarigo* (Padua 1897).

[3] G. ALESSI, *op. cit.*, p. 173.

[4] L. GÉNICOT, *Les lignes de faîte du moyen âge*, 2nd ed. (Tournai 1952), p. 176.

Bishop Bonnard wrote regarding the French scene :

> This country, at the end of the eighteenth century, was certainly not, from the religious point of view, as bad off as the real or apparent defections of the following years might make one believe. The ancient monastic orders such as the Benedictines of Morteau and Vancluse, the Minims of La Seigne, seemed, it is true, to resemble slowly flickering lamps devoid of light and heat. Nevertheless, there were many good and zealous pastors among them. Proof of this may be found in the fact that they called for help to make up for what they referred to as the insufficiency of their ordinary ministry. [1]

Although the revolution did in fact cause many religious to abandon their monasteries and priories and did result in a diminishing of vocations during this period, [2] the record of the diocesan clergy is nevertheless, on the whole, quite commendable: " The majority of the secular clergy, " according to Leflon, " remained worthy of respect and admiration and even surpassed in the sphere of religious influence the regular clergy, as both Tocqueville and Taine report. " [3]

It is also worth noting that the French clergy produced a great number of martyrs during the dark days of the Revolution. Although the political upheaval did bring about some defections, nevertheless the great majority of priests remained loyal to the faith, as is evidenced in the number of those whose causes have been investigated and approved by Rome for beatification. Several of these causes have already been decided. Of the 191 September martyrs, beatified in 1926, 130 of them were secular priests. Among the 19 martyrs of Laval beatified in 1955, there were 14 secular priests, and mention should also

---

[1] Msgr. F. BONNARD, *Le Vénérable Père Antoine-Sylvestre Receveur* (Lyon 1936), p. 68.

[2] M. PEIGNÉ-DELACOURT, *Tableau des Abbayes et Monastères d'hommes en France, á l'époque de l'Edit de 1768 relatif á l'Assemblée du Clergé, accompagné de la liste des abbayes royales de Filles* (Arras 1875).

[3] J. LEFLON, *La crise révolutionnaire 1789-1846* (Paris 1951), p. 28. See also DANIEL-ROPS, *L'Eglise des Révolutions*, Vol. I (Paris 1960), pp. 13-34.

be made of that exemplary pastor from Anjou, Noël Pinot, beatified in 1926.   A great majority of the diocesan priests up for
beatification were victims of the Revolution.   There were also
many confessors of the Faith, such as Andrew Hubert Fournet,
who suffered heroically for their religion without actually
undergoing martyrdom.   The French diocesan clergy at this
time were indeed a credit to the Church.   The same can also
be said of the diocesan clergy in other countries.   The reaction
in Belgium against the dechristianization policy of the Revolution
was due in great measure to the faith and courage of its clergy.
It would be extremely interesting to make a complete study
of all the tribulations experienced by the Belgian priests during
the French occupation.   In the Diocese of Namur alone, there
were about forty secular and thirty religious priests who were
deported to French Guiana or the islands of Ré or Oléron.
Many others were imprisoned; and some still carried on their
priestly ministrations in secret, although they were in constant
danger of being betrayed.   As a matter of national pride we
need only recall the stirring death march of the seminarians
of the Diocese of Ghent, who " out of loyalty to their bishop "
resisted the harsh decrees of Napoleon and were exiled to Wesel,
on the Rhine, where 43 of them died of hunger and mistreatment.[1]

---

[1] F. CLAEYS-BOUUAERT, *Le diocèse de Gand pendant les dernières années de la Domination française* (Ghent 1913), pp. 119-49.   J. DE SMET, " Het bisdom Gent onder Napoleon I, " *Collationes Brugenses et Gandavenses*, Vol. I (1955), pp. 240-44.

Chapter 3

From the French Revolution
to the Present

The various attempts to replenish the depleted ranks of the parochial clergy after the Revolution were generally successful. Vocations increased to such a degree in Belgian dioceses, for example, that within one generation most parishes and important positions in the diocese were being entrusted to a youthful and very zealous clergy. There was also greater concern shown for the quality rather than for the quantity of the clergy, and this concern eventually increased to such a point that it has been alleged : " The raising of the spiritual level of the clergy is one of the least spectacular but nevertheless one of the most important aspects of the Church's history during the second half of the nineteenth century. " [1] At the same time as the major religious orders and societies reorganized themselves in order to offer young people the means of tending towards perfection by observing the evangelical counsels in religious life, the secular clergy became more greatly concerned with the sanctification of their members. Once again, great emphasis was placed on securing a form of life flexible enough to guarantee mutual assistance and spiritual progress to diocesan priests engaged in the various activities of the ministry. Canon Gaduel, the Vicar General of Orleans, published in 1861 a life of Bartholomew Holzhauser and his own bishop, Dupanloup, wrote the preface for it and indicated that he desired to see the institute founded by Holzhauser revived in France. [2] In 1862, Msgr. Lebeurier,

---

[1] R. AUBERT, *Le Pontificat de Pie IX* (Paris 1952), p. 452. For Piedmont see P. T. PIATTI, *Pio Brunone Lanteri, op. cit.*, p. 66.

[2] J. GADUEL, *La perfection sacerdotale ou la Vie et l'Esprit du Serviteur de Dieu Barthélemy Holzhauser, réformateur du clergé en Allemagne* (Orléans 1861).

Canon of Orleans, founded the *Diocesan Oratory of Orleans*. The constitutions of this Oratory were the same as those of the *Institute of Secular Priests Living in Common*. [1] In 1869, Bishop Dupanloup wrote a book entitled *De La Vie Commune et des associations sacerdotales dans le clergé séculier*. This work was extremely well received and achieved wide recognition. Msgr. Lebeurier's society was later known as the *Apostolic Union of Secular Priests of the Sacred Heart*, and it was given a constitution more in keeping with the needs of the clergy at that time. The members of the Union are protected against the dangers arising from individualism and aloofness by means of regular meetings with fellow priests and by frequent contacts among themselves, as well as by a definite rule of life and spiritual direction given by one of the diocesan directors. Such a program did much to establish a moral community among priests for whom life in common was often impossible.

About the same time, in 1868, R. Loller founded at Vienna an association for priestly perseverance, *Forderung der Priesterliche Beharrlichkeit*, which soon achieved great success in German and Slavic speaking countries. Interestingly enough this society is open both to secular and religious priests. At Paris in 1875, the *Society of Priests of St. Francis de Sales* was founded by the Servant of God, Henri Chaumont. Drawing its inspiration from the spirituality of the Bishop of Geneva, it is careful not to impose any authority between priests and their bishop. The purpose of the society is to extend assistance to its members and to help priests achieve sanctification by the proper performance of the duties of their priestly and diocesan state of life. The German speaking countries have several associations for priests. Besides those already mentioned, such as the *Apostolic Union*, the *Society of Priests of St. Francis de Sales*, the *Association for Priestly Perseverance* and the *Confraternity of Priests of Good Will*, there is also the *Schönstattbund* or *Apostolische Bewegung* founded in 1919 at Schönstatt, near Vallendar-am-

[1] Msgr. F. DUPANLOUP, *De la vie Commune et des associations sacerdotales dans le clergé séculier* (Paris-Orléans 1869).

Rhein. This last group has its headquarters at the House of Studies of the Pallotines, followers of Saint Vincent Pallotti. It is open to priests and members of Catholic Action groups and is under the patronage of the *Mater admirabilis*, venerated at Schönstatt. [1]

There are two stages in the history of the *Society of the Heart of Jesus*. In 1791, the Servant of God, Pierre Joseph de la Clorivière, a former member of the then suppressed Society of Jesus, founded this group for the sanctification of priests. [2] The society died out after having existed for about fifty years, but it arose again in 1918. Its members take the three vows, and the society is now a secular institute. The diocesan director is necessarily chosen from the ranks of the local diocesan clergy, and obedience can only be imposed in those matters which in no way detract from the bishop's authority. [3] The purpose of the society is simply to help secular priests to live according to the spirit of the evangelical counsels in whatever canonical mission they have been given by their bishop.

There have always been priests Tertiaries and Oblates who follow the spirituality of a particular religious order. *The Union of the Brothers of Jesus*, which extends the influence of Charles de Foucauld to the realm of the diocesan priesthood, is very similar to such groups. Erected as a *pious union* in 1955 by Archbishop de Provenchères, of Aix, it is now awaiting official approbation by Rome as a secular institute. Its essential features are : " first of all, complete fidelity to the vocation of the diocesan priesthood in all the duties that this includes, and secondly, a call to achieve perfection in this state by means of the practices common to the spirituality of Charles de Foucauld. " Belonging to a diocese is considered a great benefit; but in order to

---

[1] J. SCHMITZ, *Von der Gemeinschaft der Schönstattpriester* (Vallendar 1960).

[2] Much could be said about the associations for priests during and after the French Revolution, especially about the influence of the Priests of the Sacred Heart and the Priests of Faith whose leaders were disbanded Jesuits. Thus, in the diocese of Namur, a spiritual environment was created which produced such great figures as Devenise, Minsart, Kinet, etc. See, for example, the remarkable book of C. DE SMEDT, *Msgr. J. B. Victor Kinet* (Namur 1899), pp. 10-42.

[3] Concerning these associations see " Le Clergé diocésain face à son idéal, " *Problèmes du clergé diocésain*, No. 3 (Paris 1949); also several articles in *Revue diocésaine de Tournai*, Vol. XIII (1958).

guarantee full effectiveness, a return to the spirit of the beatitudes is strongly emphasized. The special practices of the Union consist in a monthly day of solitude, an hour devoted each day to Eucharistic adoration, daily meditation on the Gospel and a regular monthly meeting of members to review their spiritual progress. [1]

* * *

There also exist a number of well established societies of priests which enjoy legal standing in their dioceses. Since it is not possible to consider each society in particular, we will be content with merely indicating some of their chief features.

There are a number of religious congregations which operate solely within their own dioceses and are therefore strictly diocesan congregations. *The Congregation of the Missionaries of the Plain and of St. Theresa of Lisieux*, canonically erected in 1928 at Luzon, was, until fairly recently, an example of this type of diocesan congregation. The members are completely at the disposal of their bishop, like any other priest of the diocese, but the congregation maintains its own noviciate, retreat house and follows its own method of spirituality. Such a linking together of the religious life with the active ministry recalls the way of life of the canons regular, but differs from it in two respects : it is the bishop who is the equivalent of the abbot, and the recitation of the office in choir is not a matter of obligation even in those houses where community life would make this possible. At present, the majority of canons regular belong to pontifical institutes and are subject to a superior general, whose jurisdiction is worldwide in extent. The evolution which began with the canons regular has led to the type of life that we now find among certain modern religious congregations, for example, the *Sons of Charity*. These pontifical institutes, established in quite a few dioceses, engage exclusively

---

[1] *L'Union des Frères de Jésus : Institut séculier en formation pour le clergé séculier. But et esprit* (1958). On the spirituality of the Fraternities see especially : R. VOILLAUME, *Seeds of the Desert,* Eng. trans. and adapt. Willard Hill (London : Burns and Oates, 1955).

in parish work. They are completely at the disposal of the diocese but are exempt from episcopal authority in regard to their formation, their reception of Orders, their internal organization and especially in regard to their selection of superiors. Their ties to a diocese are similar to those of other pontifical religious institutes except that their function, the parochial ministry, is the same as that of the secular clergy.

In 1860 Venerable Anthony Chevrier, priest of the Diocese of Lyon, founded the *Society of Priests of Prado*. About ten years ago, Msgr. Ancel, the superior general, wrote : " The society is comparable to societies of common life without vows. It is a diocesan institute and fully subject, by law, to the authority of the local ordinary. The superior general and his council exercise their authority in each diocese, dependent, nevertheless, upon the local ordinary. " [1] Since then, however, the society has undergone a complete transformation; and by 1954 it had developed into a secular institute. The two main concerns presently facing the superiors of Prado are : the desire to remain faithful to the ideals of Venerable Chevrier and the desire to maintain the diocesan character of the society. The founder did not wish to establish a religious congregation but rather " an association of priests, who while remaining as secular priests, would nevertheless all follow a definite way of life and would endeavor to live a life of poverty in the midst of the poor, particularly by caring for the parishes entrusted to them. " Since the priests of Prado " always have to consider their status as a community of diocesan priests bound to their bishop before considering the obligations of their own society, " it was very difficult for them to observe the rules, customs and way of life proper to their institute. In August 1959 a meeting was held to study the problems involved in reconciling these two demands. [2]

---

[1] Msgr. A. ANCEL, " La Société des Prêtres du Prado, " *Le Clergé diocésain face à son idéal, op. cit.*, pp. 40-45.

[2] " Le caractère diocésain de l'Institut des Prêtres du Prado, " *Prêtres du Prado* (Lyon 1959), special issue.

Also about this time, a desire similar to that of the founder of Prado inspired the foundation of Dom Gréa. A priest of the Diocese of Saint-Claude, he was imbued with a strong love for religious life and the liturgy and possessed a clear understanding of the importance of the local Church as well. Dom Gréa founded in 1871 *The Canons Regular of the Immaculate Conception.* In his view they were to be completely integrated with the diocesan clergy, under the authority of the local bishop, and were to enjoy a minimum number of exemptions. He realized that if they were spread throughout several dioceses they would only be able to form a loosely knit federation, and thus each house would be completely diocesan in purpose. Dom Gréa also wrote a book entitled *De l'Eglise et de sa divine constitution* [1] which masterfully sets forth his views. His foundation was not able to function along the lines that he had originally proposed for it. However, by the twentieth century it was in operation once again.

In fact, Dom Gréa's plan has influenced, to some extent, the Norbertines of Mondaye in Normandy. These canons regular are attempting to revive St. Norbert's original plan for combining the religious life with the active ministry. The community is part of the Order and therefore is not autonomous. In order to comply with Canon Law they respect their exemptions but, nevertheless, undertake a number of activities which are not essential to the purpose of the abbey. Although it is juridically linked to the Holy See because it belongs to an Order, the individual community nevertheless is primarily noted " for the close attachment that it has both to the bishop and to the Church, his spouse. It is precisely this which makes of the canon regular such a profoundly hierarchical individual possessing a definite canonical mission in a definite place. This is the real meaning of stability *in loco.* By vocation, the canon regular remains firmly rooted in one place. " This description was given by the former Abbott of Mondaye, Dom Bossière, who believed that this type of life is most in

---

[1] Dom GRÉA, *De l'Eglise et de sa divine constitution* (Paris 1885).

keeping with the early Church's idea of the *Presbyterium*, the community of priests united around the bishop. [1] It is generally agreed that there was an unfortunate separation made in the original idea of the *Presbyterium*, a separation which was certainly unknown to the members of the early Church, and one which Cardinal Mercier wished to destroy.

The great Cardinal of Malines was actually quite impressed with Dom Gréa. He knew him personally and had given much consideration to his writings when he sought to investigate the possibility of a state of perfection for his diocesan priests. However, he wanted above all to avoid changing the slightest detail of his priests' way of life; and he particularly strove to avoid grouping them together apart from the rest of the clergy. Shortly before his death Cardinal Mercier submitted to Rome the statutes for his *Fraternité sacerdotale des Amis de Jésus*. He died before approval came from Rome, but his successor, Cardinal Van Roey, canonically erected the society on the 27th of December 1926. The Fraternity is only open to secular priests of the diocese; and its members are directly and completely subject to the local ordinary, who canonically receives their vows of poverty, chastity and obedience. The vow of victim in union with the Sacred Hearts of Jesus and Mary may also be taken. The purpose of the society is to allow its members " to respond to the call of friendship with our one High Priest, Our Lord Jesus Christ, and to fulfill the conditions for friendship by conforming their personal lives as well as their activities in the ministry to the ideal of apostolic living proposed by our divine Savior to the apostles who perfectly realized it. " The *Friends of Jesus* understand their dependence upon the local ordinary to such an extent that the majority of them do not see how it would be possible for their Fraternity to function as a secular institute. In short, the obligation of obedience binds each member to the bishop independently of any other commitment. Although there is a delegate of the bishop to

[1] Y. Bossière, *Les Chanoines réguliers de Prémontré* (Mondaye 1945), pp. 52 ff., 128 ff.

oversee the everyday life of the Fraternity, it is, nevertheless, the bishop whom they directly obey. [1]

We will observe further on in our study that many priests prefer neither to take vows nor to follow the prescribed way of life of a particular society. It is indeed quite surprising that Cardinal Mercier chose to found a Pious Union with vows, especially since his spirituality did not seem to incline him to such a form of life. A number of those who knew the great archbishop agree with this observation. We must also add that Cardinal Mercier spearheaded a great theological movement concerned with the problems of clerical spirituality. A great number of theologians after him also considered this problem. Naturally, some writings have not avoided every excess, but instead of reproaching those [2] who have honestly attempted to find the truth in a particularly delicate field of investigation, wouldn't it be more valuable to recall the advice of Cardinal Mercier? : " Those who attempt nothing are never wrong, but their lives are a total waste. Rather let us recognize that an exchange of views has shed much light on what Msgr. Duperray refers to as a leading problem, namely that of creating a spirituality of the secular clergy. " [3] A similar desire " to bring to light the nobility and character of the diocesan clergy in union with their bishops " [4] was expressed at the meeting of French Cardinals and Archbishops in 1944.

---

[1] Card. D. J. MERCIER, *La Fraternité sacerdotale des Amis de Jésus* (Bruges-Paris 1927). See also F. VAN STEENBERGHEN, " Le prêtre diocésain d'après le Cardinal Mercier, " *Le Cardinal Mercier, fondateur de séminaire* (Louvain 1951), pp. 50-109.

[2] The critics can be helpful because they manage to avoid pitfalls and encourage reflection. The most frequently cited treatments of this subject are those of R. CARPENTIER, " La spiritualité du clergé diocésain, " *Nouvelle Revue théologique*, Vol. LXVIII (1946), pp. 192-217; " Autour de la spiritualité du clergé diocésain, " *ibid.*, Vol. LXXVI (1950), pp. 1063-69. See also the recent articles of O. MÉLANÇON, " La Sainte Messe, fonction principale du prêtre, " *Revue eucharistique du clergé*, Vol. LX, p. 606 — Vol. LXI, p. 293 (1957-58).

[3] Text cited by Msgr. E. GUERRY, *Le clergé diocésain en face de sa mission actuelle d'évangélisation* (Paris 1944), p. 50.

[4] Msgr. E. GUERRY, *ibid.*, p. 151.

* * *

Union with the bishop! How well Abbott Chevrier and Dom Gréa had understood the importance of this factor for the life of the Christian Community, and particularly for the apostolate as well as for priestly spirituality. As forthright a defender of the Pope's primacy and infallibility as he was during the period of the Vatican Council, Dom Gréa had written so much on the episcopacy that he earned the title " theologian of the local Church. " [1] He appears in the role of a prophet when he wrote to one of his spiritual sons : " The nineteenth century was the century of the Papacy and the Universal Church. It was first of all necessary that the pre-eminent position held by the Supreme Pontiff be brought to light. The twentieth century will be the century of the local Church. The time will soon come when the true mission of the episcopacy, in union with the Head of the Church and in submission to his authority, will be understood by both clergy and faithful alike. " [2] Over the course of centuries the doctrine of the episcopacy has weathered many storms not unlike those weathered by the doctrine of the primacy. Even though the Vatican Council did not have sufficient time to consider directly questions relating to the episcopacy, a number of the views set forth there served to point out the important aspects of this question. [3] Certain reactions to the Council, especially in Germany, as we shall see, led Pope Pius IX himself to correct some of the excessive interpretations regarding papal primacy. [4] This was a great source of encouragement for those who were attempting to promote a greater theological awareness of the mission and the authority of the bishops as successors of the apostles.

We should not consider this an innovation. The eighteenth century, and even more so the nineteenth century, tended to

---

[1] R. Aubert, *op. cit.*, p. 453.

[2] Text cited by Msgr. E. Guerry, *op. cit.*, p. 50.

[3] T. Granderath, *Histoire du concile du Vatican*, French trans. 3 vols. (Brussels 1908-19). See especially J. P. Torell, *La Théologie de l'épiscopat au premier concile du Vatican* (Paris 1961).

[4] On this entire question see O. Rousseau, " La vraie valeur de l'Episcopat d'après d'importants documents de 1875, " *Irénikon*, Vol. XXIX (1956), pp. 121-42.

describe the bishop's rights in strict canonical terms and to treat the relations between the bishop and his priests solely from the aspect of the jurisdiction exercised by him and the obedience owed him.   There is no need to go far back into the past to discover a number of important writings on the theology of the episcopacy. [1]   Although Berullian spirituality is based on the contemplation of the great mysteries of the Trinity and the Incarnation, its greatest exponents speak eloquently of the fatherhood of the bishop and the relations existing between him and his priests.   Olier wrote :

> In the same manner as God begot His Son and became a Father to Him, and carried Him, so to speak, in His own womb as if He were His Mother, nourishing Him with the very same substance with which He had begotten Him, so it is with the bishop, who, like a divine Father, in the Church begets children in his womb, and as a Mother, nourishes them with the food of divine life. [2]

Our present-day writers, because of the great concern that they show for the reappraisal of the bishop's mission, may be said to be re-echoing the sentiments expressed by the great sixteenth century reformers and by the Fathers of the Council of Trent. The work of Msgr. Jedin, professor of Church History at Bonn University, entitled *The Bishop in the Pastoral Tradition of the 16th Century* need only be read in order to convince one of this. In this work we read that the Catholic Reform of Trent was aimed at a complete interior renewal of the Church and that this objective appears nowhere more clearly than in the great stress placed by Trent upon the role of the bishop.   At this time there were quite a few treatises and exhortations on the nature and duties of the bishop's pastoral office as well as a number of biographies of outstanding prelates that were being published.   However, the ideal had been realized to a great

---

[1] Even during the nineteenth century, there were solid dogmatic treatises on the episcopate.   For example, the 83rd conference of Fr. Monsabré on " *Le générateur du sacerdoce* " : J. M. L. MONSABRÉ, *Conférences de Notre-Dame* (Carême, 1886), 7th ed. (Paris 1900), pp. 173-214.

[2] Cited by P. BROUTIN, *La Réforme pastorale, op. cit.*, Vol. II, p. 252.

extent in such outstanding bishops as Charles Borromeo, Francis de Sales and many more.

Father Broutin declares :

> With the firm conviction that comes from possessing the truth, the Church, at Trent, went to the very core of the supernatural mystery of its hierarchical constitution. All the major themes such as the apostolate, the episcopacy, the primacy and fullness of the priesthood, the fatherhood of the bishop, and his pastoral mission were treated and blended together into a perfectly coherent synthesis.

This resulted in a " tremendous step forward in the discipline and the theology of the episcopacy. " [1]

* * *

In 1946 there appeared a short but extremely valuable treatise, entitled *De l'évêque*, by Canon A. G. Martimort. At first it seemed to be an innovation, and it is indeed interesting to observe that Cardinal Saliège expressed in his enthusiastic preface to this work a desire to have the theological sources of this subject more closely investigated. [2] There has recently been a renewed interest manifested in the theological tract *De Episcopo*. Interest in this question has continued to grow, and it is a frequently discussed subject in the Church today. This should be a source of great encouragement not only to those concerned with priestly spirituality, but also to those currently engaged in the leading movements of the Church. Consider the effect that this will have upon the ecumenical movement since, as we know, the East has always placed great stress upon the role of the individual bishop and the importance

---

[1] P. BROUTIN, *L'évêque dans la tradition pastorale du XVIe siècle*. French adaptation of Msgr. H. Jedin's *Das Bischofsideal der Katholischen Reformation* (Bruges-Paris 1953), p. 132.

[2] A. G. MARTIMORT, *De l'évêque* (Paris 1946).

of the local Church. [1] It is also extremely encouraging to the Church's missionary activity which is seeking to establish dioceses in every part of the world by first establishing the hierarchy and then eventually nominating members of the native clergy as bishops. [2] This will also have an effect upon the liturgical movement since the bishops will come to realize " that a dynamic pastoral liturgy ties in completely with the nature of the episcopacy because it is derived solely from the bishop and performed in his name. " [3] Consider also the effect that this will have upon Catholic Action and upon all the various lay apostolic movements whose members the bishop is expected to guide through the many real difficulties involved in the apostolate. [4] We should add that the proof for what we have been saying is to be found in the fact that the attacks of the Church's enemies against the Shepherds of the Christian people have never before been as violent and insidious as they are today. [5] Indeed this is the age of bishops! So true is this today that we can speak of " a movement springing from within the Church which is attempting to revive the original notion of the episcopacy. " [6]

---

[1] J. MEYENDORFF, " L'Eglise et la communauté des fidèles dans l'Eglise Orthodoxe," *L'évêque et son Eglise : Cahiers de la Pierre-qui-vire* (Paris 1955), pp. 94-103; O. ROUSSEAU, *La vraie valeur de l'épiscopat, loc. cit.*, pp. 128-29.' Of particular interest are the reactions of Orthodox theologians, notably F. Florovsky, to the announcement of the coming council. See O. ROUSSEAU, " Le prochain concile et l'unité de l'Eglise, " *Irénikon*, Vol. XXXII (1959), pp. 318-23.

[2] Pope PIUS XII, Enc. *Evangelii Praecones* (June 11, 1951), *AAS*, Vol. XLIII (1951), p. 507. Pope John XXIII, Enc. *Princeps Pastorum* (Nov. 28, 1959), *AAS*, Vol. LI (1959), p. 837.

[3] " Qu'est-ce qu'un évêque? " *Paroisse et liturgie*, Vol. XL (1938), p. 310.

[4] Pope PIUS XII, *Discourse to the Bishops* (May 31, 1954), *AAS*, Vol. XLVI (1954), p. 314.

[5] Msgr. M. KELLER, *Das Bischofsamt in der Kirche* (Münster 1955), p. 4.

[6] Editorial of *Irénikon*, Vol. XLVI (1956), p. 3.

Chapter 4

Some Conclusions and
the Teaching of Recent Popes

At the end of this historical survey, it seems worthwhile for us to enumerate the main features of clerical spirituality as set forth during the last few centuries :

1) Union to Our Lord Jesus Christ, especially in the mysteries of His priesthood;
2) A more precise understanding of the spiritual treasures of the Sacrament of Holy Orders;
3) The collaboration of every priest of second rank in the work of the bishop;
4) The stress placed on the pastoral ministry by the Council of Trent and, as we shall see, by recent Popes;
5) The added obligation to seek sanctity because of the great powers of the priesthood and the duties inherent in this state;
6) The great importance of the duties of the priestly and diocesan state of life in insuring this sanctification;
7) The realization by priests of the need to draw their inspiration from the Gospel and therefore to live, according to their state, at least in the spirit of the evangelical counsels which is also the spirit of the Beatitudes.

* * *

The light shed by Church history is quite valuable since it allows us to interpret faithfully the Church's point of view. We are not attempting merely to set forth our own views :

Mea doctrina non est mea. [1]   We must always be particularly attentive to the teaching of him who is, in the Church, the " Column and foundation of truth, " [2] and who, despite whatever name he chooses to take, is nevertheless the Pope, the successor of St. Peter.   The Popes have always shown great interest in the priesthood; but recent Popes have repeatedly exhibited this interest to such an extent that Bishop Veuillot recently was able to publish two volumes containing more than 90 documents on the priesthood culled from the pontificates of Leo XIII, Pius X, Benedict XI, Pius XI and Pius XII.   Since it was written nine years ago, this work naturally does not include the later documents of Pius XII and the recent writings of John XXIII. [3]

Cardinal Montini has written that all of these documents clearly give " eloquent and moving testimony to the paternal, enlightened and sustained concern which the supreme teaching authority of the Church has shown for the Catholic clergy. This work comes at the right time, since it brings the answer to that pressing problem of our own day : what is the true notion of the priesthood?   Under the exterior pressure of modern needs, and the interior stimulus which comes from the incessant activity of the mind and the action of divine grace, the answer to that question is being urgently sought. " [4]

Three of the more important documents comprise a charter of the priestly life : the exhortation to the clergy *Haerent Animo* of St. Pius X (August 4, 1908), the Encyclical *Ad Catholici Sacerdotii Fastigium* of Pius XI (December 20, 1932) and the

---

[1] Jn 7, 16.

[2] 1 Tm 3, 15.

[3] Msgr. Pierre VEUILLOT, *The Catholic Priesthood* (Newman Press : Westminster, Md. 1955).   For the last years of Pius XII one will find some material in the article of E. BERGH, " Pie XII et le sacerdoce, " *Nouvelle Revue théologique*, Vol. LXXXI (1959), pp. 3-24.   Above all, in the collection : *Documents pontificaux de Sa Sainteté Pie XII*, published first by R. KOTHEN and then by Msgr. S. DELACROIX, successively at Louvain, Paris and Saint-Maurice (Switzerland) from 1948 on.

[4] Card. J. MONTINI.   Preface to the book of Msgr. P. Veuillot cited above pp. XIII-XIV.

Apostolic Exhortation *Menti Nostrae* of Pius XII (September 25, 1950). [1]

These documents have greater relevance for diocesan priests than for religious. Cardinal Van Roey felt no hesitation in writing :

> The priesthood that they consider — and everything points to this being true — is the secular priesthood; the priest that they have in view is the priest who is subject to his bishop and exercises under his direction the diocesan ministry although there are certain primary considerations, such as the exalted dignity of the priesthood, which equally apply to religious priests. [2]

As we will later see, Pope Pius XII went to the very heart of the most delicate problems of priestly spirituality particularly those applying to the secular clergy. It was our pleasure to be able to discuss this subject with Pius XII and to receive some valuable insights from him regarding it. It was shortly after one of these audiences that we received a *Note on the Perfection of the Secular Clergy*. [3] It has been said that the direct approach taken in the note by the Pontiff will certainly lead to a better understanding of the nature of both the priesthood and the religious life. [4] In the course of this treatment many other documents will be cited. We have already sufficiently stressed to our own priests, the importance of the Discourse to the Second General Council of the States of Perfection given in December, 1957. [5] More than any other Pontiff, Pope Pius XII

---

[1] See *AAS*, Vol. XLI (1908), pp. 555-77; Vol. XXVIII (1936), pp. 5-53; Vol. XLII (1950), pp. 652-704.

[2] Card. J. E. VAN ROEY, " Le prêtre diocésain d'après les encycliques pontificales, " *Collectanea Mechliniensia*, Vol. XXII (1952), pp. 565-86; Vol. XXIII (1953), pp. 5-33. The same view is held by Card. M. CEREJEIRA, " L'unité du clergé séculier et du clergé régulier, " *La Documentation catholique*, Vol. XLIX (1952), col. 282.

[3] This *Note* was published in our *Lettres Pastorales*, Vol. II (1952), pp. 121-23. It appears in the collection of Msgr. P. VEUILLOT, *op. cit.*, Vol. II, pp. 241-44. It may also be found in Appendix I of this volume.

[4] J. C. FENTON, " Priestly Perfection and the ' Status Perfectionis ', " *The American Ecclesiastical Review*, Vol. CXXVIII (1953), p. 52.

[5] Pope PIUS XII, *Discourse to the Second General Congress on the States of Perfection* (Dec. 9, 1957), *AAS*, Vol. L (1958), pp. 34-43.

attempted to stress the importance of the episcopacy in the
Church by placing great stress on obedience to the bishop and
by showing that in a diocese the bishop must be the center of
unity.   Truly unforgettable are the discourses that he delivered
on this subject at the time of St. Pius X's canonization. [1]   How
truly significant also is the account of the audience that Bishop
Théas of Tarbes and Lourdes had with Pius XII on December 2,
1944.   The bishop describes it as follows :

> It was during that period in France when a wave of
> antiepiscopalism had arisen.   During the course of a visit
> to Rome at this time, I sensed the great anxiety of the Holy
> Father over the opposition which certain French bishops
> were experiencing.   The Pope spoke to me of the
> episcopacy in terms of great trust, respect and esteem :
> Never before had I heard such sentiments expressed.
> " We place all of our supreme authority behind the defense
> and protection of the authority and rights of the bishops
> and also strongly emphasize the submission which is owed
> to them. "   On several occasions during the audience, the
> Holy Father quoted from the *Acts of the Apostles* : " The
> Holy Spirit has placed bishops over the government of
> the Church of God. "   The Church cannot exist without
> obedience to and respect for her bishops.   The Holy Father
> stressed, moreover, that the type of submission required
> is a submission of love.   Whoever does not love his bishop
> cannot obey him as he ought. [2]

It is quite clear that the pontificate of John XXIII was
inspired by the very same principles.   As proof of this, we
need only refer to the study begun in 1906 by Father Angelo
Roncalli which was recently published in the *Fontes Ambrosiani*
of Milan.   This work, in five volumes, is devoted to the
apostolic visitation made by St. Charles Borromeo to Bergamo
in 1573.   The final volume appeared in 1959. [3]

---

[1] Pope Pius XII, *Discourse to the Bishops* (May 31, 1954) and (Nov. 2, 1954), *AAS*, Vol. XLVI (1954), pp. 313-17, pp. 666-77.

[2] Msgr. P. M. Théas, *L'évêque dans l'Eglise* (Toulouse 1953).

[3] *Gli Atti della Visita Apostolica de S. Carlo Borromeo* (1575), 2 vols. in 5 tomes (Florence 1936-59).

As a proof of Cardinal Roncalli's pastoral zeal in the Diocese of Venice, we need only read the discourse that he delivered to his priests on the occasion of the diocesan synod in November, 1959. He refers there enthusiastically to *L'Évêque* by Bishop Guerry. [1] As further proof, we need only mention the many allocutions new Pope John and particularly his recent Encyclical on the Curé of Ars. Like the aforementioned documents of St. Pius X, Pius XI and Pius XII on the priesthood, we may also claim that Pope John wrote this one especially for secular priests who, like John Vianney, belong to the diocesan clergy. The Sovereign Pontiff clearly indicated this when he declared to the bishops of the world :

> And you, Venerable Brethren, will easily see that in this letter our concern and our thoughts are especially directed to men in Holy Orders, who are certainly our most beloved sons, and especially those engaged in the pastoral ministry. We wish to have them consider attentively the marvelous example of this holy man, who once shared in their own priestly ministry and who now is constituted as their heavenly patron. [2]

---

[1] *Acts of the 30th Diocesan Synod of Venice, Discourse of Nov. 25, 1957.* The text has been reproduced in *La Documentation catholique*, Vol. LV (1958), cols. 1619-24.

[2] Pope JOHN XXIII, Enc. *Sacerdotii Nostrii Primordia* (July 31, 1959), *AAS* Vol. LI (1959), p. 547.

2

The Bishop

Chapter 5

The Bishop in the Light
of the Faith and Teaching
of the Church

" Bishops, " according to the Code of Canon Law, " are successors of the apostles and by divine right are placed over individual Churches which they govern, with ordinary power, under the authority of the Roman Pontiff. [1] " As J. F. Noubel, a noted canonist, says, the juridical life of the Church depends, as does its mystical life, on the divine positive law established for all time by Christ. Institutions will come and go as will their legal systems, but the divine constitution of the Church always remains fundamentally and pre-eminently canonical. It is constantly necessary to return to

> this basic legal system, given once and for all; an expression of divine wisdom, it is, we venture to say, a juridic marvel. What is said of Christ, its source, may also be used to describe the Church's legal system. *Virtus de illo exibat et sanabat omnes* (Lk 6, 19). The legal force of the divine positive law, and especially the constitutional and administrative law derived from the precepts of Christ, the Founder of the Church, is backed up by divine authority since its purpose is to provide for the very transmission of divine life. [2]

We will now examine in greater detail the Church's teaching on the episcopacy and bishops.

[1] *Codex Juris Canonici*, can. 329, § 1.
[2] J. F. Noubel, " L'Eglise diocésaine, sa construction juridique actuelle, " *L'Année canonique*, Vol. I (Paris 1952), p. 142.

* *
*

"All power in heaven and on earth has been given to me.
Go therefore and make disciples of all nations, baptizing them
in the name of the Father, and of the Son, and of the Holy
Spirit teaching them to observe all that I have commanded you,
and behold I am with you all days even unto the consummation
of the world." [1]

This important text should be recalled whenever the Gospel
is read. The Messianic mission of the Son of God is perpetuated
for all times through the mission of the apostles. Scriptural
references regarding this abound. If the proper distinctions
are made, it can even be said that the apostles are, like Jesus,
the foundation of the Church. [2] Like Jesus, they are the light
of the world. [3] Like Jesus, they are the shepherds of the Christian
people [4] and the door through which the flock will enter into
the Holy City. [5] Like Jesus, they also possess the keys of the
kingdom. [6] Certainly, these collective attributes are ordinarily
used to describe the personal and sovereign rights of Peter,
the Head of the Apostles and the Vicar of Jesus Christ.

The fundamental and first thesis of the tract *De Episcopis*
is that bishops are, by divine right, the successors of the apostles.
"Bishops," wrote Pius XII, "are to be honored by the Christian
people as the successors of the apostles by divine right." [7]
"It is particularly necessary," Leo XIII wrote, "that the
authority of Peter permanently reside in the Supreme Pontiff,
and thus, since bishops are successors of the apostles, they
thereby derive from them their ordinary power, *horum potestatem
ordinarium haereditatis capiunt*. Consequently, the episcopal order
pertains to the very constitution of the Church, *ita ut intiman*

---

[1] Mt 28, 18-19.
[2] Eph 2, 20-22. Compare 1 Cor 3, 11 and 1 Pt 2, 4-8.
[3] Mt 5, 14. Compare with Jn 8, 12.
[4] 1 Pt 5, 2. Compare with Jn 10, 11-15; 21, 15-17; 1 Pt 5, 4.
[5] Ap 21, 14. Compare with Jn 10, 9.
[6] Mt 18, 18. Compare with Ap 1, 18; 3, 7.
[7] Pope Pius XII, Enc. *Mystici Corporis* (June 29, 1943), *AAS*, Vol. XXXV (1943), p. 212.

ecclesiae constitutionem ordo episcoporum necessario attingat. " [1] This belief has been professed by the Church from the earliest times. At the center of its unity in space and time there is the special mission of the bishops united together by means of the *Ordo Episcoporum* which, in the plan of God, succeeded the *Collegium Apostolorum*. The writings of the Apostolic Fathers, particularly those of St. Ignatius of Antioch, bear witness to this as do also the earliest liturgical texts, [2] the history of the early councils [3] and the laws and customs current in the early Christian community. The Council of Trent cited this constant tradition of the Church regarding the episcopacy when it solemnly declared : " The bishops are successors of the apostles and as such belong to the Hierarchical Order in a very special way since they were constituted by the Holy Spirit to govern the Church of God. " [4] These first principles serve as a firm basis for the theology of the episcopacy, upon which the teaching of Pius XII was so often based. [5]

The Council of Trent also has defined as a truth of faith that bishops are superior to priests. It condemned those who taught that bishops are not superior to priests, or that they do not possess the power to confirm and to ordain, or that the power that they do possess is common to bishops and priests alike. [6] The conciliar texts give no further details. At any rate, the superiority of bishops over priests is particularly

---

[1] Pope Leo XIII, Enc. *Satis Cognitum* (June 29, 1896), *AAS*, Vol. XXVIII (1895-96), p. 732.

[2] A. Béraudy, " Les effets de l'Ordre dans les Préfaces d'ordination du Sacramentaire léonien, " *La tradition sacerdotale, Etudes sur le sacerdoce* (Le Puy 1959), pp. 96-97. On the doctrinal richness of the Leonine Sacramentary see A. Rose, " Aspects de l'épiscopat selon les prières consécratoires du sacre des évêques et des ordinations, " *Revue monastique*, 156 (1959), pp. 81-92.

[3] H. Marot, " Conciles anténicéens et conciles œcuméniques, " *Le Concile et les conciles* (Chevetogne-Paris 1960), pp. 19 ff.

[4] *Concilium Tridentinum*, sess. 23, cap. 4 : Denz., No. 960. Compare *Codex Juris Canonici*, can. 329.

[5] Cf. the later writings of Pius XII : *Discourse to the Bishops* (May 31, 1954), *loc. cit.*, p. 314; *Exhortation to the Participants of the Second World Congress of the Lay Apostolate* (Oct. 5, 1957), *AAS*, Vol. XXXIX (1957), pp. 924-25; Enc. *Fidei Donum* (April 21, 1957), *AAS*, Vol. XLIX (1957), pp. 235-37.

[6] *Concilium Tridentinum*, sess. 23, can. 7. Denz., No. 967.

evident in the administration of Confirmation and Holy Orders.
It is worth noting that the above-mentioned condemnation was
given at the time when the Fathers of the Council were
considering the Sacrament of Holy Orders and recognized the
privileged position enjoyed by bishops with regard to this
sacrament.

Precisely how does the Church view Episcopal Consecration?
It is true that the sacramentality of the episcopacy has
never been defined.   In fact, the Council of Trent endeavored
to avoid any consideration of this question.   Yet, St. Robert
Bellarmine did not hesitate to teach, as a truth of faith, the
existence of a special sacramental character in the episcopacy.
Since the great majority of theologians ever since then have seen
fit to consider this view as theologically certain, we may conclude
that this doctrine has made great progress during the last four
centuries. [1]   Despite recent controversies and the unfortunate
recriminations produced thereby, the sacramental character of
Episcopal Consecration appears more and more to be a truth
firmly rooted in Catholic Tradition.   Some of the best theologians
are now espousing the view of Bellarmine.   In my opinion,
this doctrine warrants definition. [2]

* *
*

We will now consider in greater detail the relation that exists
between Episcopal Consecration and the prerogatives of the
bishops as regards : apostolic succession, the fullness of the
priesthood, their doctrinal and pastoral mission, jurisdiction over
a particular flock and their relations to the Pope and the Universal
Church.

Theologians have always agreed that Episcopal Consecration
imparts the ability to exercise the fullness of the priesthood,

[1] M. Schmaus, " Bischof, " *Lexicon für Theologie und Kirche*, 2nd ed. (Fribourg 1958),
col. 493.
[2] See especially J. Lécuyer, " Le sacrement de l'épiscopat, " *Divinitas*, Vol. I (1957)
p. 246.

but this is so only because Episcopal Consecration is truly sacramental. Since the sacramentality of Episcopal Consecration is certain, instead of stressing the juridical qualifications of a bishop, we should rather stress that, by virtue of Episcopal Consecration, the bishop receives a new aptitude, a special charism, or more precisely, a sacramental *character*.

In considering apostolic succession, Franzelin wrote : *Successio, haec perennis non, sicut in veteri Testamento, generatione carnali, sed generatione spirituali propagatur per sacramentalem manuum impositionem.* [1] It goes without saying that apostolic succession is frustrated in its authority when Episcopal Consecration is illicitly conferred. In other words, the bishops may only exercise their rights of apostolic succession as long as they are in union with the Head of the Episcopal Order, the Pope, the successor of St. Peter. The late Holy Father pointed this out quite forcefully in June, 1958 when he considered the case of the Chinese bishops who had been consecrated without the approval of Rome. [2] However, such an illicit consecration will fully produce its effects in the meantime and even prior to the Supreme Shepherd's receiving the schismatic bishops back into union with the Church.

* *

By incorporation into the Episcopal Order every bishop is a member of the Hierarchical College of the Universal Church. Yet, it does not follow that he is thereby the head and shepherd of a definite flock. In order to lay claim to this, a bishop must possess a definite title to govern a particular church. [3] However,

---

[1] Card. J. B. FRANZELIN, *De Ecclesia Christi* (Rome 1887), p. 262.

[2] Pope Pius XII, Enc. *Ad Apostolorum Principis* (June 29, 1958), *AAS*, Vol. L (1958), pp. 601-14.

[3] The text in the Code of Canon Law (can. 329, § 1) already cited (p. 59) specifically distinguishes between apostolic succession and the governing of a diocese. The term *title* can cause difficulty because of the division of bishops into *titular* and *residential* in present-day practice. Actually, all bishops receive a title at their nomination; but those who are only titular are assigned, as it were, to churches which no longer exist, and thus they do not possess a flock of their own. On this question see J. F. NOUBEL, *op. cit.*, pp. 145-46; J. CHELODI— P. CIPROTTI, *Jus Canonicum : De Personis*, 3rd ed. (Rome 1942), p. 289.

the jurisdiction resulting from this title is closely bound up with Episcopal Consecration. Thus Dom Gréa declares :

> Whenever it is given, this title is not derived solely from the fact that the bishop is a member of the Episcopal Order in union with the Supreme Shepherd. Rather, it extends back to the time of the bishop's consecration, at which time it is like a fruit contained germinally in the roots and branches. [1]

Episcopal jurisdiction is firmly rooted in the nature of divine institutions and in the Sacrament of the Hierarchy. This fact must be well understood.

The episcopacy and apostolic succession were divinely instituted for the purpose of governing the Church. The Code of Canon Law states that the Sacrament of Holy Orders was instituted for the governing of the faithful, *ad fidelium regimen* and to provide for divine worship, *et cultus divini ministerium*. [2] The Council of Trent declares : " The bishops, successors of the apostles, were set up, as the Apostle says, to govern the Church of God. " [3] From the beginning, the bishop's mission was conceived as that of a *pastor*, a *prelate* and an *overseer*. These expressions refer more to the powers of governing and carrying out the pastoral ministry than to the powers of Orders. Since it is a matter of faith that bishops are the successors of the apostles, it therefore follows that the episcopal character sets a man apart for the purpose of governing the Church.

As we have already stated, there is no reason to conclude that each bishop must be at the head of a diocese and exercise ordinary episcopal jurisdiction over a particular section of the

---

[1] Dom GRÉA, *op. cit.*, p. 288. J. Creusen says also : " Cum potestate ista connectitur potestas saltem radicalis... regendi populi Dei " (*Epitome Juris Canonici*, 6th ed., Vol. II, Rome 1940, pp. 157-8).

[2] *Codex Juris Canonici*, can. 948. While canon 107 only makes the distinction between clerics and the laity, canon 948 determines the twofold purpose of the hierarchy before treating the question of Orders. See C. DE CLERCQ, " Des Sacrements, " R. NAZ, *Traité de droit canonique* Vol. II (Paris 1947), p. 273.

[3] *Concilium Tridentinum*, sess. 23, cap. 4 : DENZ., no. 960. The council is treating of bishops in the theological sense apart from an exegesis of the text from the Acts of the Apostles.

Church. By instituting the episcopacy for the government of the Church, Christ gave supreme and monarchical authority to Peter and His successors. This Church, aided by the Holy Spirit, who leads it towards the perfect understanding of revealed truth, demonstrates, by its history, that the Pope can allow a situation to exist in which bishops function without possessing their own flocks, and that he can even entrust, for a time, the government of a church to a priest who does not possess the episcopal dignity. Such is the case of prefects apostolic, apostolic administrators and residential bishops prior to their consecration. [1]

As numerous as vicars apostolic are today, we know that they only exercise their authority in the name of the Pope, as his vicars. This system began in the seventeenth century when the Popes saw fit to reserve the governing of mission territories to themselves. [2] Yet, this is only a temporary measure since, as has already been pointed out, Rome seeks to establish the Hierarchy as quickly as possible in these countries by creating dioceses and entrusting them to residential bishops. [3] The importance of this step in mission countries is not to be found solely in the fact that these dioceses now possess their own Shepherds to govern them according to the provisions of the monarchical episcopate. What is especially important is that the grouping together of these dioceses into ecclesiastical provinces allows the activities of the bishops of the area to be more closely coordinated. Isn't it true that a number of recent apostolic constitutions have spoken of the establishment of the *Order of Bishops?* One of these texts reads as follows : *In Unione Federali Birmana Ecclesiarum atque Episcoporum Ordo constituitur quae est Episcopalis Hierarchia.* [4] Father Gy writes regarding

---

[1] F. WERNZ—P. VIDAL, *Jus Canonicum*, Vol. II, *De Personis* (Rome 1943), pp. 719-21.

See J. CREUSEN, *op. cit.*, Vol. I, 7 th ed. (1949), p. 326.

[3] See especially Card. J. E. VAN ROEY, " L'Episcopat et la Papauté, " *Au Service de l'Eglise*, Vol. I (1939), p. 180; " Eeuwfeest van de kerkelijke Hiërarchie in Nederland " *ibid.*, Vol. VIII (1955), pp. 343-62.

[4] Constitution *Dum Alterna Vicissitudine* (Jan. 1, 1955), *AAS*, Vol. XLVII (1955), p. 263. See the earlier Constitution *Quemadmodum ad nos* (May 25, 1853), *AAS*, Vol. XLV (1953), p. 705.

this subject : " Although in some mission countries there may be a few bishops presiding over certain dioceses, it cannot be maintained, however, that they comprise an *Ordo Episcoporum* in the same way as this exists in Italy, France and in those countries where the Hierarchy is established. " [1] Is the tenor of these Roman documents seeking to emphasize the collegial and organic nature of the Episcopal Order, as Father Gy contends? Who can say? However, it is quite true that this manner of speaking is certainly in keeping with the sentiments currently being expressed by a number of recognized theologians.

* * *

Some may wonder whether the system of the monarchical episcopate is based on divine law. It is true that the diocesan organization, as we know it today, is governed by the Code of Canon Law. [2] However, in this particular regard, we might well ask if the legislator hasn't simply legalized an existing situation. Papal documents are silent on this matter. Although they never fail to point out that bishops are, by divine right, the successors of the apostles and that, as such, they are endowed with the powers of teaching, ruling and sanctifying the Church, these same documents never consider the divine institution of the monarchical episcopate, the system according to which a single bishop governs a definite part of the Church's flock. This silence is especially significant in view of the recent Encyclical, *Fidei Donum*, in which Pius XII clearly affirmed

---

[1] P. M. GY, " Remarques sur le vocabulaire antique du sacerdoce chrétien, " *Etudes sur le sacrement de l'Ordre (Lex Orandi,* 22), (Paris 1957), pp. 132-33.

[2] *Codex Juris Canonici,* can. 329, § 1.   In commenting on this canon MATTHAEUS CONTE A CORONATA writes : " If in this canon the Code says that bishops by divine institution are to be appointed to their own churches, this must be understood correctly. It is not as if a local organization, which exists ' de facto ' in the Church, were of divine institution. It means that bishops, by the power of their consecration are ' radically ' and ' aptitudinally ' qualified to rule the church assigned to them by the Roman Pontiff. " (*Institutiones Juris Canonici,* 2nd ed., Rome 1939, Vol. I, p. 468, no. 3).   Likewise, E. REGATILLO, *Institutiones Juris Canonici,* 4th ed. Vol. I (1951), p. 317.

the divine institution of the Pope's universal jurisdiction. [1] However, one must be particularly careful not to conclude hastily that the monarchical episcopate was not instituted by Christ. We must also bear in mind that ordinarily Popes do not consider questions which are still being freely discussed by theologians.

Do early Christian writings shed any light on this matter? Unfortunately, they are not as clear as we would like them to be. Do they permit us to maintain that from the beginning the episcopate was always and everywhere monarchical? Would it not have been possible for a particular church, such as Alexandria, for example, to have been under the joint direction of several bishops? [2] At any rate, St. Ignatius of Antioch apparently knew of only one bishop for each church; and he based his spiritual doctrine of the episcopacy precisely on this unity. How can one explain his manner of speaking if this notion of the bishop as the center of unity had not been perfectly realized by the end of the first century, at least in Asia Minor? The New Testament itself directs us to such an understanding of the monarchical episcopate.

It is consistent with the spirit of the Gospels to combine, in the working of the Church, unity and plurality, the universality of the Church's mission and its mission to establish the Church on the local level, the substantial identity of the message of Christ and the manner in which it is presented to men. Although Christ placed a superior, His own Vicar, over the apostles, He nevertheless commissioned each one of them to go forth into every corner of the earth to establish a Church and minister to men. The figures of the *Shepherd* and the *Watcher*, found especially in the pastoral epistles, suggest the idea of a special charism " for the establishment and organization of local communities rather than for a circuit riding type of missionary

---

[1] J. LÉCUYER, " La dignité apostolique de l'épiscopat, " *Les Missions catholiques*, Vol. XC (1958), pp. 48-49.

[2] See especially J. COLSON, *Les fonctions ecclésiales aux deux premiers siècles* (Paris 1954). See also his recent article " Evangélisation et collégialité apostolique, " *Nouvelle Revue théologique* Vol. LXXII (1960), pp. 349-72 which attempts to number among the first successors of the apostles certain itinerant preachers not attached to any particular Church.

apostolate. " [1]   In an extremely penetrating study that was
recently published, Karl Rahner maintains that the *localization*
of the Christian Mystery is an essential characteristic of the
celebration of the Eucharist and that the Church, a permanent
and universal social institution, is intended, by its very nature,
to function in a determined place.   To use the expression
of Rahner, the Church truly becomes an *event* (ereignis) and,
in the full sense of that term, is actualized in the local church
and fully exercises its spiritual activity, thereby manifesting
its historical spatio-temporal character. [2]   This is why the
establishment of a native Hierarchy, whose members are more
greatly aware of the problems of their people, is such an important
event in a mission country. [3]

It is not surprising then that history attests to the early
existence of the monarchical episcopate.   The earliest sacramentaries, whose tradition is expressed in our present-day Roman
Pontifical, view Episcopal Consecration as the conferment of
the power to rule a particular Church : *Tribuas ei, Domine,
Cathedram episcopalem*, the consecrators say, *ad regendam Ecclesiam
tuam et plebem sibi commissam*. [4]   The practice still remains of
never consecrating a bishop without giving him a title to a
particular diocese even though the titular diocese no longer
exists.   History, liturgy and law, as well as the constant practice
of the Church, clearly attest that Episcopal Consecration entails
the governing of a definite flock.

Another problem must now be considered.   Does jurisdiction come to the bishops directly from Christ or directly
from the Pope?   The Council of Trent did not give a solution

---

[1] P. BROUTIN, " Le Pasteur d'Eglise au cours de l'histoire, " *Le Courrier de Mondaye*
Feb. 1957), No. 49, p. 3.

[2] K. RAHNER, *The Episcopate and The Primacy* (Herder and Herder, 1962) p. 27.

[3] Pius XII said that this was the chief purpose of the missions. Enc. *Evangelii
praecones loc. cit.*, p. 507. Likewise, Pope JOHN XXIII, Enc. *Princeps Pastorum AAS*, Vol. LI
(1959), p. 337; *Radio message to the Catholics of Africa* (June 5, 1960), *AAS*, Vol. LII (1960),
p. 476. In this last document we see his concern to give the Churches of Africa ' pastors
of their own flesh and blood. '

[4] A. BÉRAUDY, " Les effets de l'Ordre dans les Préfaces d'ordination du Sacramentaire
léonien, " *La Tradition sacerdotale, op. cit.*, pp. 94-5.

to this question. The majority of the Fathers of the Council were, apparently, favorable to the second opinion. However, in view of the declarations of Pius XII, it appears that the issue has been settled. [1] In 1943, the Encyclical *Mystici Corporis* stated : " If they enjoy ordinary power of jurisdiction, this power is immediately communicated to them by the Sovereign Pontiff. " [2] The Encyclical *Ad Sinarum Gentem* (1953) put it this way. " The power of jurisdiction, which is conferred upon the Supreme Pontiff directly by divine law, flows to the bishops by the same law, but only through the successor of St. Peter, to whom not only the simple faithful, but even all the bishops must be constantly subject, and to whom they must be bound by obedience and the bond of unity. " [3] Msgr. Journet observes :

> To say that the bishops' jurisdiction comes down to them from the Sovereign Pontiff is not to say that it comes down to them by the mere will of the latter or in virtue of a free canonical provision . . . . Their jurisdiction, although fully subordinated to that of the Sovereign Pontiff, nevertheless belongs to them by divine law, not merely by ecclesiastical law, in an ordinary and proper way, not in a delegated and vicarious way, as an indispensable degree of the Hierarchy, not as an institution revocable by the Sovereign Pontiff. [4]

The universal and supreme jurisdiction of the Bishop of Rome in no way interferes with the subordinate and local jurisdiction of other bishops.

[1] A. MICHEL, " Les décrets du Concile de Trente, " in C. J. HEFELE—H. LECLERCQ, *Histoire des Conciles*, Vol. X, Part 1 (Paris 1938), pp. 473-93. Eng. trans. (Edinburgh: T. and T. Clark, 1872-96), 5 vols.

[2] Pope PIUS XII, Enc. *Mystici Corporis, loc. cit.*, p. 212.

[3] Pope PIUS XII, Enc. *Ad Sinarum Gentem,* (Oct. 7, 1957), *AAS*, Vol. XLVII (1955), p. 9.

[4] C. JOURNET, *Church of the Word Incarnate*, Vol. I : *The Apostolic Hierarchy* (New York : Sheed and Ward, 1954), p. 405. This recalls the neat distinction advanced by P. Laynez at the Council of Trent : " The power of jurisdiction of the bishops, *considered in general*, is immediately of divine right. But this is not the question. It is rather a question of the power of jurisdiction of each local bishop. Now, there is no doubt that this power derives immediately from the universal jurisdiction of the Sovereign Pontiff. " (A. Michel, *op. cit.*, p. 474).

According to the Council of the Vatican, there is no reason why the authority of the Sovereign Pontiff should interfere with the bishops' ordinary and immediate power of jurisdiction since they have been commissioned by the Holy Spirit and have succeeded the apostles as the rulers of the flocks entrusted to their care. On the contrary, the episcopal power is affirmed, strengthened and defended by the Supreme and Universal Shepherd. [1]

Leo XIII likewise states : " Although the authority of the bishops is neither complete, universal nor supreme, they should not be considered merely as vicars of the Roman Pontiffs since they possess an authority proper to them alone and truly fulfill their role as prelates of the people they govern. " [2] " The bishops, " according to Cardinal Van Roey, " are neither the vicars nor the delegates of the Sovereign Pontiff in the ordinary governing of their dioceses. They do not merely appear before their people as the representatives of the Pope, but of Christ Himself. " [3]

* *
*

On Good Friday the Church invites the faithful to pray for the Pope, " that Our God and Lord, who chose him to the Order of the Episcopacy, may preserve him in health and safety for the good of His Holy Church to govern the holy people of God. " The great dignity and awesome mission of the Sovereign Pontiff could be expressed in no more fitting a way.

[1] *Conc. Vaticanum*, sess. 4, cap. 4; DENZ., no. 1828.

[2] Pope LEO XIII, Enc. *Satis Cognitum* (June 29, 1896), *loc. cit.*, p. 732. On this matter, J. Chelodi (*op. cit.*, p. 287) writes : " Thus the episcopal office in general rests on divine right. It cannot be abolished or made subject to suppletion by the Supreme Pontiff. Nor can it be changed or restricted in its essentials. Bishops are true leaders, endowed with ordinary, not just delegated jurisdiction in the external and internal form. They are pastors of their own flock, distinct from priests and superior to them. However, as long as these substantial elements of their office remain intact, there is nothing to prevent the supreme ruler from increasing or decreasing their prerogatives or even from adding to or taking away from their delegated faculties. " Compare the words of Pope Pius XII, Enc. *Mystici Corporis, loc. cit.*, pp. 211 ff.; *Discourse to the Bishops* (1954), *loc. cit.*, p. 314.

[3] Card. J. E. VAN ROEY, *L'Episcopat et la Papauté, loc. cit.* p. 179. " Le sacerdoce d'après l'encyclique de S.S. Pie XI, " *Au service de l'Eglise*, Vol. II (1939), pp. 225-26.

Risen in the glory of His Father, Christ, Himself the Head, the Chief of His Church, governs it by means of the Hierarchy which He established.   In order to allow the salvific economy of the Incarnation to function in the temporal sphere, Christ first chose a Vicar from among the apostles and now chooses one from among the bishops.   As a successor of St. Peter, the Pope governs all the people of God as the Vicar of Jesus Christ.   The office of the Papacy does not constitue, in the hierarchy of Orders, a new and distinct rank of the episcopate. [1] The Pope is the head of his brothers, the bishops, because he represents Christ in their midst and receives directly from Him all the powers necessary for the realization of his supreme and universal mission.   Just as the Vicar General of a diocese usually remains a priest, but shares in the bishop's powers to such an extent that he forms together with him a single moral person, so the Pope, still only a bishop, shares in the powers of Christ necessary for ruling the Church and thereby becomes one with Him.   This is what is meant by his title, *Vicar of Jesus Christ* on earth. [2]   The Pope is not outside the episcopal college, but he concentrates its powers in his own person.   Father Liégé writes :

> The primacy of St. Peter was a primacy in the episcopate, *within the apostolic college*. What Christ conferred in equal measure on the twelve apostles, he gave to Peter in a special way so that in his person the apostolic powers would be unified and summed up. Thus, the Pope, as President of the Episcopal College, has the task of expressing authoritatively the unity of that college, whose members are spread throughout the world. [3]

The Pope is personally and in a special way the Foundation

---

[1] It is significant that the Preface of the Apostles is no longer said in the Mass *Pro Summis Pontificibus*, although it appeared there when this Mass was placed in the Missal in 1942.   Certainly apostolic succession is common to all bishops.

[2] On the history of this title see M. MACCARONE, *Vicarius Christi, storia del titolo papale* (Rome 1952).

[3] P. A. LIÉGÉ, " Evêque, " *Catholicisme*, Vol. IV (1956), col. 795.

of the Church, the Shepherd of Shepherds, the Custodian of the Keys of the Kingdom of God. [1]

When the Pope is elected by the Conclave and accepts the results of the election, all power immediately comes to him directly from the Lord in virtue of the promise made to Peter that He would establish the Church upon him. This divine investiture is final and unrestricted in all that pertains to the Pope's ruling of the Church and his pastoral solicitude for the faithful and their shepherds. When other bishops are placed over their dioceses, they receive their jurisdiction, which belongs to them by divine law, immediately from the Pope. Noubel has written that the bishop's power in his diocese is complete in itself — its restrictions being secondary. [2] It is the task of the sovereign authority to determine just what restrictions are demanded by the common good of the Church. In all points, however, rigid barriers do not exist between the powers of the Pope and the powers of the bishop.

When we consider the fact that the episcopacy is of divine right and that it must continue to exist and fulfill its mission, it does not seem possible to limit the Sovereign Pontiff's right to restrict episcopal jurisdiction. We should not lose sight of the Holy Spirit's assistance in those questions of positive law which have a direct bearing upon the Hierarchy. In the final analysis, it is His assistance which is the surest guarantee against any excesses which may eventually arise. We firmly believe that the Popes are divinely assured of sufficient wisdom to maintain the necessary balance that must exist between the primacy and the episcopacy if the Church of Christ is to function effectively. Father Rahner declares :

The Holy Spirit's assistance is the final and decisive guarantee

---

[1] Texts concerning St. Peter : the foundation : Mt 16, 18; the pastoral mission : Jn 21, 15-17; the power of the keys : Mt 16, 19.

[2] J. F. NOUBEL, *op. cit.*, p. 144. Explaining canon 334, § 1, this author writes : " Their powers are, then, plenary powers which are exercised officially by the very fact that they are appointed, except for restrictions imposed on the exercise of their powers by the general law or by the particular terms of their letters of nomination. Their power is plenary; the restrictions are subsidiary. "

of the sensible balance that must exist between the two powers. Whatever the problem facing the Church at a particular time may be, it is this balance which will avoid either an excessive concentration of power or a mode of action, on the part of bishops, which might jeopardize the unity of the Church.

He adds that juridic norms might seem to hamper the free rein of the Spirit but that in the last analysis it would be the Spirit who would safeguard these norms. " The reason why there can never be an adequate constitution for the Church is because account must be taken of the Spirit who alone can guarantee the unity of the Church in the face of two powers, neither one of which is capable of being adequately limited by the other. " [1] Moreover, according to the mind of Rome, the powers of the bishops cannot be restricted to such a point that they would be merely reduced to the status of functionaries, vicars of the Pope or mere executors of Roman decisions. Theologians, like philosophers, should not profess a sort of cockeyed optimism as though everything in the Church was always perfect in every respect. The Church cannot err in faith and morals, but this does not mean that everything is necessarily the best in the best of all possible worlds! Doesn't the present concern of the Popes to center the various phases of the apostolate more closely around the bishop make this readily understandable?

---

[1] K. RAHNER, *loc. cit.*, pp. 35-6.

Chapter 6

The Bishops
and Their Universal Mission

Are the bishops merely competent in their own dioceses? Yes, in matters of ordinary jurisdiction; no, in matters of shared or common jurisdiction, in union with the Vicar of Christ. " The bishops, " according to Msgr. Freppel at the Vatican Council, " are judges in their own dioceses and they are also judges for the entire Church if they are called to a council. They also function as judges whenever the Pope sees fit to ask their advice before defining a matter of faith and morals. " [1] The bishops take part in the ecumenical councils, not as mere advisors, but as judges and legislators. [2] It is erroneous to contend either that this power can be exercised independently of their Supreme Head, or that their collective authority is superior to the authority of the successor of Peter, or that the intervention of the bishops conditions papal infallibility.

A typical example of the consultation of bishops apart from a council took place before the definition of the dogma of the Assumption. In the Constitution *Munificentissimus Deus* of November 1, 1950, Pope Pius XII recognized the agreement of the *Magisterium* in the fact that " those whom the Holy Spirit has established as bishops to govern the Church of God have almost unanimously expressed their agreement. " This document also appeals to the faith of the Christian people and this is so only because the universal Magisterium sustains and directs it, " *quam idem Magisterium sustinet et dirigit.* " [3] The bishops, therefore, are not only the specially authorized witnesses of the Church's faith, but truly the organs of its faith; and their teaching

[1] Cited by T. GRANDERATH, *Histoire du concile du Vatican, op. cit.*, Vol. III, Part 2 (1913), p. 84.

[2] *Codex Juris canonici*, can. 223, § 1, 2.

[3] Pope PIUS XII, Const. *Munificentissimus Deus* (Nov. 1, 1950), *AAS*, Vol. XLII, p. 756.

has a universal value in so far as it represents the teaching of
the Sovereign Pontiff who is its foundation stone and surety.
Msgr. Journet states :

> Besides this particular jurisdiction which they possess as
> properly theirs, the bishops, taken as a college, in virtue
> of their close union with the Sovereign Pontiff, participate
> in the universal jurisdiction proper to the Pontiff.... The
> collegiate jurisdiction of the bishops is not numerically
> added to the universal jurisdiction, but is one with it. [1]

Besides the *exceptional activity* of the bishops, as when they
are assembled in council, there is also the *regular activity* of
the bishops :

> The bishops scattered throughout the world rule their
> local churches. They do more. Because they are closely
> united to the Supreme Shepherd and act with his tacit or
> expressed consent, they contribute to the preserving and
> explaining of the deposit of revealed truth all over the
> world, to the maintaining and formulating of the rules
> of the common discipline, and, in a word, to the ruling
> of even the Universal Church. [2]

Pope St. Celestine declared :

> This concern for maintaining the truth is generally expected
> of all bishops. It is an inherited and indispensable
> obligation which all of us, who represent the apostles in
> various parts of the world, take upon ourselves. The
> apostles were told : Go and teach all nations. Realize that
> we have received a general command and therefore it
> must be carried out by all since it was given to all. [3]

* * *

---

[1] C. Journet, *op. cit.*, p. 413.

[2] C. Journet, *ibid.*, p. 415.

[3] Text cited by P. Broutin, *La Réforme pastorale en France au XVII* siècle, op. cit.*, Vol. II
pp. 344-45.

Since they are the organs of the Hierarchy, the bishops are not merely executors of Roman decisions. Naturally they should be attentive and submissive more than others to the teachings and directives of the Supreme Authority. They should scrupulously observe, for example, all the recommendations that are now being made regarding the liturgy. There are, nevertheless, many areas in which the bishops can and should speak out and provide the necessary impetus and direction for various activities in their dioceses. Their pastoral endeavors will thereby be extended even beyond their dioceses and will have an effect upon the entire Church. In this particular regard, we are reminded of such men as Ketteler in Germany, Mercier in Belgium and Suhard in France.

Moreover, every bishop should have a deep concern for the entire Church. "A bishop," according to St. John Chrysostom, "should not only have an interest in the church confided to his care, but this interest should also include all other churches. He should extend his charity to all areas in which the Church and her faithful are to be found." [1] Recent Popes have reminded bishops of this obligation especially in regard to the Church's missionary activity throughout the world. Pius XI stated :

> It was not only to Peter, whose See we occupy, but to all the apostles whose successors you are, that the Master enjoined the obligation of going throughout the world to preach the Gospel to every creature. *It clearly follows from this* that since it is our task to propagate the Faith, you must also have a share in our labors and assist us in this task to whatever extent your individual endeavors on local level allow. [2]

The bishop's obligation to be concerned with the evangelization of the world does not spring solely from that degree of charity

---

[1] J. CHRYSOSTOM, *Eulogy on St. Eustachius, Bishop of Antioch* in MIGNE, *P.G.*, Vol. L, col. 602.

[2] Pope PIUS XI, Enc. *Rerum Ecclesiae* (Feb. 28, 1926), *AAS*, Vol. XVIII (1926), p. 69.

which is expected of each member of the faithful, but stems from the bishop's status as a legitimate successor of the apostles.

An encyclical by Pius XII caused something of a sensation. It will achieve great fame in mission history as well as in the theology of the episcopacy. The Encyclical *Fidei Donum* of April 21, 1957 devotes three paragraphs to an urgent call to bishops in behalf of the missions.

> It is therefore not without reason that we turn to you, Venerable Brethren, in an hour which is important for the expansion of the Church. If, in our mortal organism, when one member suffers, all the others suffer with it (Cfr. 1 Cor 12, 26), the sound members providing the sick members with the proper help, likewise in the Church every member does not live for himself alone, but helps the others and all help each other for their mutual consolation, as well as for a better development of the whole body. (Encyclical, *Mystici Corporis*, *Acta Apostolicæ Sedis*, XXXV, 1943, p. 200). In truth are not the bishops "the most eminent members of the Universal Church, those who are joined to the Divine Head of the entire Body with a very special bond and therefore are justly called 'the first members of the Lord' (St. Gregory)? " Is it not of them more than any other that Christ, the Head of the Mystical Body, "requires the help of His members : because the Sovereign Pontiff takes the place of Jesus Christ and must, in order not to be crushed by the weight of his pastoral duties, call upon many to share his anxieties? " (*ibid.* p. 213). United in closer bonds to Christ and His Vicar, Venerable Brethren, you will take to heart this sharing, in a lively spirit of charity, of the solicitude for all the Churches which weighs upon our shoulders (Cfr. 2 Cor 11, 28). Stimulated by the charity of Christ (Cfr. 2 Cor 5, 4), you will be happy to experience with us the pressing duty of propagating the Gospel and of establishing the Church throughout the entire world, you will be happy to develop among your clergy and your people a spirit of prayer and mutual help, in dimensions as great as the Heart of Christ. " If you want to love Christ, " said St. Augustine, " spread charity

all over the earth for the members of the Christ are all over the world. " (*In Epist. Ioannis ad Parthos*, Tr. X, n. 8, Migne P.L. XXXV, 2060).

There is no doubt that Jesus has entrusted His entire flock solely to the Apostle Peter and to his successors, the Roman Pontiffs; "*Pasce agnos meos, pasce oves meas* — Feed my lambs, feed my sheep " (Jn 21, 16-18). But, if every bishop is the proper pastor only of that portion of the flock entrusted to his care, his quality as a legitimate successor of the apostles by divine institution renders him jointly responsible for the apostolic mission of the Church, according to the words of Christ to His apostles " as the Father has sent me, I also send you " (Jn 20, 21). This mission which must embrace all nations and all times (Cfr. Mt 28, 19-20) did not cease with the death of the apostles. It continues in the person of all the bishops in communion with the Vicar of Jesus Christ. " The dignity of the apostles, which is the foremost in the Church, " as St. Thomas Aquinas asserted (*Expos. in Epist. ad Rom.*, C.1, Lect. 1), resides in the fulness in them who are the envoys and the missionaries of the Lord, par excellence. This apostolic fire, brought upon the earth by Jesus, must communicate itself from their hearts to the hearts of all our sons, and it must incite in them a new ardor for the missionary action of the Church throughout the world. [1]

It would doubtless be an exaggeration to say that this passage from the Encyclical *Fidei Donum* is revolutionary in importance [2] since it reiterates the appeal of Pius XI and expresses the teachings of the Fathers. It is nevertheless incontestable that this document, which is extremely precise, destroys the narrow conception that many people have of the episcopacy. Regarding this encyclical, it has been said : " Never before had a Pope emphasized so strongly the missionary solidarity of the bishops throughout the world. Never before had a Pope so closely linked the missionary apostolate with the title of successor

---

[1] Pope PIUS XII, Enc. *Fidei Donum loc. cit.*, pp. 236-37. See also Pope JOHN XXIII, *Radio message to the Catholics of Africa, loc. cit.*, p. 475.

[2] *Missi*, Vol. VIII (Oct. 1957) p. 270.

of the apostles, which is the title of every bishop in Christendom. Never before had the Pope so clearly reminded the bishops that they are, for the entire world, the missionaries par excellence, and that the most important dignity that they possess is the dignity of the episcopacy. " [1]

The scope and application of this document is quite extensive. It provides an excellent insight into the *Discourse to the Bishops* delivered by Pius XII in 1954, the year of the canonization of Pope Pius X. The bishops are joined to the Pope as the apostles were joined to Peter. As successors of the apostles by divine right, the bishops must share in the Pope's care and vigilance for the Universal Church. Under his supreme authority, they comprise the apostolic college to which Christ has entrusted His Church, with the triple prerogative and mission of teaching, ruling and sanctifying the Church. [2] This is why in the Mass we pray for the Pope, the local ordinary, and all bishops who collectively have the task of " cultivating " the Orthodox, Catholic and Apostolic faith. [3]

* *

At the time of the Vatican Council a great outcry against the decrees of the Council arose because of an extreme interpretation of papal infallibility, which reduced the bishops' role to that of mere executors of Roman decisions " whose prerogatives were completely absorbed by the Pope's jurisdiction. " [4] This was the occasion for a conflict between Church and State in Germany. Bismark maintained that the position of the bishops

---

[1] *Ibid.* On this subject see the thought-provoking article of J. FRISQUE " Pour une théologie de la mission, " *La Revue nouvelle*, Vol. XXXII (1960), pp. 257-69.

[2] Pope PIUS XII, *Discourse to the Bishops* (May 31, 1954 and Nov. 2, 1954), *AAS*, Vol. XLVI (1954), pp. 313-17, and pp. 666-77.

[3] See Dom B. CAPELLE, " Et omnibus orthodoxis atque apostolicae fidei cultoribus, " *Miscellanea historica in honorem Alb. de Meyer*, Vol. I (Louvain 1946), pp. 137-50. The eminent Abbé establishes that this text refers to all bishops throughout the world, the universal episcopal body.

[4] *Journal de M. Icard.* Cited by R. AUBERT, *Le Pontificat de Pie IX, op. cit.*, p. 342.

had completely changed since the Council and that this would necessarily result in a deterioration of relations between the Pope and the heads of State. In 1875 the German bishops published a forceful and clear refutation of this view. Nevertheless, since some objected that this document did not faithfully represent the viewpoint of the Vatican Council, the Pope intervened twice within two weeks and stated that he enthusiastically approved the " brilliant declarations and protestations of the German bishops. " The Pope also stated that they had expressed the " true meaning of the decrees of the Council " and that this document expressed " the authentic Catholic doctrine established and developed by sound and irrefutable arguments, " and that therefore " the Pope did not need to add anything further to the discussion. " [1]

Exactly what was stated in this document of the German Episcopate? The following is an important extract from it :

According to the teaching of the Catholic Church, the Pope is the bishop of Rome, but not the bishop of any other diocese, nor any other city; he is neither bishop of Breslau, nor bishop of Berlin, etc. But in his capacity as bishop of Rome, he is at the same time Pope, that is to say, the Shepherd and Supreme Head of the Universal Church, head of all the bishops and faithful; and his power as Pope must always be respected and heeded everywhere, not merely in special and exceptional cases. In this position the Pope must make sure that each bishop fulfills his task in all details. Should a bishop be unable to do this, or should some special need arise, the Pope has the right and obligation — not in his capacity as bishop of the diocese, but in his capacity as Pope — to prescribe everything that is necessary for the administration of the diocese. [2]

[1] Texts cited by O. Rousseau, " La vraie valeur de l'épiscopat dans l'Eglise d'après les documents de 1875, " *Irénikon*, Vol. XXIX (1956), pp. 137-41. On this entire question see the article of Dom O. Rousseau.

[2] O. Rousseau, *ibid.*, p. 133. The significance of this statement by the German bishops has previously been pointed out by Dom L. Beauduin, " L'Unité de l'Eglise et le concile du Vatican, " in L. Beauduin, A. Chavasse, P. Michalon, M. Villain, *Eglise et unité, Réflexions sur quelques aspects fondamentaux de l'unité chrétienne* (Lille 1948), pp. 13-61.

The German bishops' statement of policy in 1875 and the resounding approbation accorded it by Pius IX hold true even today.   Recently, the Secretariate of State of His Holiness lost no time in branding as erroneous a number of theories on the nature and prerogatives of the episcopacy, similar to those which appeared shortly after the Vatican Council.   The following is an account of what led to the Secretariate's intervention.

According to the published text of a conference given in 1955, a professor of theology declared to a group of young Catholic Actionists :

> In a world which is continually being drawn more closely together and in which problems have a universal reference, it is important to avoid different attitudes and contradictory approaches to these problems.   This can easily happen as long as the bishops continue to act solely in the interest of their own dioceses.   Likewise, at a time when States are disappearing, it is necessary that dioceses also lose their sovereignty.   The Pope must directly assume the direction of those matters which up until now were in the hands of the bishops in their dioceses.   Henceforth, it is the task of Peter and his successors to assume the general direction of every Catholic movement, of every phase of Catholic Action and the apostolate. [1]

Undoubtedly, this text contains many elements of sheer improvisation; but we can readily understand from these " erroneous interpretations " why the Hierarchy cannot allow them to be spread. [2]

Certainly, the current trend in the world today poses many problems which the Church must resolve by making the necessary adaptations while at the same time continuing to safeguard her unity.   No one will deny that Rome should oversee the

---

[1] See O. ROUSSEAU, *loc. cit.*, p. 128, n. 2.   See also our article " L'Evêque dans l'Eglise," *loc. cit.*, p. 10.

[2] Msgr. A. DELL'ACQUA expressed himself in somewhat the same terms in a letter to us (Feb. 21, 1957) after the publication of our article on " L'Evêque dans l'Eglise. " See *Revue diocésaine de Namur*, Vol. XI (1957), pp. 1-13, 119.   *La Documentation Catholique*, Vol. LIV (1957), cols. 629-36.

various phases of the apostolate, but there is nothing new in this. Indeed, at this time, more frequent interventions by Rome are desired and to be expected. But it is nevertheless true that an excessive centralization ought to be avoided, and on this particular point we should realize that sociology should not be a determining factor in theology. The transitory and even permanent systems of civil society cannot determine the policies and systems which the Hierarchy, established by divine right, should follow.

Pius XII considered this very point in November, 1954 in his second *Discourse to the Bishops* in which he repeated the constant tradition of the Church. The Pope stated on that occasion:

Frequent and mutual communication among bishops is very helpful for the faithful and effective exercise of the pastoral office. Thus one perfects the other in assaying the lessons of past experience; government is made more uniform, the wonder of the faithful is avoided, for often they do not understand why in one diocese a certain policy is followed, while in another, which is perhaps a neighboring diocese, a different or even a quite contrary policy is followed. To realize these purposes general meetings of the bishops, which are now held almost everywhere, are very helpful, as are also the more solemnly convened Provincial and Plenary Councils, for which the Code of Canon Law provides, and which are governed by definite laws. In addition to this union and communication between brothers in the episcopacy, there should be added close union and frequent communication with this Apostolic See... not only in doctrinal matters, but also in affairs of government and discipline.... There have also been instances in which the Roman Pontiffs, without having been asked, have settled disputes that had arisen or commanded that doubts be brought to them to be resolved. [1]

The Pope concluded:

This union and harmonious communication with the Holy

[1] Pope Pius XII, *Discourse to the Bishops* (Nov. 2, 1954,) *loc. cit.*, pp. 675-76.

See arises not from a desire to centralize and unify everything,
but by divine right and by reason of an essential element
in the constitution of the Church of Christ. The result
of this is not detrimental but advantageous to the bishops
to whom is entrusted the governing of individual dioceses. [1]

To counteract the problem which arose nine months later,
in August, 1955, no better solution could be given than what
has just been cited.

* * *

According to St. Cyprian, [2] " The episcopate is one, the
individual members each have a part, and the parts make up the
whole. " The bishops are closely united, engage in the same
tasks, and therefore possess the same responsibilities. Each
bishop rules his own diocese, but his concern for the universal
good of the Church always enters into and even predominates in
all that he does. Each bishop is aware that he is governing
a part of the universal flock and that he shares this same common
purpose with every other bishop. Pope Pius XII's encyclical
on the missions reminds the bishops that their local and personal
mission must first be accomplished in their respective dioceses.
Yet, they still have the responsibility of devoting themselves
to the care of the Universal Church as well as the obligation
of being of mutual assistance to one another and of uniting
themselves fraternally around their common Father in order
to accomplish their common mission.

Bossuet's statement, which nowadays could not be said
to contain the slightest trace of Gallicanism, seems to sum this
up perfectly :

All the bishops have but one flock; and each of them leads

---

[1] Pope Pius XII, *ibid.*, p. 676.

[2] St. Cyprian, *De Catholicae Ecclesiae unitate* in Migne, P.L., Vol. IV, col. 501. On
this text see M. Kuppens, " Notes dogmatiques sur l'Episcopat, " *Revue ecclésiastique de Liège*,
Vol. XXXVII (1950), pp. 80-93.

a part which is inseparable from the rest, so that actually all the bishops are involved in the very same task and are therefore as one. They are given a distinct portion of the flock to govern merely in order to facilitate the accomplishment of their mutual task. [1]

More light will be shed upon the collegial nature of the episcopacy when the Second Vatican Council considers the question of the universal mission of the episcopacy. [2]

---

[1] Bossuet, *Oraison funèbre du P. Fr. Bourgoing,* éd. Lebacq, Vol. IV (Paris 1921), p. 415

[2] See especially J. Hamer, " Note sur la collégialité épiscopale, " *Recherches des sciences philosophiques et théologiques,* Vol. XLIV (1960), pp. 40-50; Y. Congar, " Conclusion, " of the volume devoted to the meetings at Chevetogne in 1959, *Le Concile et les conciles* (Chevetogne-Paris 1960), pp. 257-69; J. Frisque, " Pour une théologie de la mission, " *loc. cit.*

Chapter 7

The Sacramental Character
of the Episcopacy

As has already been pointed out, the Council of Trent did not pronounce upon the sacramentality of the episcopacy. The controversy was indeed an ancient one. While the East was almost always unanimous in considering the episcopacy as an Order distinct from the priesthood, [1] the West was for a long time divided on the question of the sacramental nature of Episcopal Consecration. The opinion opposed to its sacramentality appealed to the authority of St. Jerome and *Ambrosiaster*. For a long time the writings of the latter were regarded as expressing the point of view of St. Ambrose and St. Augustine, and we know that the Scholastics certainly held these writings in high regard. In fact, St. Thomas himself never really abandoned them entirely. Nevertheless, the reaction was such by the time of the Council of Trent that, as we have seen, St. Robert Bellarmine did not hesitate to teach, as a truth of faith, the existence of a special sacramental character in the episcopacy. [2] From then until now the majority of theologians have more and more come to consider this teaching as at least theologically certain. [3] In 1953, in a study devoted to Episcopal Consecration, Father Boularand concluded by stating that its sacramentality is " fast becoming a Catholic doctrine, " and that the " negative thesis is becoming untenable. " [4] Recently,

---

[1] M. JUGIE, *Theologia Dogmatica Christianorum Orientalium*, Vol. III (Paris 1930), p. 406.

[2] D. BOUIX, *Tractatus de Episcopo ubi et de Synodo dioecesana* (Paris 1859), pp. 96-98.

[3] D. BOUIX, *ibid.;* F. M. CAPPELLO, *De Sacramentis*, Vol. IV: *De Sacra Ordinatione*, 3rd ed. (Turin-Rome 1951), pp. 44-47; M. SCHMAUS, " Bischof, " *loc. cit.*, p. 493.

[4] E. BOULARAND, " La consécration épiscopale est-elle sacramentelle? ", *Bulletin de littérature ecclésiastique*, Vol. LIV (1953), pp. 7-34.

this question was considered by his colleague, Father Beyer, and resolved in the negative. [1]   According to the view of this canonist, the distinction between priests of the first and priests of the second rank does not arise from the essence of the Sacrament of Holy Orders.   Describing Episcopal Consecration, he writes that " It is not a sacramental rite, but a sacramental, or, if you will, an act jurisdictional in character, which is conferred through a liturgical ceremony. " [2]   According to this author, Episcopal Consecration is always the basis for the full exercise of the priesthood, since a priest thereby receives the fullness of jurisdiction.   However, it cannot be said that the fullness of the priesthood belongs to the bishop by virtue of his own Order.   *In the line of Order*, therefore, there is no superiority of the episcopacy over the priesthood. [3]

This rather severe and extreme position has disturbed quite a few theologians and the Hierarchy itself.   Criticism was not lacking; and, only four years after the publication of Father Beyer's thesis, Father Lécuyer concluded his studies on the sacramentality of the episcopacy as follows : " We are faced here with one of the most solidly attested truths found in Catholic Tradition.   Tradition has always considered it a truth of faith, based on Scripture; for it has always viewed the *charism* given to Timothy as a grace proper to the episcopacy. " [4]   This is nothing but a return to the position of Robert Bellarmine.

---

[1] J. BEYER, " Nature et position du sacerdoce, " *La Nouvelle Revue théologique*, Vol. LXXVI (1954), pp. 356-73, 469-80; *Les Instituts séculiers* (Bruges 1954), pp. 152-180.

[2] J. BEYER, *Les Instituts séculiers, op. cit.*, p. 158; " Nature et position du sacerdoce, " *loc. cit.*, p. 369.

[3] Father Beyer mistakenly seeks to construct his theology of the episcopacy on the basis of a certain limited body of data, namely the concessions granted in a few papal documents. However, the traditional understanding of this question must also be considered.   Even before the writings of Father Beyer, the limited collection of data had been examined and evaluated differently by several reputable theologians and canonists such as Y. Congar, E. F. Regatillo, F. M. Cappello, E. Boularand, C. Journet, H. Lennertz, J. Lécuyer, etc.   Since then we have had the interpretations of such men as Dom O. Rousseau, P. A. Liégé, Bishop E. Guerry, J. Colson, B. Luykx, H. Bouëssé, M. Schmaus.   Some of these have already been cited in this book. — On the other hand, as has been said, the powers of the bishop or the priest are not the full measure of the priesthood, so that one risks making a mistake if he defines the priestly character on this basis alone.   H. LENNERTZ, *De Sacramento Ordinis*, 2nd ed. (Rome 1954), p. 105.

[4] J. LÉCUYER, " Le sacrement de l'épiscopat, " *loc. cit.*, p. 246.

The opposition cited the so called tradition of St. Jerome; but, as we know, this is nothing but a pseudo-tradition. Lécuyer shows how even St. Thomas' later writings exhibit an altogether different understanding of the episcopacy from what he originally maintained in his *Commentary on the Sentences*. [1] It is not always an easy task to interpret the texts of St. Jerome who taught at a time when the theology of the episcopacy was still in the process of developing. [2] Nevertheless, just what do his views, and the views of all who followed him, represent in the face of the almost unanimous opposition expressed by the Eastern Church and the early tradition of the Western Church? Father Broutin writes :

> Let there be no mistaking the fact that during the first eight centuries the priest as such was the bishop. In official documents, in laws, writings and common opinion the word *sacerdos* was primarily applied to the bishop. The shepherd is the bishop. Prior to St. Martin and his work of rural evangelization, the parish and the episcopal see were one and the same. The bishop, aided by his presbyterium, administered it. The whole of Patristic literature and the early history of the Church is unintelligible if this system is not considered. St. Cyprian's letters clearly stress this point. They tell us that the bishop acts through the Church and the Church through the bishop. The *De Sacerdotio* of St. John Chrysostom should more accurately be entitled *De Episcopatu*. [3]

Especially important is the extremely clear evidence of the earliest sacramentaries of the Western Church. Dom Bernard Botte recently made a careful study of them, and he shows how clearly they express the distinction in Order between

---

[1] J. Lécuyer, " Aux origines de la théologie thomiste de l'épiscopat, " *Gregorianum*, Vol. XXV (1954), pp. 56-88; J. Lécuyer, *Le sacerdoce dans le Mystère du Christ* (Paris 1957), pp. 475-87. See also the annotations of L. Ciappi in the new Italian edition of Monsabré, *Esposizione del Dogma cattolico* : Vol. XIV, *Ordine* (Turin-Rome 1951), p. 209, No. 4.

[2] P. A. Liégé, " Evêque, " *loc. cit.*, col. 801.

[3] P. Broutin, " Le Pasteur d'Eglise au cours de l'histoire, " *loc. cit.*, p. 4. See also P. M. Gy, " Remarques sur le vocabulaire antique du sacerdoce chrétien, " *loc. cit.*, pp. 144-45.

the episcopacy and the priesthood. He even believes that the later texts of the Roman Pontifical express a definite reaction against the views attributed to St. Jerome.

Dom Botte writes :

> The true tradition is not to be found exclusively in extremely precise statements on the subject. It is rather to be found quite concretely in attitudes, customs and actions prior to any definite formulization. In the statements of ecclesiastical writings we must be quite selective. All do not have the same value. The words of St. Augustine, who speaks as a bishop in the name of a tradition he guards, have more weight than the theories of St. Jerome or of Pseudo-Dionysius who are only expressing their own opinion. A point developed in a sermon does not have the same value as a sentence spoken in a Council. To avoid any misunderstandings we should be careful not to attempt to blend all these different ideas.

However, it is necessary to keep these views in mind whenever an evaluation of the Church's understanding of her priesthood is being considered. This understanding is more faithfully manifested in her laws and practices than in theories that have been proposed from time to time. Dom Botte continues :

> This understanding has two roots : the Church's realization of being apostolic as well as one and Catholic. The Church is apostolic because her bishops have handed down from age to age, along with the deposit of tradition, a *charism* which comes to them from the apostles and, in the last analysis, from Christ. The Church is one and Catholic because her bishops are joined one to another and the *Ordo episcoporum* maintains, by its fellowship, the unity of the Church spread throughout the world. This leads us to base our synthesis not upon the power possessed by each priest in particular, but, from an ecclesial perspective, upon the priesthood, as a principle of the growth, organization and unity of the Body of Christ. Our study of the prayers of the Liturgy have led us to the same conclusion. . . . The *presbyterium* is not an autonomous organization placed

alongside the bishop. The *presbyterium* partakes of the priesthood of the bishop by submission to and union with him.... [the bishops] realize that they belong to the Order of bishops upon whom the apostolicity and the unity of the Church depend, not merely in the strict juridicial sense, which would view this only as an external discipline, but in the full theological sense of the word. Due to a *charism*, transmitted by the imposition of hands, the bishops, assisted by their *presbyterium*, have built up the Church. Through them it must continue to grow and increase. [1]

Referring to the earliest Christian liturgies which express " the priestly and apostolic character of the episcopacy in a truly impressive and unanimous manner, " Father Lécuyer concludes : " Successors of the apostles, the bishops are on the same plane as the priesthood of which they have the fulness. " [2] In short, the episcopacy requires the supreme consecration of the priesthood and the character of the fullness of the priesthood : in the Church the bishops are the Heads and the High Priests.

Reference may be made to the Bulls which grant to simple priests the faculty of conferring Major Orders including the priesthood. It appears difficult to maintain the interpretation of those who see in this only the faculty of promoting candidates for the priesthood to Orders independently of the diocesan bishop. [3] Nevertheless, among those who recognize in this the power to ordain, there are those who maintain a clear distinction between the episcopacy and the priesthood *in the line of Orders*. [4] Thus Father Lennertz recently concluded the study of the problem in these terms : *Quoad ordinationem episcopalem statuimus thesim ut certam et nunc communiorem.* If, he adds, the note on this thesis is not sufficiently strong, it is only so

---

[1] B. Botte, " Presbyterium et Ordo Episcoporum, " *Irénikon*, Vol. XXIX (1956), pp. 23-27; also " L'Ordre d'après les prières d'ordination, " *Etudes sur le sacrement de l'Ordre* (Lex Orandi, 22) (Paris 1957), pp. 13-35.

[2] J. Lécuyer, *Prêtres du Christ, Le Sacrement de l'Ordre* (Paris 1957), p. 29.

[3] However, this is still the opinion of F. M. Cappello, *De Sacramentis, op. cit.*, pp. 206-9.

[4] See especially Y. Congar, " Faits, problèmes et réflexions à propos du pouvoir d'Ordre et des rapports entre le presbytérat et l'épiscopat, " *La Maison-Dieu* (1948), fasc. 14, pp. 107-28; Msgr. E. Guerry, *L'évêque* (Paris 1954), pp. 54-56, 126-28.

propter auctoritatem externam illorum theologorum qui tenent vel tenebant ordinationem episcopalem non esse sacramentum. [1]

Assuredly, the " theological evidence " of these ancient Bulls concerning ordinations serves as evidence; and evidence must be evaluated by theologians in the same way as it is evaluated by scholars in other fields. But if it is admitted that the theological meaning of the evidence is certain, and that simple priests at one time did possess the power of conferring Major Orders, including the priesthood (but excluding the power of conferring the episcopacy), what are we to conclude? Must we qualify our treatment of episcopal prerogatives from now on? Must we henceforth treat the powers of the bishops any differently from the way in which they have ordinarily been treated? It in no way follows that the sacramentality of the episcopacy, which is firmly based on the tradition of apostolic succession, must be denied. The specific grace of the episcopacy constitutes the bishop in apostolic succession, in the priestly and pastoral mission of the twelve apostles. This grace is derived from the imposition of hands, and fully confers the Holy Spirit given to the Son by the Father and transmitted by Christ to the apostles and their successors. [2]

However, some will say that the episcopacy and priesthood are radically equal in the line of Order, since a simple priest can be called upon to confer the priesthood. Yet it still remains true that the episcopacy can only be transmitted by bishops. And therefore, as Father Liégé says, " it is necessary to guard against any quantitative notion in this particular regard. " The episcopacy and the priesthood " qualify men for functions which are different but still organically united in the mission of the Church : they are therefore distinct in the order of *ministerial intensity.* " Whatever the powers of the Church relative to the minister of Holy Orders may be, the priesthood is a parti-

---

[1] H. LENNERTZ, *De Sacramento Ordinis, op. cit.*, p. 110.

[2] See J. LÉCUYER, " Mystère de la Pentecôte et apostolicité de la Mission de l'Eglise, " *Etudes sur le sacrement de l'Ordre, op. cit.*, pp. 167-208. Also the remarks of A. G. MARTIMORT and Dom B. CAPELLE, *ibid.*, p. 213.

cipation in the episcopacy, not a mere aptitude to do whatever the bishop does. The priesthood is derived from the episcopacy; and thus it is not a question of trying to see what the episcopacy can add to the priesthood, but rather of determining just what it can share with it. " Many false problems will be avoided, " writes Father Liégé, " if this descending perspective is adopted. " [1] On this subject, it is important to refer to the teaching of the recent Apostolic Constitution of Pius XII, *Sacramentum Ordinis*, which rendered an authoritative solution to the controversies regarding the form of the Sacrament of Holy Orders as applied to the episcopacy, the priesthood and the diaconate. " This document, " Msgr. Journet wrote, " represents a major event in the history of the Sacrament of Holy Orders, " and it should be carefully examined by theologians and should result in their re-examining their own teachings. [2] Father Beyer, naturally, can dismiss this by saying that the Pope's intervention only concerns the power of jurisdiction; but it is easy to answer this by showing that the document quite definitely contains considerations and presuppositions of a doctrinal nature.

It goes without saying that the form of a sacrament clearly specifies the type of grace to be conferred. [3] How truly indicative of the sacramentality of ordination are the words which were declared to be the essential form necessary for the bestowal of the priesthood! [4] " Almighty Father, we beseech you to give to your servants here present the dignity of the priesthood. Renew in their hearts the spirit of holiness so that they may receive from you, O God, the charge befitting those in the second degree and that they may inspire a reform of morality

---

[1] P. A. Liégé, *loc. cit.*, cols. 802-3. See also J. Colson, " L'évêque et l'ordination au presbytérat, " *Prêtres diocésains* (1957), pp. 7-85, 103-4.

[2] C. Journet, " Vues récentes sur le sacrement de l'Ordre, " *Revue thomiste*, Vol. LIII (1953), p. 81.

[3] M. Schmaus, " Bischof, " *loc. cit.*, col. 493.

[4] Pope Pius XII, Const. *Sacramentum Ordinis* (Nov. 30, 1947), *AAS*, Vol. XL (1948), p. 7. According to this Constitution, the form of the priesthood is the Preface in which one can further ascertain the essential words : " *Forma constat verbis Praefationis, quorum haec sunt essentialia ideoque ad valorem requisita : Da quaesumus...* "

by the example of their own conduct. " [1]   What tremendous doctrinal riches are to be found in this text.   God is envisaged as operating in the souls of the new priests and renewing them in the spirit of holiness.   It is a consecratory transformation which confers upon them the character and dignity of the priesthood as well as the mission and powers of those in the second degree, or according to the context, those subordinates of the bishop, who are his collaborators : *cooperatores Ordinis nostri.*   They are also given the grace of a holy life, by which they will be able to promote, through their good example, the reform of morality.   Let us only stress here that the distinction between the two ranks in Holy Orders is attested to by the very form of the sacrament in which priests are specifically ordained as the collaborators of the bishops, the priests of first rank.

Since they are successors of the apostles, the bishops inherit the triple prerogatives of teaching, governing and sanctifying.   Pius XII developed this at length in 1954 on the occasion of the canonization of Pius X.   Two years later he described the Hierarchy in the same terms in an address which he delivered to the delegates to the International Congress on Pastoral Liturgy at Assisi : " The Hierarchy is the custodian of the *Depositum fidei* and the *Depositum gratiae :* sanctifying grace, the virtues, the gifts, the power to baptize, to confer the Holy Spirit, to forgive sins through the sacrament of Penance and to ordain priests. " [2]   The expression *Depositum gratiae,* we believe, had never been used prior to this occasion; in any case it is unusual.

Consequently, greater attention should be given to the relation existing between the *Depositum gratiae* and the *Depositum*

---

[1] Ordination Pontifical, Preface for the Ordination of Priests.   The meaning of " *secundi meriti munus* " is certain in the immediate context of the Preface where one reads the expression " *sequentis ordinis viros et secundae dignitatis* " *;* the ancient texts also had " *secundis praedicatoribus* " instead of the current " *secundis praedicationibus.* "   See B. BOTTE, " L'Ordre d'après les prières d'ordination, " *Les Questions liturgiques et paroissiales,* Vol. XXXV (1954), p. 169.   See also L. CIAPPI, *op. cit.,* p. 209, no. 4; A. BÉRAUDY, " Les effets de l'Ordre dans les Préfaces d'ordination du Sacramentaire léonien, " *La tradition sacerdotale, op. cit.,* pp. 92-107.

[2] Pope PIUS XII, *Discourse to the Participants in the Congress of Pastoral Liturgy at Assisi* (Sept. 22, 1956), *AAS,* Vol. XLVIII (1956), p. 713.

fidei. Just as the truths of faith are transmitted by every priest, so the grace of Christ is also transmitted through them; but the full measure of these great treasures has been given, according to the Pope, to the apostles and to their successors, the bishops. Is it not necessary, therefore, to conclude that the full exercise of the sanctifying mission, like the ruling mission of the bishops, is to be found first of all in the Apostolic College and therefore in the College of Bishops? On this very point Pope Pius XII, speaking to the Second World Congress of the Lay Apostolate in October 1957, stated that the bishops derive the *plenitude of their priestly power* from the apostles, but that they " transmit to others through ordination, *in a determined measure*, the power to consecrate. " [1] Could anything be more definite?

In the light of the important documents that we have just cited, two other texts of Pius XII are significant. On the very day of the consecration of Cardinal Montini, December 12, 1954, the late Holy Father sent his benediction " to his faithful collaborator, who today has become his brother in the Episcopal Order. " [2] In June, 1955, Pius XII spoke of Msgr. Fontenelle as " he who only yesterday was invested by the Holy Spirit with the fullness of the priesthood. " [3] It is only by consecration that bishops are invested with the fullness of the priesthood and that they belong to the Episcopal Order.

* *

If there is a distinct sacrament, there is also a specific grace. According to the Council of Trent, it may be held that a liturgical rite is a sacrament provided this rite confers a specific grace. [4]

[1] Pope PIUS XII, *Allocution to the 2nd World Congress of the Lay Apostolate* (Oct. 5, 1957), *AAS*, Vol. XLIX (1957), p. 924.

[2] Pope PIUS XII, *Allocution on the Occasion of the Consecration of Bishop J. Montini* (Dec. 12, 1954), *AAS*, Vol. XLVI (1954), p. 728.

[3] Pope PIUS XII, *Allocution on the Occasion of the Consecration of Bishop J. Fontenelle,* *L'Osservatore Romano* (June 10-11, 1955).

[4] *Concilium Tridentinum*, sess. 23, c. 3 : DENZ., 1959.

And next there is the question of the resulting sacramental powers : even though a bishop has no more power than a simple priest with regard to his priestly functions, the fact that he has received a specific new grace to carry them out is enough to constitute a sacrament.   Confirmation is certainly a sacrament, although it adds no new power to those already conferred by baptism. [1]   It is therefore false to maintain that Episcopal Consecration has no effect upon the priestly powers of the bishop.   The bishop receives through this consecration a charism, let us frankly say, a character, which allows him to act in a proper and definite way as a successor of the apostles in matters pertaining to the government and worship of the Church, as well as the administration of the sacraments.   The sacrament of the episcopacy *structures* the Church of Christ in a marvelous manner.   Let us consider once again what Pope Pius XII, decidely the theologian of the episcopacy, has to say.

The Pontiff stated that the bishops enjoy a privileged and incomparable position in the Church.   The bishops, according to *Mystici Corporis* in 1943 and *Fidei Donum* in 1957, are " the most eminent members of the Universal Church, those who are united to the Divine Head of the entire body by a very special bond and are therefore rightly called the first members of the Lord." [2]   Also, since they are the legitimate successors of the apostles, " the dignity of the apostles which is foremost in the Church, " as St. Thomas Aquinas asserted, " resides in its fullness in those who are first and foremost the envoys and missionaries of the Lord. " [3]   Pius XII endeavored to describe the three chief prerogatives which bishops possess by divine right, namely those of teaching, ruling and sanctifying. [4]   These prerogatives stem from the very status of the bishops as

[1] J. Lécuyer, " Le sacrement de l'épiscopat, " *loc. cit.*, p. 222; T. Camelot, " La théologie de la confirmation à la lumière des controverses récentes, " *La Maison-Dieu*, No. 54, pp. 79-90.

[2] Pope Pius XII, Enc. *Mystici Corporis, loc cit.*, p. 200. Enc. *Fidei Donum, loc. cit.*, pp. 236-37.

[3] Pope Pius XII, Enc. *Fidei Donum, loc. cit.*, p. 237.

[4] Pope Pius XII, *Discourse to the Bishops* (May 31, 1954 and Nov. 2, 1954), *AAS* Vol. XLVI (1954), pp. 313-17, 666-77.

successors of the apostles, and the most eminent members of the Body of Christ, the Heads of the Church. This great mystery is evident in the consecration of a bishop, when the three consecrators pronounce the words comprising the sacramental form of the episcopacy : *Fill up in Thy priest the perfection of Thy ministry and sanctify with the dew of Thy heavenly ointment this Thy Servant decked out with the ornaments of all beauty.* [1] Before the bishop engages in his sacred ministry, he undergoes the rite of consecration, which completes his priesthood and effects an ontological transformation in him. This consecration brings with it certain corresponding rights and privileges and will always be a source of grace to him for the fulfillment of his mission. As Father Lécuyer writes : " The nature of the episcopacy, far from being able to be expressed simply in terms of apostolic succession or juridical powers, can only be fully understood in terms of the presence of a charism, a spiritual power in which the permanent action of the Spirit guiding the Church is to be found. " [2] It is this character of the fullness of the priesthood, with the supernatural graces that it produces, which is the specific grace proper to the episcopacy.

* * *

As the sacrament of the Hierarchy, Episcopal Consecration therefore constitutes the bishops as overseers of the mysteries of Christ [3] and the most outstanding members and leaders in Christ's Mystical Body. [4] If the bishops truly establish and *structure* [5] the Church, it is not because of the geographical position of their dioceses, but rather because through their sacred mission they act in the name of Christ at the very center of the Christian community. Through them Christ teaches,

---

[1] Pope Pius XII, Const. *Sacramentum Ordinis, loc. cit.,* p. 237.
[2] J. Lécuyer, " Le sacrement de l'épiscopat, " *loc. cit.,* p. 250.
[3] 1 Cor 4, 1.
[4] S. Gregory, cited by Pope Pius XII, Enc. *Fidei Donum, loc. cit.,* p. 237.
[5] Eph. 2, 20.

governs and sanctifies His Church. It is impossible to be
joined to the Lord without being united to the Hierarchy.
It is principally in regard to bishops that the following words
are to be understood : " Who hears you, hears Me; who despises
you, despises Me. " [1]   The bishops are the source of the contact
between Christ and His Church as well as the source of the
Church's unity.

Thus, the episcopacy is ordered to the Eucharist, the
sacrament of unity and of communion in the Christ life. [2]   The
plenitude of the Church's apostolic mission is contained in
the fullness of the priesthood.   As the bishop oversees by
divine right the Mystical Body of Christ, he likewise overeess
His real Body.   All other priests have their priesthood only
through a share in his priesthood.   Despite whatever duties
the Church may entrust to them, whether it be to confirm,
or to ordain deacons or even priests, they only perform this
in a restricted and limited sense.   Bishops, on the contrary,
have the power to confer all Orders up to and including the
episcopacy; and it is usually they who act as the ministers
of Confirmation since this sacrament prepares the faithful
for the apostolate and enjoins upon them the defense of the
faith.   According to the precise notion of the sacramental
character, the episcopacy confers a participation in and
a conformation to the priesthood of Christ, which sets a man
apart for divine worship and the governing of the Church.
Consequently, the bishop is on the highest level of those leaders
divinely established by God for the Church. [3]

In conclusion, let us say that the sacramental character
of the episcopacy is not sufficiently distinct from that of the
priesthood.   If it were, there would then be an eighth sacrament.

---

[1] Lk 10, 16.

[2] H. De Lubac, *The Splendour of the Church*, Eng. trans. Michael Mason (New York :
Sheed and Ward, 1956), pp. 87-112.

[3] A. M. Roguet, *The Sacraments*, Vol. IV, Theology Library, ed. A. M. Henry (Chicago :
Fides, 1955-58), p. 24.   See the same author's " La théologie du caractère et l'incorporation
à l'Église " *La Maison-Dieu* (1952), N⁰ 32, pp. 74-89; J. Lécuyer, " Le sacerdoce dans le
mystère du Christ, " *op. cit.*, pp. 404-7.

According to scholastic terminology, there is only a real *modal* distinction. The episcopal character may therefore be considered as the intrinsic perfecting of the priestly character or, according to our view, the simple priest only incompletely shares in the priestly character of Christ, of which the bishop receives the fullness. [1] It seems to us that the manner is descending rather than ascending. Nevertheless, episcopal ordination increases grace and perfects the priestly character and therefore is really and properly speaking a sacrament.

[1] Our discussion of the ancient liturgies and the teaching of Pius XII (p. 94-95) permits us to conclude that the fullness of the priesthood resides in the bishop alone, not only in regard to the Mystical Body but also in regard to the real Body of Christ. Thus, the priestly *character* is more fully achieved in episcopal consecration than in priestly ordination. H. Bouëssé, *Le sacerdoce chrétien* (Bruges 1957), pp. 121-23, 194, argues against this thesis with the authority of St. Thomas who thinks that the simple priest has the same power over the Eucharist as a bishop. But doesn't St. Thomas himself direct us to correct his doctrinal teaching on the episcopacy when a further study of the sources warrants it? In the present state of theological discussion would not he himself consider his view superceded?

Chapter 8

The Bishop, the Shepherd and Father
of His Diocese

As soon as a bishop is entrusted with his own flock, he is fully established in his mission as a bishop. Let us consider this more closely by examining the imagery of the Gospels. Pius XII stated :

> You know well how Holy Scripture, in describing the Church, frequently uses images taken from architecture and man's social life and from man himself. Thus, the Church is a *building* constructed upon a corner stone, so solid that no attack by man or the devil will bear it away. [1] It is a *kingdom*, the keys of which are in the hands of him to whom Jesus, the eternal King, has given the power to bind and loose in heaven and on earth. [2] It is a *body* whose members are the faithful and whose actions are governed by the Head, Jesus, but a body which is nevertheless represented on earth by His Vicar. [3] There is one comparison upon which Jesus seems to insist particularly. The Church is *a sheepfold*, with Christ Himself as the invisible Shepherd; and since there must be a visible shepherd, the Pope takes His place on earth. [4]

If the proper distinctions are made, we can say that the doctrine of the episcopacy is also contained in these excellent Gospel texts. If the Pope is the head of the Church because he is

[1] Mt 16, 18.

[2] *Ibid.,* 16, 18-19.

[3] Rom 12, 4-6; 1 Cor 12, 12-27; Eph 4, 4.

[4] Pope Pius XII, *Discourse to the Pastors of Rome* (March 27, 1953), *AAS*, Vol. XLV (1953), pp. 238-39.

Vicar of Jesus Christ, and if, as such, he alone possesses transcendent powers, it therefore follows that, under the authority of the Sovereign Pontiff, the entire Hierarchy prolongs the " apostles' foundation, " [1] governs the Mystical Body of Christ, the Church, [2] and each residential bishop rules, as a true pastor, the flock committed to his care. [3]

The parable of the Good Shepherd is of prime importance for understanding the role of bishops in their dioceses. Like Christ, the bishop can say to his subjects, " I have come so that you may have life and have it more abundantly. " [4] This is the chief aim of all of the powers, responsibilities, duties and concerns of the bishop. He is to be a good shepherd in imitation of Jesus, whose place he takes; to know his flock, to live in their midst, to have no other concern than to lead them to Christ and to seek in Him the way and the life for his flock; to protect and defend the sheepfold, even at the price of his own life and at the expense of his own popularity; to dedicate his entire being to the salvation of souls and to redeem them by offering himself in their behalf; to be concerned over the lost sheep and those not yet in the fold, as well as those who are weak and spiritually dead although still in the fold. [5] Such is the program outlined by Pius XII, who adds this important bit of advice :

> And when his thoughts turn to the sheep who are living, the good pastor, the parish priest, should not think that he can rest content. It is true that, in particular circumstances, it may be necessary to leave the ninety-nine sheep in the safety of the fold to go in search of the one sheep that has strayed. Ordinarily, however, it will be necessary to preserve life in those who possess it, taking care lest anyone should want for the appropriate spiritual nourishment. [6]

[1] Eph 2, 20; Ap 21, 14. See Card. J. E. VAN ROEY, " Eeuwfeest van de kerkelijke Hierarchie in Nederland, " *loc. cit.*, pp. 350 ff.

[2] Acts 20, 28.

[3] *Concilium Vaticanum*, sess. 4, cap. 3; DENZ., No. 1828.

[4] Jn 10, 10.

[5] Jn 10, 1-19.

[6] Pope PIUS XII, *Discourse to the Pastors of Rome* (March 26, 1953), *loc. cit.*, p. 243.

Another Gospel image goes to the heart of the mystery of the episcopacy. This is the image of Christ, the Spouse of His Church. [1] Too often we forget that the restoration brought about by the Redeemer is accomplished in this mystical union, *In Ecclesia et in Christo Iesu*, as St. Paul so beautifully expresses it. [2] The supreme revelation of the Apocalypse ends with the triumph of the Spouse of the Lamb, and by spouse is meant a collaborator in His life's work. [3]

Tradition is clear on the question of the union existing between the bishop and his particular Church, the diocese. Bishop Guerry writes : [4]

> This is a union which is complete and indissoluble, and which makes a diocese his spouse, as is symbolized by the ring he wears, with all the duties this mystical union implies : solicitude, fidelity, total self-oblation. The bishop alone has a personal right to be in charge of his people. The others, his cooperators in the diocese, receive that right as shared, partial and dependent upon his. [5] As a successor of the apostles, the bishop has the immediate responsibility of organizing the apostolate in his diocese. He is therefore responsible — to God, to the Pope and to the Church — for all those who live in his diocese, faithful Christians, the indifferent, the unbelieving, the hostile, the pagan. [6]

Therefore, if the Church is the mother of the faithful, the bishop, in his relations with them, acts as their spiritual father. Next we will consider those texts which describe the *family of God*

[1] See our articles entitled, " In Ecclesia et in Christo Iesu, " *Collationes Namurcenses* Vol. XXXII (1938), pp. 385-400; Vol. XXXIII (1939), pp. 93-111.

[2] Eph 3, 21.

[3] Ap 21, 9-14.

[4] Bishop E. GUERRY, *In the Whole Christ*, Eng. trans. M. G. Carroll (New York : Society of St. Paul), pp. 261-62. Indeed, the union of a bishop with his own church is linked to the deeper, more basic union which he has contracted with the one great Church of Christ in the unity of the apostolic college. See page 107 of this book.

[5] St. THOMAS, *Summa Theologica*, II-II, q. 184, a .6.

[6] *Codex Juris Canonici*, can. 1350.

and the *fatherhood of God*. We find great insight in the texts
of St. Ignatius of Antioch: " You must come to reverence
the very power of God the Father in your bishop. " Even
though the bishop is a young man, the Magnesians are overjoyed
at receiving him, since they are aware that in obeying him they
are obeying " the Father of Jesus Christ, the Universal
Bishop. " [1] If the Father is referred to as the universal bishop,
this is only because St. Ignatius is so imbued with the notion
that every bishop appears before his subjects as one who manifests
and incarnates in himself the fatherhood of God. " This
representation and continuation, " writes Bishop Guerry, " is
the mystery of the Hierarchy, which is the sacrament of divine
paternity, the visible sign manifesting and embodying the
paternity of God in relation to mankind. " [2]

In November, 1957, at the opening of the Diocesan Synod
of Venice, Cardinal Roncalli, the late Pope John, developed
the theme of the bishop as father and shepherd, *pater et pastor*,
in his diocese. He insisted that the attribution to the bishop
of the name of father is not based on the great kindness and interest that he displays to those closely associated with him, nor
even on the conscientiousness that he manifests in fulfilling his
duties. Rather, this is based on his belief in the mystery of
divine paternity that he incarnates in himself. [3]

In order to understand the mystery of the Church, and
consequently the mystery of the Hierarchy, it is necessary to
start not with men but with God. Right from the start, the
mystery of the Holy Trinity shines forth; and it is in the Trinity
itself that the Incarnation is determined. The Incarnate Son,
on the Cross, gives Himself the Church for a spouse, thereby
associating it in the Trinitarian life through the paternity of the
Father and joined to the Holy Spirit. According to another
image, Christ is the Head of the Church, living in it in and

---

[1] St. IGNATIUS OF ANTIOCH, *Ad Magnesios*, III, 11.

[2] Bishop GUERRY, *op. cit.*, p. 257.

[3] Card. A. G. RONCALLI (Pope John XXIII), *Priest and Pastor of Souls*, discourse to the
thirtieth diocesan synod of Venice (Nov. 25, 1957), *La Documentation catholique*, Vol. LV (1958),
cols. 1619-21.

through the Spirit, the Soul of the Church. But even though He is always the Head and the Life of His Church, Christ established the hierarchy of apostles as bishops, in whom He is visibly present in the world, and through whom He prolongs His espousals with the Church and continues His life-giving work. In this way, there is established the divine family of grace for all those who become children of God. The priestly prayer of Christ is realized : " That they all may be one, as You, Father, in Me and I in You... and thus, I in them and You in Me they may be perfected in unity. " [1] In this great mystery of the fatherhood of God we find the raison d'être of the Hierarchy through which God wished the work of grace to be entrusted to a visible Church.

It is not surprising then that from the earliest centuries the bishop was given the truly expressive name of *father*. The faithful were so conscious of his spiritual fatherhood that the Eastern monks, for example, had this in mind when they specified the rights and duties of the Superior, the *abbas*, in their monasteries. [2]

As has been said, theologians currently divide the bishop's mission into the three categories of teaching, ruling and sanctifying. Canonists distinguish, on the other hand, between the powers of Order and jurisdiction. The latter includes power to legislate, to judge and to punish. [3] They usually also include in this the powers of teaching by which the bishops are the " true doctors or masters of the faithful entrused to them. " [4] However, does not the fatherhood of the bishop include duties which go beyond these categories?

Indeed, canonists list under the general title of obligations and powers of *administration* a great number of directives which are concerned with the more important aspects of the life of the soul. The Code of Canon Law obliges bishops to promote

---

[1] Jn 17, 21-23.
[2] P. SCHMITZ, *Histoire de l'Ordre de saint Benoît*, Vol. I (Maredsous 1942), pp. 18-19.
[3] C. PESCH, *Praelectiones dogmaticae*, 5th ed., Vol. I (Freiburg-im-Br. 1915), p. 308.
[4] *Codex Juris Canonici*, can. 1326.

and to encourage all that is necessary or useful for the spiritual well-being of the faithful. This concern is particularly evident with regard to priests, their special collaborators. They must make sure that they regularly go to confession and that they are faithful to their spiritual exercises of mental prayer, visits to the Most Blessed Sacrament, recitation of the rosary and daily examination of conscience. [1] Since we are dealing here with a spiritual society organized for the salvation of souls, it is of little importance whether we consider this concern a matter of jurisdiction or a duty incumbent upon the bishop. The important thing is to realize that the Hierarchy acts in the Church in an altogether different manner from the way in which secular authorities act in civil matters. Beyond the visible realm of organizations and laws, there is to be found, at the very heart of the Church, the mystery of the sacred Hierarchy, the mystery of the Holy Spirit's presence given in plenitude to the apostles and their successors. We will return to consider once again what has been said about the fatherhood of the bishop. The truth of this is only perceived in all its fullness in Episcopal Consecration which makes of the bishop, according to a Byzantine prayer used at consecrations, " the dispenser of the grace of the High Priesthood. " [2]

The bishop is in every sense the sanctifier of his people since he is the confector of the Eucharist par excellence, towards which the ministry of the Word and all pastoral activity converge. [3] It is actually through the bishop and the Eucharist that the bonds uniting the diocesan community to God are tied together. [4] For this reason, then, the Pontifical High Mass of the residential bishop has an unparalleled religious significance.

[1] *Codex Juris Canonici*, can. 335, § 1.

[2] This phrase is cited by B. BAZATOLE, " L'évêque et la vie chrétienne au sein de l'Eglise locale, " *Le Courrier de Mondaye* (May-Aug., 1958), No. 54, p. 7.

[3] On the necessity of combining the preaching ministry with the sacrificial ministry of the priesthood see J. LÉCUYER, " Théologie et sacerdoce chrétien, " *La tradition sacerdotale*, *op. cit.*, pp. 248-63; Y. CONGAR, " L'Evangile, le sacerdoce aaronique et les sacerdoces anciens, " *Evangéliser*, Vol. XIII (1959), pp. 288-304.

[4] J. FRISQUE, " L'évêque dans la vie chrétienne, " *Église vivante*, Vol. VI (1954), pp. 277-82.

The center of the diocese is less the Chancery Office than the Cathedral in which are to be found the bishop's throne, his *cathedra*, and above all, his altar. [1] At the altar the bishop is shown by the liturgy to be " the very heart of his presbyterium, " the center of all the clergy laboring in his diocese. [2] At the altar he is also shown to be the *Pontiff* given by God to his people to rule them and to dispen e the mysteries of God [3] as the accredited representative of his Church, which he personifies before God. [4]

* *
*

The relationship that exists between the diocese and the Universal Church is very striking. It is by means of this relationship that the local Church fully accomplishes its mission. Bishop Guerry writes :

> This union of a bishop with his diocese has such fecundity and carries such responsibility only because it is *a particular case of the general union of the Universal Church with Jesus Christ*. The Universal Church is not the sum total of all the particular dioceses; on the contrary, indeed, the dioceses proceed from the Church. The Church has preceded them, and it is she who contains them and gives them significance. She has been entirely founded on the episcopate, which is *one* as the Church herself is one. How admirable, therefore, is the unity of the episcopate which embodies the entire mystery of the *unity* of the Church.

[1] U. BERLIÈRE, " La dévotion à l'église cathédrale, " *Cours et Conférences des Semaines liturgiques*, Congress of Malines, 1924 (Louvain 1925), pp. 111-16.

[2] This neat phrase is by Canon A. ROSE, cited above on p. 61 footnote 2. Concerning the place of the bishop in sacramental life, see the article of A. NOCENT, " L'évêque et la vie sacramentelle des fidèles, " *Revue monastique*, (1959), No. 156, pp. 100-6.

[3] 1 Cor 4, 1.

[4] The bishop is not delegated by men in a democratic way. He is given to them by God as pastor and father. He has a perfect right to act in the name of his Church just as the father of a family has a perfect right to represent his children before the authorities. See J. HAMER, " Le Concile œcuménique, engagement de toute l'Eglise, " *Lumière et Vie* (1960), No. 45, pp. 50-59.

It follows that each bishop is not primarily the pastor
of a single flock. He is primarily a pastor of the Universal
Church, in union with the Pope and with the other bishops,
under the authority of the Pope, the Supreme Head and
the center of unity. By virtue of the Priesthood of Christ
which the bishop possesses in plenitude, he is a source of
spiritual fecundity spread throughout the entire Church.
*And the Mystery of Christ, which the Universal Church possesses,
exists whole and entire in each particular diocese,* because this
mystery is contained whole and entire in the grace and the
priesthood of its bishop. This tremendous doctrine of the
unity which exists between the Church and the episcopate
protects individual dioceses against the dangers of particularism and of selfish concern for their own interests alone. [1]

However, since the Church universal is not, as we have
said, the sum total of each and every local diocese, it should
not be thought that the local dioceses are only like tiny pieces,
and small unformed fragments or atomic molecules in relation
to the Universal Church. This last description was coined
by Father Rahner who, on the contrary, views the local diocese
" as a *concentration* of the Church seeking to realize its
mission. " [2] A diocese, he maintains, is " the holy community
of Christ's disciples assembled together for worship with an
apostle or a successor of the apostles at their head. " [2] This
understanding is a return to St. Cyprian's idea which we have
already cited : *Plebs adunata Sacerdoti et grex suo Pastori adhaerens.* [4]

In order to explain in more detail the conception that he
has of the local Church, Rahner refers to the notion of the
Remnant of Israel. When the Chosen People apostatized en
masse, the future of their nation remained safe provided there
still existed a group, sometimes reduced merely to a few persons,
in whom the promises resided, and through whom these promises

[1] Bishop GUERRY, *op. cit.*, p. 262.
[2] K. RAHNER, *The Episcopate and the Primacy, loc. cit.*
[3] K. RAHNER, *ibid.*
[4] St. CYPRIAN, *Epist. LXIX,* MIGNE, *P.L.,* Vol. IV, col. 406.

could be handed on to succeeding generations. Thus the entire mystery of the Church, the fulfillment of these promises, is present in such a way in the bishop, and through him in the Church, that, hypothetically, should everything else in the world disappear, it alone would remain and would be capable of being spread throughout the world once again. [1]

This comparison only has value because the salvation of the *Remnant*, in our hypothesis, only guarantees the continuance of that Church which was assured of perpetuity, the Pope's Church, specifically the Roman Church, the source of unity and the custodian of infallibility.

* * *

We have considered at great length the privileged place that the bishop holds. This was only proper since to consider him is to consider his church, his diocese. It is not only the bishop's task to consider his role and responsibilities, but this is likewise incumbent upon his collaborators, his priests. It would indeed be wonderful if all the members of the Christian community were more conscious of just what the bishop represents in their lives.

One of the main concerns of the Council of Trent was to center all of the Church's strength and vitality around the bishop. This concern characterizes, as we shall see, the pontificates of Pius XII and John XXIII. The chief concern, in both of these pontificates, has been to assure more unity in the apostolate. The bishop must always be the center of unity in a diocese. Unfortunately, this was not always the case. However, it is not sufficient for the flock merely to have a shepherd. It is also necessary that the flock follow its duly appointed leader and that the voice of the shepherd not be drowned out by and confused with other voices lacking the requisite authority.

---

[1] K. RAHNER, *loc. cit.*, pp. 23 ff. For a similar treatment see Msgr. P. M. THÉAS, " Qu'est-ce qu'un évêque? " *Lourdes, terre de Marie* (Lourdes 1958), pp. 251-52.

It is sometimes maintained that it is as meritorious to have faith in the Hierarchy as it is to believe in the Eucharist! In the Hierarchy also appearances are sometimes deceiving! There is yet another mystery : Why has God entrusted His work to weak and sinful men? All the more reason why the faithful should pray for the bishops so that, despite their weaknesses, they may lead their flocks according to the ideal of the messianic Shepherd, with the powerful assistance of the Holy Spirit. " May he stand and feed his flock in Thy strength, O Lord, in the sublimity of Thy name. " [1]

As for the bishop himself, let him constantly recall these words contained in the Preface of Episcopal Consecration : *Give to him, O Lord, the keys of the kingdom of heaven, so that he may make use of, not boast of, the power which Thou hast given unto edification, not unto destruction. May he be untiring in his solicitude, fervent in spirit. May he detest pride, cherish humility and truth, and never desert it, overcome either by flattery or fear.* Anything besides this is meaningless and futile. What matters is in the soul : *The brightness of souls rather than the splendor of vestments commends the Pontifical glory unto us.*

Each year, on the anniversary of his Consecration, the bishop reads these words : *Take heed, watch and pray, for you do not know when the time is. Watch, lest coming suddenly he find you sleeping. Watch.* [2]

---

[1] *Breviarium Romanum*, " Prayer for the Bishop of the Place, " in the *Preces* for Lauds and Vespers, Mi 5, 4; Is 11, 1 ff.

[2] *Missale Romanum*, " Mass on the Anniversary of the Election and Consecration of a Bishop, " Mk 13, 33-37.

3

The States
of Perfection
and the Priest

Chapter 9

Preliminary Notions

In treating of the bishops, we have also constantly had in mind priests, their very special collaborators. It can be said of the bishop and his priests that their cause is common in the diocese : *causa communis existit.* [1] This is so not only because they must together edify the Lord's Church and lead her flocks, but also because their own sanctification is dependent upon the proper fulfillment of their state of life, which for them is the sacred ministry.

However, it is not possible to speak of holiness and perfection without touching upon the very delicate question of the *states of perfection.* This we must do, and we sincerely hope that our readers will accord our treatment the same respect which is accorded to all other approaches of grace. Our aim is not to contrast the secular clergy with the religious clergy. We simply wish to be able to answer a few of the important questions facing our priests : are they bound to seek perfection, can they attain it, and if so, by what means? [2]

* * *

What is a state of life? What is a state of life in relation to evangelical perfection? It is important to be extremely precise since we are in an area in which misunderstandings frequently arise because of inaccuracy in the use of terms.

---

[1] *Pontifical*, Admonition in the Ordination of Priests.

[2] On the problems of perfection, see especially Msgr. E. RANWEZ, *Morale et perfection* (Tournai 1959).

A state of life is a stable way of life in which the whole person is engaged in a definite mode of existence. As the basis of this, there must be a permanent element, or in any case, an element usually not subject to change. If it is an obligation freely incurred, it must be final and irrevocable. [1]

A state of life can be either private or merely internal, either public or social, thereby having a definite relation to society as is the case in the married or clerical state. The state of life can be, moreover, either completely social, or, at the same time, juridical, in so far as the rights and duties of this state are or are not recognized and sanctioned by law.

These distinctions are also valid for the religious society. The juridical state of life, called canonical, the state of life which has meaning not only before God but also before the Church, *coram Ecclesia*, requires an external and visible act. This was understood by the ancients to be a sort of *solemn oath*. This is the case in the married state in which a contract is made according to definite prescriptions set down in the Code of Canon Law. [2]

In the order of Christian perfection, a state of life exists as long as there is a stable way of life engaging the person in definite obligations necessary for the attainment of perfection. These obligations, however, can be considered from two aspects : either from the aspect of the end in view, which is the perfection to which all must tend according to their vocation, or from the aspect of the means used in tending towards perfection. In scholastic terminology, this would mean that the different states of life are in the first case considered in terms of the final cause, and in the second case in terms of the *dispositive*, material or instrumental cause.

Note — The word perfection did not always have exactly the same meaning even in papal documents. The Encyclical *Casti Connubii* of Pius XI, uses it as a synonym for sanctity. [3]

---

[1] St. Thomas, *Summa Theologica*, II-II, q. 183, a. 1.

[2] *Codex Juris Canonici*, can. 1094-1103.

[3] Pope Pius XI, Enc. *Casti Connubii* (Dec. 31, 1930), *AAS*, Vol. XXII, (1930), p. 548.

In one of the last discourses of Pius XII perfection is clearly linked to the practice of the evangelical counsels. It exists when these counsels are practiced over and over again, and when there is an oblation or complete and total giving of self, which will more easily guarantee perfect union to God through charity. [1] This is what St. Thomas refers to as instrumental perfection leading to the perfection of charity.

Using this term Pius XII more often spoke of the tending to perfection as the habitual disposition of a soul to follow the way of the counsels, even if this striving toward perfection is not sanctioned by the taking of vows.

In order to avoid confusion, we will simply use the term *perfection* and mean by this the perfection of charity as well as sanctity. The expression *tending to perfection* will therefore signify the constant and effective practice of the evangelical counsels. This distinction, as we have just remarked, is constantly evident in the writings and speeches of Pius XII. [2]

* * *

At baptism, the foundation of the Christian state of life, the obligation to seek sanctification is imposed. All God's children, each according to his state in life, are expected to be as perfect as their heavenly Father. In any case, all must live in conformity with the dignity of the Christian life with which the sacrament of Christian rebirth has invested them. [3] If difficulty is had in understanding this point, consider this statement of Pius XII : " We must not only admire the heroism of the saints, as we do now, on the occasion of the canonization of a humble

---

[1] Pope PIUS XII, *Allocution to the 2nd General Congress on the States of Perfection* (Dec. 9 1957), *AAS*, Vol. L (1958), p. 35.

[2] Observe how greatly this is stressed in the Note of July 13, 1952, published in my *Lettres Pastorales*, Vol. II (1952), pp. 121-23. Cfr. also the *Allocution to the 2nd General Congress on the States of Perfection* (Dec. 9, 1957), *loc. cit.*

[3] Gustave THILS, *Christian Holiness*, Eng. trans. John L. Ferrand, S. J. (Tielt : Lannoo, 1961), p. 4.

parish priest, St. Andrew Herbert Fournet, but we must also realize that everyone is called to sanctity. *Usually people do not consider sanctity as a vocation incumbent upon all men. This is an error. All men have the vocation to become saints.* Even though all are not called to achieve sanctity in the same way or reach the *same exalted heights,* all are called *to be saints.* " [1] This same call was also issued by Pius XI to married people. " Regardless of their condition or state of life, all can and must imitate the perfect exemplar of all holiness which God has presented to men in the person of Our Lord, and with the help of God, *attain the realization of Christian perfection.* " [2] In the very first year of his pontificate, on the occasion of the centenary of the death of St. Francis de Sales, Pius XI stated : " Be perfect as your heavenly Father is perfect. No one should think that this command is only addressed to a few chosen souls and that it is enough simply for the rest to tend to a lower degree of virtue. This law, as is evident from the text, binds *all* men without exception. " [3] Pope Pius XII spoke in exactly the same manner. [4] Moreover, St. Peter, the first Pope, did not consider a way of life worthy of the name Christian unless it was a life obedient to God in all things. Christians, bound to obedience, *filii obedientiae,* as he referred to them, must tend to sanctity, thereby following the command of Him who called them to the faith : " You shall be holy, because I am holy. " [5]

*   *
   *

Charity, in which perfection essentially consists, unites a person to God and joins him to His holy will. It tends to love

---

[1] Pope Pius XI, *Discourse,* after the approval of two miracles for the canonization of Blessed Andrew Hubert Fournet and Blessed Marie de Sainte-Euphrasie Pelletier (Jan. 8, 1933), *L'Osservatore Romano* (Jan. 9-10, 1933).

[2] *Ibid.,* Enc. *Casti Connubii, loc. cit.,* p. 548.

[3] *Ibid.,* Enc. *Rerum Omnium Perturbationem* (Jan. 26, 1923), *AAS,* Vol. XV (1923), p. 50.

[4] Pope Pius XII, *Allocution to the First General Council of Religious* (Dec. 8, 1950), *AAS,* Vol. XLIII (1951), pp. 26-36; " Note " (July 13, 1952), *loc. cit.* — On the texts of Pius XI and Pius XII see Msgr. E. RANWEZ, *Morale et Perfection, op. cit.,* pp. 85-90.

[5] 1 Pt 1, 1-2; 14-16.

God more than all, to prefer nothing to God, to do nothing which is contrary to the love of God and to love also one's neighbor for the love of God.   There are certainly degrees in this charity, and the highest degree possible here on earth is when God is loved as much as He can be by a mortal creature.   The entire process of seeking this union of love with God must be sought in Christ and with Christ.   Beginning with baptism and according to the measure of grace providentially imparted to each person, each Christian is called to the perfection of charity. Nevertheless, there are states of life which by their very nature impose a new title and a more definite obligation to seek perfection; and these states also guarantee the graces necessary for the fulfillment of this obligation.   Such a state of life is that of the priesthood.   Because of the reception of the sacrament of Holy Orders, which consecrates priests for the important task of worship and the salvation of souls, *intuitu munerum quibus dedicantur*, priests must live a life in keeping with their vocation. According to the Code of Canon Law, they, even more than the laity, must lead a holy life. [1]

More than anyone else, the bishop is held to the obligation of perfect charity since he has been constituted as a successor to the apostles in order to represent Christ in the Church and to exercise among men, until the end of time, His office as High Priest, Teacher and Shepherd.

With the sole exception of the Blessed Mother, whose divine maternity is the supreme and incomparable example of collaboration with God, the bishop is, we repeat, more than anyone else, bound to perfection.   The humble and docile Virgin of Nazareth was predestined to be the Immaculate Queen of Angels and Saints.   In regard to Christian perfection, Mary is in a truly exalted state of life which is, as it were, a beacon for all states of life intent upon achieving perfection.   The more closely a vocation enters into collaboration with the redemptive and sanctifying work of Christ, the more it partakes of the graces

---

[1] *Codex Juris Canonici*, can. 124.

guaranteed for the attainment of this end. The bishop's and the priest's program of sanctification is therefore inspired by the lessons drawn from the contemplation of her whom we rightly call the Queen of the Clergy.

* * *

The relations between the religious life and evangelical perfection are of a different order. Whether cleric or lay, the religious pledges himself to be receptive to every divine grace given to him to regulate his life according to the evangelical counsels, and is thereby constituted in a stable way of life with all the means which will help him to tend toward the perfection of charity. From the point of view of the *means of perfection,* we must stress that the only canonical states of tending to perfection are those which include the obligation officially accepted by the Church of practicing the three counsels of poverty, chastity and obedience. [1] Quite frequently the religious life alone is thought of when mention is made of the states of perfection.

Actually, the Church presently recognizes three states of perfection, or more precisely, three states of tending to perfection, *status perfectionis acquirendae.* As we shall observe, this area is undergoing a development. In another section we will consider separately the bishop's state of perfection, the *status perfectionis acquisitae et communicandae,* the state of acquired perfection which is to be communicated.

We must also mention that the approval of the Church canonically constitutes a state of perfection. It is not, however, this intervention on the part of the religious authority which constitutes the state of perfection in itself and obliges a man to seek perfection. " Theology, " remarks Father Henry, " does not set down as a requirement of marriage the assistance of the

---

[1] See pp. 119-120. Before the 13th century, the monks only vowed conversion of life, obedience and monastic stability.

parish priest, but this is nevertheless a necessary canonical conditions which the theoligian does not exclude. Canonical conditions are quite different from theological realities. " [1]   Suarez understood this when he spoke of a state of perfection, not in the sight of the Church, but in the sight of God : " Through an interior vow anyone may be said to be in a state of perfection in the sight of God, although not in the sight of the Church. " [2] And thus, even before their official recognition as states of perfection, various associations, today known as lay institutes, existed and possessed all the essential elements necessary for their receiving approval.

The three canonical states presently recognized by the Church are : [3]

1. The religious state properly so called. Of necessity, it includes the profession of public vows, that is to say, vows recognized by the Church and received by her. Each member officially assumes a definite and perpetual obligation to practice the evangelical counsels of poverty, chastity and obedience. [4] This religious state demands the common life.

2. The societies of common life, such as the Vincentians or the White Fathers. The members of these societies pledge themselves also to the practice of the counsels, but by means other than public vows — either by private vows, or an oath of stability or in other ways. These pledges or promises are recognized by the Church. However, since they are not merely manifestations of individual piety, a dispensation can only be granted in virtue of powers specially delegated by the Church for this purpose. The principal and characteristic element of this second state of perfection is the common life and

---

[1] A. M. HENRY, review of the book by P. BEYER, *Les Instituts séculiers, La Vie Spirituelle*, Vol. XCII (1955), p. 216.

[2] SUAREZ, *De statu religionis et perfectionis*, Vol. I, chap. XII, p. 8.

[3] *Annuario Pontificio per l'anno* 1959 (Rome), pp. 869-949; J. BEYER, *Les Instituts séculiers op. cit.*, pp. 144-49.

[4] There are many counsels in the Gospels, but the three great counsels are viewed as including all the others. In fact, they are so comprehensive that they cover practically every aspect of life. G. THILS, *op. cit.*, pp. 324-25.

submission to a superior. The practice of the common life and the vow of poverty is less strict than in the religious life properly so called. This is why the members of these groups very often have a certain amount of control over their own possessions.

3. The secular institutes. In them we discover what Pius XII called the essence of the states of perfection, namely a tending toward perfection stablized by a pledge to practice the evangelical counsels. The common life is not demanded and only rarely exists. Instead, these are " groups of chosen souls " who, while remaining in the world, gather together in associations easily adaptable to the needs of the special apostolate in which they are engaged. [1] The Motu proprio *Primo Feliciter* of 1948 placed these institutes under the Sacred Congregation of Religious in order to assure unity in direction as well as to safeguard the spirit of the recognized states of perfection. [2]

*   *   *

Clerics, priests, and above all bishops, are bound to do all that they can to attain the perfection of charity. Actually, they have more of an obligation to seek perfection than religious. [3] Although they are not bound to make a profession of religious vows, they are nevertheless able, by living at least according to the spirit of the evangelical counsels, to avoid anything which might possibly hinder their spiritual progress. In this way, then, they will be sanctified by the very exercise of their sacred ministry, which, in itself, has tremendous possibilities for individual sanctification. On this point, it is particularly worth quoting

---

[1] Pope Pius XII, Const. *Provida Mater* (Feb. 11, 1947), *AAS*, Vol. XXXIX (1947), p. 117.

[2] *Ibid.*, Motu proprio *Primo Feliciter* (March 12, 1948), *AAS*, Vol. XL (1948), pp. 285-86.

[3] A truth which Pope John XXIII has recently reiterated in his Encyclical *Sacerdotii Nostri Primordia, op. cit.*, p. 550.

the following statement of E. Masure : " There is to be found an entire spirituality in the active ministry in the sense that this ministry is not only sanctified but sanctifies since it is charity in action. " [1]

Regarding the bishop whose specific state of perfection has been recognized from the earliest times as the *status perfectionis acquisitae et communicandae*, it may be said that his self-oblation is only sanctifying to the extent that the spirit of the evangelical counsels prevails in his life. If this spirit is truly rooted in him, the bishop will then certainly be sanctified through the performance of his special mission since the pastoral office, as St. Thomas points out, operates in the realm of perfection. [2] The following text of St. Hilary, cited by Pope Pius XII, is worth recalling.

> If the bishop is faithful to his duties, if by word and deed he strengthens those who are weak, if he assists those who are wavering and converts the erring, if he dispenses the word of life to those whom he is obliged to nourish with the food of eternity, when death comes and finds him engaged in such activity, he will receive from the Lord the glory promised to the loyal administrator and the diligent overseer. Thus he will partake of heavenly glory near God since there is nothing greater nor anything better. [3]

Historical Note on the States of Perfection

The history of the Church attests that the Hierarchy has always been concerned with helping souls to attain evangelical perfection. Likewise, in our own time, the Holy See, with the assistance of the Holy Spirit, is engaged in developing and

---

[1] E. MASURE, " Trends in Contemporary Spirituality in France " in J. GAUTHIER, *Some Schools of Catholic Spirituality*, Eng. trans. Kathryn Sullivan, R.S.C.J. (New York : Desclée, 1959), p. 347. See G. THILS, *op. cit.*, p. 20. He shows how the duties of a state of life also demand of every priest a personal response to his Christian and priestly vocation.

[2] St. THOMAS, *Summa Theologica*, II-II, q. 184, a. 8.

[3] Pope PIUS XII, *Homily for the canonization of St. Vincent-Maria Strombi* (June 11, 1950), *AAS*, Vol. XLII (1950), p. 518.

adapting the states of perfection to present day needs. On a number of occasions Pius XII spoke explicitly on this very point. [1]

From the earliest days of Christianity, the most fervent Christians were intent upon following the Lord more closely : " *Come follow Me.... These follow the Lamb wherever he goes.* " [2] This can be done either through a life of asceticism or through the active ministry. [3] Both of these approaches are inspired by faith and animated by love. In both ways souls can consecrate and dedicate themselves to a life of total self-renunciation. Such renunciation of self found its greatest expression in martyrdom. Baptism of blood was so great an ideal in early Christian spirituality that those not called to undergo it sought to achieve the same effect — either through what they referred to as the martyrdom of the ascetical life, or through a total dedication of themselves to the active ministry.

In the teaching and example of Jesus and His apostles, we find all the principles necessary for tending to perfection through the ascetical life. Soon, however, many lay Christians began to leave the world to live the eremitical life in the desert. Being thus cut off even from the Christian communities, they endeavored to live only for the next world. The cenobitical way of life was the next to arise. This offered more possibilities for the practice of the social virtues, particularly humility, obedience and fraternal charity. In these groups, which were originally composed of isolated groups of hermits, St. Basil emphasized charity and the spirit of spiritual brotherhood. Nearer still to this ideal, St. Benedict placed more emphasis upon the familial character of these communities. This is especially evident in the paternal authority of the superior, the *abbas*. In order to achieve perfection, Benedict's monks pledged themselves to a conversion of life, stability and obedience. For quite a long period of time, these communities

[1] Pope Pius XII, Const. *Provida Mater, loc. cit.*, p. 115.

[2] Mt 19, 21; Ap 14, 4.

[3] G. Thils, *op. cit.*, pp. 525-26.

only had as many priests as were necessary to provide for the spiritual needs of the community.

We should not forget that the apostolic life led by those great initiators and pioneers, the apostles of Christ, was essentially a life of dedication to the work of spreading the Gospel throughout the world. More than anyone else, they were conscious of being the imitators of the Master and of being possessed by His Spirit. Instead of fleeing from the world, they went forth after Pentecost intent upon living in it and upon spreading Christ's grace and truth. They practiced the asceticism of the Gospel and total self-renunciation according to their own vocation. What they considered most important in the evangelical counsels was their spirit. This fact is clearly brought out in the account of the property held in common by the members of the Jerusalem Church, and it serves as a lesson in the exegesis of the words of the Master. The apostles handed on their spirituality to their collaborators, the bishops, priests and deacons. They also employed it in giving direction to the early virgins and widows, the precious helpers of their ministry. [1]

Both of these states of life, the contemplative and active, which were to continue up until our own day and which were to result in two vocations and two spiritualities, [2] were, before very long, being effectively combined. In the East, from the fourth century on, there was a constant coming and going between the solitude of the monasteries and the activity of the Episcopal Sees. Many priests lived as monks for a number of years, and it soon became common for monks to be chosen as bishops. In the West, several bishops, among whom St. Augustine was the most famous, established communities of priests and lay helpers to assist their dioceses. Quite frequently these communities were given a

---

[1] 1 Tim 5, 3-16; see, for example, the commentary of G. BARDY in L. PIROT, *La Sainte Bible*, Vol. XXII (1938), pp. 225-27.

[2] When Pope Pius XII addressed himself to the secular and religious clergy in Spain, he spoke of *religious perfection* and *sacerdota perfection* — *Letter to Cardinal V. Valeri*, on the occasion of the Congress on Perfection t Madrid, *AAS*, Vol. XLVIII (1956), p. 662. Perfection and the apostolate are proposed or both but according to the distinct orientation of each. See also the important document on perfection and the secular clergy which is reproduced here in the Appendix, pp. 301-303.

constitution which was, in many ways, similar to that of the monastic communities. Thus, by the end of the fourth century, there existed episcopal communities and schools as well as monastic communities and schools. Although the rule attributed to St. Augustine only dates from the Middle Ages, it is nevertheless true that it is imbued with the spirit of the great Bishop of Hippo. His patronage has justifiably been invoked ever since by other groups of canons regular. Thus, there arose a type of life situated midway between the traditional clerical way of life and the monastic life. The Premonstratensian Order, whose members are not monks but *regulars*, is but one example of this type of life. The distinction between regulars and seculars dates from the eleventh century. The monastic way of life also underwent a further development. To the life of asceticism and manual life there was soon added the Divine Office and the *lectio divina*. As the number of priests in each community continued to increase, apostolic activity quickly tended to be exercised outside the cloister and at times far beyond the monastery. Toward the end of the sixth century, Gregory the Great selected Benedictine monks for the missionary conquest of England. However, the parochial ministry was always viewed as secondary and exceptional by monasticism. Thus, the monastic way of life was in principle quite distinct from the Orders of Canons and the active religious societies which were soon to arise in great numbers.

The diocesan way of life also underwent a development which had an effect upon the relations between the local bishop and his priests. The presbyterium, according to St. Ignatius, is united to a bishop as strings to a lyre. [1] The presbyterium was the college of priests associated in the sacred ministry and the pastoral activity of the bishop. The idea of collaboration in the work of the bishop was fundamental, whereas the idea of the common life was secondary. Thus, when the rural parishes were created, and when priests were of necessity spread out far and

---

[1] St. IGNATIUS, *Ad Ephesios* 4, 1.

wide, this change in the diocesan way of life presented no difficulties. Communities of priests differing from the episcopal communities were also established. They were under the direction of a local superior who was called the abbé, the *abbas*. These were the collegiate chapters, which were established at the time when the veneration of important relics began, and the cathedral chapters, whose members served as the bishop's principal advisors. This evolution was complete and irreversible. The Council of Trent was later to sanction this system of having the clergy spread out in different areas — a result of the ever-increasing number of parishes that were being established in cities and rural areas.

It is indeed a remarkable fact that up until the ninth century every aspect of the religious life of the diocese was centered around the bishop. In fact, all priests, whether members of a cathedral chapter, or diocesan priests serving in rural areas, or monks living in an abbey, were all diocesan priests. The Carolingian period, however, marked a definite turning point in the relations existing between priests and bishops. There were many reasons for this. The feudal system regarded bishoprics, abbeys and chapters as temporal powers; and this gave rise in the Church to conflicts of interest and influence. As a result of such a climate, serious moral disorders arose and the situation progressively worsened to such an extent that priests laboring in rural areas found it quite easy to abandon their ministry. Religious societies became interdiocesan and then universal. The law of exemption was introduced and applied to practically all of the abbeys and chapters. Faculties of theology in universities were created since the cathedral and monastic schools, which from the time of St. Augustine had served as seminaries, lost their best members during this period and rapidly declined. This is why a great many priests were ordained without sufficient preparation. Because of these conditions it was only a matter of time before the role of the bishop was lessened. This had a damaging effect not only upon the secular clergy but also upon the entire Church.

It is not surprising then that the Council of Trent, desirous of spiritual restoration, sought to re-establish the bonds uniting priests to their bishops and to guarantee clerics a better formation by means of well organized seminaries. [1]

The moral crisis experienced by the Church from the ninth to the eleventh century took its toll in all areas of the Church, the parish clergy, cathedral chapters and monasteries.

This decadence has been particularly exaggerated in regard to the canons and the secular clergy. [2] By the beginning of the eleventh century, a resurgence of Christian life which was more in keeping with the Gospel began to be noticed. Even prior to the disorders which arose because of the huge benefices and the ever-increasing attachments to riches, many reformers preached at great length about the need of renouncing wealth and of returning to what was referred to, in different terms, as the *apostolic way of life*. The reform of many chapters and monasteries ensued and a number of new institutions arose. The most famous of the twelfth century institutions were those founded by St. Bernard and St. Norbert for monks and canons respectively.

The reform of the chapters took different forms. While certain chapters were merely content with a return to the observance of their original rules and way of life, others, as we have observed, took on the status of religious. Some were subject to the bishop in the same way as they had always been while others functioned as a more or less autonomous organization within the diocese, while others even extended beyond a particular diocese and were exempt in law.

As a result, the terms canons regular and canons secular were employed to distinguish the two main types of canons.

For a long time monks had been the only religious in the Church. The emergence of chapters of canons regular is the

---

[1] On the question of the seminaries and institutions which preceded them see J. A. O'DONOHOE, *Tridentine Seminary Legislation, Its Sources and Its Formation, op. cit.*, pp. 1-14.

[2] See especially the studies of C. DEREINE, " Chanoines " (Des origines au xiiie siècle), *Dictionnaire d'histoire et de géographie ecclésiastiques*, Vol. XII (1951), cols. 353-405, *passim ; Les chanoines réguliers au diocèse de Liège avant saint Norbert* (Bruxelles 1952), pp. 18-30.

beginning of a long development which will dominate the entire history of religious from the Middle Ages until modern times. Actually, the parochial ministry was not primarily stressed by Robert d'Arbissel or St. Norbert, but their disciples did devote much time to preaching and parish work. The idea soon caught on and by the thirteenth century the Mendicant Orders, such as the Dominicans, Franciscans and Carmelites, had been founded. Along with the definite obligations and observances of their respective rules, these orders also engaged in preaching and missionary work. They had no relation to any particular diocese but were directly subject to a superior general endowed by Rome with extensive powers. Their very name indicates that they professed a more radical type of poverty, which, at least in principle, did not even permit the community to possess any property.

In the sixteenth century the clerics regular, such as the Theatines, Jesuits and Barnabites *et al.*, arose. The priesthood was for them so important a part of their spirituality that they saw fit to sacrifice whatever was not essential to their religious state of life for the sake of the active ministry in whatever form it existed.

Up until 1900, these religious societies were the only ones recognized by the Church as religious societies properly so called. On December 8, 1900, Pope Leo XIII, in his apostolic Constitution *Conditae a Christo Ecclesiae*, extended the status of religious to congregations of simple vows which by the end of the sixteenth century had arisen in the Church. Up until that time they were only considered pious associations.

The present Code of Canon Law, however, includes among religious societies properly so called, at least in many regards, societies of common life without vows, such as the Vincentians, the Oratorians, the White Fathers. These societies either do not take any vows, or if they do, they only take them privately. Yet they live a community life which is very similar to that of religious; and they are dedicated, as are religious, to striving for perfection and engaging in apostolic and charitable works.

This is, as we have already stated, the second state of perfection now recognized by the Church. [1]

Since 1947, the secular institutes have been considered as constituting the third state of perfection. The obligatory practice of the three evangelical counsels and the dedication of one's life to the work of the apostolate in whatever form this exists are included here, but there is no obligation to lead a common life or to take public vows. The term secular indicates that the members in no way intend to change the social status that they had or would have had in the world had they not joined these institutes.

As a result of this long development, the Church only recognizes as states of perfection those states of life which include the three vows of poverty, chastity and obedience, or at least promises establishing canonically moral equivalents to the vows.

*   *   *

Has this development come to an end? Is it not possible that other states of perfection will be accorded recognition? Several authors believe this possible and even probable. [2] Do not some of the later statements of Pius XII lead us to believe that this will soon be so?

When I met the late Holy Father in 1957, he appeared to me to be particularly concerned with the desires of priests and lay people who wished to undertake a perfect way of life which would lack, even more so than the secular institutes, any special external framework. Was not this the concern which, in

---

[1] On the development of the religious life and the states of perfection see C. DEREINE, *loc. cit.*; P. PISANI, *Les Compagnies de prêtres du XVI° siècle au XVIII° siècle* (Paris 1927); Dom O. ROUSSEAU, *Monachisme et vie religieuse* (Chevetogne 1957). See also " Stati di perfezione (maschili di diritto pontificio), " *Annuario Pontificio per l'anno 1959* (Città del Vaticano), pp. 839-918.

[2] J. GOEYVAERTS, " De seculiere Instituten, " *Collectanea Mechliniensia*, Vol. XL (1955), p. 206; A. HAYEN, " Les Instituts séculiers, " *Evangéliser*, Vol. X (1956), p. 320.

December 1957, resulted in the address of Pius XII to the Second General Congress of the States of Perfection?

There can be, the Holy Father stated, " a real tending to perfection " apart from the canonical states of perfection. This tending to perfection is an habitual disposition of the Christian soul to devote itself entirely to God through the continuous practice of the evangelical counsels for the purpose of loving and serving God. It likewise includes a dedication of self to the service of one's neighbor for exactly the same purpose. According to the Holy Father :

> The ideal of Christian perfection is derived from the teachings of Christ and in particular from the evangelical counsels. It is derived from the life of Christ, from His passion and death — the inexhaustible fonts in which the heroism of all Christian generations finds its inspiration. It also includes the work of Christ, that is to say, the service of the Church performed out of love for Christ, in the position and according to the function that devolves upon each one in the Mystical Body.

> Every Christian is called upon to strive to attain this ideal of perfection with all his strength, but it is fulfilled in a more complete and definite way in the three states of perfection according to the manner described in Canon Law and in the aforementioned Apostolic Constitutions. In particular the Constitution *Provida Mater* of February 2, 1947 on " Secular Institutes " gives to the greatest possible number of souls, who eagerly aspire today to a more perfect life, access to the states of perfection. Although this Constitution states that associations which do not meet the prescribed requirements do not constitute " states of perfection, " it does not claim in any way that there do not exist real tendencies to perfection outside of these associations.

> We are thinking at this moment of all those men and women from all walks of life who, assuming the most varied professions and functions in the modern world, out of love for God and in order to serve Him in their fellowmen,

dedicate their person and all their activities to Him. They pledge themselves to the practice of the evangelical counsels by private and secret vows known only to God and allow themselves to be guided in matters of obedience and poverty by persons whom the Church has judged fit for this purpose and to whom she has entrusted the task of directing others in the exercise of perfection.

None of the constitutive elements of Christian perfection and of a real tendency to achieve it are lacking in these men and women. They therefore really take part in it although they are not committed to any juridic or canonical state of perfection.

It is clear that in the essential elements of its definition and its realization, Christian perfection does not allow for any revision or adaptation. But, since the conditions of modern life undergo deep changes, modifications will be required in one's application of it.

These modifications will affect those who live in states of perfection and those who do not participate in them, but even more so the latter, especially if they hold a high social rank and even higher functions. Are they not compelled then to surround themselves with a certain wealthy apparel, take part in official functions and utilize costly means of transportation : all things that would seem to be hard to reconcile with the constant preoccupation with the mortification of one who wishes to follow and imitate the humble and poor Christ?

And yet, in the midst of material goods, they do not depart in any manner from the entire dedication of themselves to God and never cease to offer to the Lord an unreserved oblation of themselves. Such is the action of grace which works in man according to the words of Christ : " Things that are impossible with men are possible with God. " [1]

These lives, whose commitment is total and whose tending to perfection is effective and lasting, include therefore all the

---

[1] Pope Pius XII, *Allocution to the Second Congress on the States of Perfection, loc. cit.,* pp. 35-37.

essential and constitutive elements of perfection. Even though in the eyes of the Church, they do not represent a state of perfection, are they not, as Suarez teaches, accepted as such by God?[1] Besides, can we not hope some day soon to see the Church recognize in these dedicated lives a state of perfection? Does it not seem that the above statement of Pius XII already suggests how to proceed? Certain persons judged by the Church to be capable of directing others in the exercise of perfection would serve as guides and even superiors in those matters concerned with poverty and obedience. Although they would not be considered superiors but only counsellors, they would nevertheless be capable, at least, of leading the way to the perfect obedience of the constituted authority. Priests whose moral and religious life is regulated by diocesan statutes could profit from this. Members of pious associations such as the Priests, the Sons and the Daughters of St. Francis de Sales or the priests of the Apostolic Union, would also find this extremely beneficial for the proper observance of the rules of their respective associations.

Having made their vows to their bishop or his delegate, they would then be part of a pious union or would simply be part of the secular clergy like other priests. However, in obeying the bishop's delegate, they would each be constituted in a canonical state of perfection.[2]

The status of those who joined the associations founded by Cardinal Mercier in 1918, such as the Fraternity of Friends of Jesus for priests and the Auxiliaries of the Apostolate for the laity, differ only slightly from what we have just described. All of these associations, although involved in special works, seek to be completely diocesan in character. The local ordinary is their only superior, and the only bonds existing between the members are those derived from their mutual friendship and collaboration in the work of the bishop. Their founders also saw fit to allow no other authority to come between the bishop and his priests

---

[1] See above p. 119.

[2] In short, this is precisely what St. Gregory Barbarigo, Bishop of Padua, did by allowing his oblates to add the vow of poverty to their vows of obedience and chastity. See above p. 36.

and lay helpers. Each member personally receives from the bishop, upon whom he totally depends for his share in the latter's work, a definite assignment and directions for his life. In this way organization is reduced to a minimum; and this exists only to facilitate the realization of the apostolic ideal in the world through close union with the bishops, the successors of the apostles. These strictly diocesan associations could not, without losing their special purpose, function as interdiocesan institutes. Although they can function in more than one diocese, they are, like the Oratories of St. Philip Neri, strictly autonomous diocesan groups. [1]

Have not preparations already been made for these new types of associations? Consider the reception given at Rome, more than twenty years ago, to the Fraternity of Friends of Jesus. Not only did Pope Pius XI, from the inception of his pontificate, [2] show himself favorable to this group, but on February 3, 1926, the Sacred Congregation of the Council issued a decree of praise, which Cardinal Van Roey published on December 27 of that year. [3] Consider also the numerous examples of " the individual profession of perfection always made in the face of the Church and in public, " in Christian antiquity. The Constitution *Provida Mater* mentions this type of profession made by virgins and widows in the early centuries. [4]

---

[1] See *Fraternité sacerdotale des Amis de Jésus, Commentaire des statuts* (Schilde-Anvers 1960).

[2] Card. D. J. MERCIER, *La Fraternité sacerdotale des Amis de Jésus* (Bruges-Paris 1927), pp. 47-49.

[3] *Ibid.*, pp. 5-8; Card. J. E. VAN ROEY, *Au service de l'Église*, Vol. II (1939), pp. 391-93.

[4] Pope PIUS XII, Const. *Provida Mater, loc. cit.*, p. 115 : " With motherly solicitude for all those who wholeheartedly and in different forms profess the life of perfection, she has never ceased to encourage them in their holy resolution. She has not only accepted and recognized the individual profession of perfection, provided it was made in the face of the Church and in public, like the ancient and venerable consecration of virgins which was formerly a liturgical ceremony, but she has wisely confirmed it and strenuously defended it, bestowing on it many canonical prerogatives. " This type of individual (*singularis*) profession is here distinguished from that which is made in a society or community established by the Church.

Chapter 10

The Episcopacy —
State of Perfection

The episcopacy was very early considered a state of perfection. [1] The reason for this is that bishops are completely dedicated by their office to the direction of souls, and consequently they must practice pastoral charity with supreme devotion in imitation of Christ, the Ideal Shepherd. [2] They are also the ambassadors of Christ par excellence, the most important missionaries of the Lord, in whom resides the fullness of the dignity of the apostolate. They are truly the most important members of the Mystical Body of Christ. Pope Pius XII frequently pointed this out to the faithful and stressed that, even more than others, bishops must have the fire of charity burning in their hearts and must never cease to spread this through the world by their pastoral and missionary zeal. [3] According to the exhortation given by St. Peter, they are to " tend the flock of God which is among you, governing not under constraint, but willingly, according to God, not for the sake of base gain, but eagerly. " [4]

This dedication of self to one's flock demands a great amount of love for Christ, but the Lord does not invite one to assume the duties of a bishop without giving an abundance of grace by which to love Christ perfectly. " The general rule, applicable to all

---

[1] SUAREZ, " De Statu Religionis et Perfectionis, " *op. cit.*, Vol. I, chap. xv, 5.

[2] " Vera et formalis ratio cur episcopi versentur in statu perfectionis est professio perpetuae curae animarum. " A. VERMEERSCH, *De Religiosis, Institutis et Personis*, Vol. I (Bruges 1902), p. 6.

[3] Pope PIUS XII, Enc. *Fidei Donum, loc. cit.*, pp. 235-36.

[4] 1 Pt 5, 1-4.

cases of special graces given to a rational creature, " states
St. Bernardine of Sienna, " is well known. Each time that divine
grace is given to someone for an exceptional task or for an
exalted state of life, this grace accords all the charisms demanded
by this task and state of life and it truly enriches it abundantly. " [1]
Certainly, the creature so chosen should correspond to the gifts
of God; but, as has been very well said, " human weakness
changes neither the demands nor the nature of God's love. " [2]
The sacramental grace of Holy Orders is also necessary for the
proper fulfillment, *digne agere*, of one's ministry. [3] Such a high
regard for the episcopacy is had by all who treat of the states of
perfection. However, in this particular field, the terminology
was somewhat elaborated with reference to the religious state
of perfection. [4] This accounts for the lack of clarity which
appears in many statements. Suarez had pointed out that the
state of perfection is different for the bishop and for the
religious. [5] Father Creusen therefore concludes that from the
start it is most important to attempt to determine a univocal
term of comparison when contrasting the episcopacy and the
religious life. [6] It was precisely for the purpose of avoiding any
confusion that we first considered the various states of life before
attempting to determine any possible relation that they might
have to perfection.

How does one go about concretely presenting the type of
life which situates, so to speak, the bishop in a state of perfection?
The following excerpt from the excellent work of Dom Lottin
provides us with just such a concrete presentation :

[1] St. BERNARDINE OF Sienna, *Sermon on St. Joseph*, read in the Breviary at the 2nd Nocturn
of the Solemnity of St. Joseph.

[2] J. J. BERTHIER, *De la perfection chrétienne et de la perfection religieuse d'après saint Thomas
et saint François de Sales*, Vol. II (1902), p. 250.

[3] See above p. 96; and also p. 166.

[4] Canon 487 of the Code of Canon Law defines only the religious state, i.e., the first
state of perfection; compare *Annuario Pontificio* (1959), p. 870.

[5] SUAREZ, *op. cit.*, Vol. I, chap. xviii, 9 : *Oportet advertere status episcopi et religiosi esse
diversarum rationum.*

[6] A. VERMEERSCH — J. CREUSEN *Epitome Juris Canonici*, 7th ed., Vol. I (Malines 1949),
p. 436.

The bishop is constituted in a state of perfection. Since he is totally dedicated to the service of God, in the person of all those he is to sanctify, is not his commitment as complete as that of the religious? The religious pledges himself to tend to perfection, but he is not asked to be perfect. Perfection is, on the contrary, expected of a bishop. The holiness that he must communicate should first be possessed by him. Service to others demands from all bishops an overflowing amount of charity which, although depriving them of the consolations of contemplation, results, through their generous activity, in the conquest of souls for Him whom they prefer above everything else. In what then is the bishop actually engaged? In the perfect practice of charity towards men.... Perfect charity seeks to extend itself beyond friends and strangers to enemies, even when these latter are not in extreme necessity. This charity reaches its full intensity, when, not merely content with putting one's goods at the disposal of others, a person exposes his body to fatigue, suffering and even endangers his safety and freedom for the salvation of his brothers.

Charity will be completely beneficial even beyond the benefits of the natural order when at the opportune time, it seeks to dispense to all people the supernatural graces derived from the Word of God and the sacraments. All these various aspects of fraternal charity are the endowment of the episcopacy. In assuming his office, the bishop pledges himself, in imitation of the apostles, to love his persecutors, to sacrifice his life and liberty in the service of his flock and to distribute to every member of his flock the graces with which he has been endowed. Such self-abnegation assumed by the bishop contains and, at the same time, far exceeds the sacrifices which the religious undertakes. [1]

This is what Cardinal Richaud has to say on this matter :

As a successor of the apostles, the bishop, in union with

---

[1] O. LOTTIN, " La doctrine de saint Thomas sur l'état religieux, " *La Vie spirituelle,* Vol. VII (1923), pp. 391-92.

the Pope, the Vicar of Christ for all mankind, is wedded to the Church. Like a husband in relation to his wife, the bishop no longer belongs to himself, but must devote himself entirely to his Church. According to the Gospel, the exercise of authority is a sort of servitude. Bossuet declared : " What is the episcopacy except a type of servitude which charity imposes upon us for the purpose of saving souls! " There is no more formidable and demanding a task than that of the episcopacy. However, there is no task which is as gratifying. Jesus told St. Peter that caring for the souls of others indicates a tremendous amount of love. When Bishop Saliège took canonical possession of his diocese at Gap, and later on at Toulouse, he expressed the sentiment of St. Paul when he declared : " Our heart is overflowing. " The heart which tries to assume the proportions of Christ's heart : what an excellent description of what a Pontiff ought to be; and this is exactly what the Cardinal (Saliège) desired when he assumed the ring and the shepherd's staff. [1]

*   *   *

The episcopal state, therefore, is designed for ministering to souls for the sake of Christ. The bishop is committed to the pastoral care of his flock; he is essentially a shepherd, *pascit oves :* " Bishops are obliged, " states St. Thomas, " to fulfill their pastoral office for the *salvation of their subjects.* " [2] As a successor of the apostles, the bishop has, by divine right, the mission and the power of representing Christ before men and of performing among them all the duties of the Good Shepherd, whose lieutenant he is. Episcopal Consecration perfects this mission and constitutes along with it the basis of the episcopal state of life.

---

[1] Card. P. RICHAUD, *Éloge funèbre du Cardinal Saliège* (Dec. 18, 1956), in the collection of pastoral works entitled *Dans les chaînes du Christ* (Paris 1959), pp. 445-46.

[2] St. THOMAS, *Summa Theologica*, II-II, q. 185, a. 5.

Dom Botte writes :

Ordination is not simply the transmission of juridical or liturgical powers; it is a sacramental act which confers a grace of holiness. The members of the Hierarchy are consecrated to the service of God. As the Syrian ritual states, they are set apart. The grace of the Holy Spirit ought to transform their souls; it should help them to fulfill their mission in preaching just as much by example as by word. Holiness — and a holiness which exceeds that of the faithful — is at the same time imposed upon them through the awareness that they have of the gift that they have received and the responsibility that they have assumed in answering the call of God... The grace of the Holy Spirit is not given them exclusively to guarantee the juridical or sacramental validity of certain acts, but allows them to acquire a holiness which can serve as an example for the Christian people. [1]

Suffice it to add that the bishop cannot, as the Gospel states, look back, [2] and that he can only be freed of his pastoral duties by the Sovereign Pontiff, the sole authority which can dispense the religious of pontifical law from the perpetual vows. [3]

Set up in order to communicate doctrine, grace and the perfection of Christ [4] to his flock, the bishop is the *perfector of others;* he is in the *active* state of perfection, in *statu perfectionis communicandae.* [5] Whereas the religious is striving for perfection and is ranked in the Church as a disciple, the bishop ranks and functions as a ruler, a master of doctrine and a sanctifier : " The episcopal state, " St. Thomas declares, " pertains to perfection as a professorship of perfection. Hence the religious state is compared to the episcopal state as the school to the professorial

---

[1] B. Botte, " L'Ordre d'après les prières d'ordination, " *loc. cit.*, pp. 177-78.

[2] Lk 9, 62.

[3] St. Thomas, *Summa Theologica*, II, q. 184, a. 6 in cor. and ad 2.

[4] Not his own perfection as Vermeersch and Creusen wisely observe *op. cit.*, p. 437.

[5] A. Vermeersch, *De Religiosis, op. cit.*, Vol. I, p. 5.

chair. " [1]   Is it not more valuable to dedicate oneself solely to
God?   Will not the bishop hesitate to devote himself more
completely to the direction of souls if he is greatly concerned
with contemplation?   No, answers St. Thomas, since his pastoral
solicitude is specifically based on love of the Lord : " It is a sign
of greater love if a man devotes himself to others for his friend's
sake than if he be willing only to serve his friend. " [2]   The scene
in the Gospel in which St. Peter receives his assignment to feed
the flock out of love for His Master applies to apostles and
bishops alike. [3]   " Be it the task of love to feed the Lord's
flock, " declares St. Augustine. [4]   St. Gregory is even more
definite : " If, then, the care of feeding is a testimony of love,
he who, abounding in virtues, refuses to feed the flock of God,
is convicted of having no love for the Supreme Shepherd. " [5]
Citing this text, Blessed Bartholomew of the Martyrs, the great
sixteenth century bishop, wrote : " If, therefore, some abandon
their pastoral duties because they desire the quiet of contemplation, let them realize that they are responsible for many souls
whom they would have been able to help, had they remained
in the world. " [6]   In a letter written to his friend Henry, Bishop
of Verdun, who was considering giving up his pastoral duties,
St. Robert Bellarmine objects to this powerful attraction for the
contemplative life :

> Regarding the desire that you have to take the wings of
> a dove and to fly away to a place of very soothing peace
> and quiet, allow me to declare what is on my mind.   I do
> not believe that there is any more pleasing quiet to be found
> than in doing the will of God with all the strength of soul
> that one possesses.   I have always had special regard for
> those words of the Lord : " Father, take away this Chalice
> from me, nevertheless, not my will but thine be done. "

[1] St. THOMAS, *Summa Theologica*, II-II, q. 185, a. 8.

[2] *Ibid.*, II-II, q. 184, a. 7, ad 2.

[3] Jn 21, 15-17.

[4] St. AUGUSTINE, " In Joannem, " tr. 123; cited by St. THOMAS, *Summa Theologica*, II-II, q. 185, a. 2, ad 1.

[5] St. GREGORY, *De Cura Pastorali*, book I, chap. v.

[6] BARTHOLOMEW OF THE MARTYRS, *Stimulus Pasto 'm* (ed. 1667), Part 2, chap. x, p. 261.

The office of the Shepherd is replete with dangers.
However, since it pleased our Redeemer to call us into these dangers, who are we to dare ask : Why have You done this? He who loved us and laid down His life for us deigned to say to St. Peter, and through him to all shepherds : " If you love me, feed my sheep. " Who, except one who loves himself instead of God, would dare to answer the Lord by saying : I do not wish to feed Your sheep for fear of losing my own soul. The true lover of God says with the apostle : I prefer to be anathema to Christ for the sake of my brothers than not to assume the burden which divine love imposes on me. Thus, there can be no danger to salvation where charity reigns. Do not be imprudent. Does not charity cover a multitude of sins? Most esteemed Prince, I have seen fit to write these things which I have very often thought about, since I perceive that you are somewhat distressed by your pastoral office. [1]

Such a high regard for the episcopacy has lasted through the centuries and was affirmed in a very concrete manner during the time of the Council of Trent. The Fathers of the Council were especially concerned with stressing the great dignity of the bishop's mission. On the occasion of the canonization of St. Pius X, Pius XII exhorted the bishops to show forth charity by devoting themselves to all that is demanded by Christ's injunction to Peter, " If you love... , feed — *Si diligis... , pasce.* " The Pope explained that these words, which are a command of our divine Redeemer to the apostle Peter, show clearly the meaning of apostolic labor, its exalted virtue, and the reason for its merit. All bishops should imitate St. Pius X who " took that command from the lips of Christ and strenuously fulfilled it : he loved and fed. He loved Christ and fed His flock. " [2]

However, since it is necessary to love Christ to such a point, since the episcopal state necessarily demands the perfection of

---

[1] St. Robert BELLARMINE, " Letter of Nov. 6, 1601 to Henry of Lorraine, Bishop of Verdun "; cited by J. FULIGATTO - S. PETRA SANCTA, *Vita Roberti Bellarmini* (Antwerp ed. 1631), pp. 212-14.

[2] Pope PIUS XII, *Allocution to the Bishops* (May 31, 1954), *loc. cit.*, pp. 313-14.

charity, since there is no other vocation which demands the attainment of this, would it not be presumptuous to accept this charge? Certainly, as St. Thomas observes, it would be imprudent to undertake this presumptuously. Nevertheless, when God issues an invitation through the voice of the Pope, all difficulty disappears since, like any other real vocation, it is accompanied with the guarantee of all the necessary graces. [1] Are we to imagine that the vocation to the episcopacy is an exception to this rule — especially since, as Pius XII stated, the bishops are the most highly esteemed members of the Lord's Mystical Body?

The active life of the apostolate, sustained by grace, is sanctifying in itself since its actions are more directly ordered to perfect charity. This is particularly true of the bishop, who, in the process of fulfilling his pastoral office, lives, as it were, in a constant exercise of perfection — *status perfectionis exercendae*. Episcopal spirituality is, therefore, on the highest level, a spirituality of the duties of one's state of life. [2]

Certainly Suarez was not wrong in saying that the episcopal state, although higher in dignity and in perfection, is more exposed and less protected than the religious state. [3] But even Suarez admitted that the bishop's ministry is eminently suited to personal sanctification since the excellence of this ministry can only have a favorable reaction on the dispositions of those who are consecrated in the spirit of Christ. [4] Bartholomew of the

---

[1] St. THOMAS, *Summa Theologica*, II-II, q. 185, a. 1, ad 2; q. 186, a. 6.

[2] J. CHELODI, referring to Suarez (*op. cit.*, Vol. I, chap. xv, 9), says that the common doctrine of the Church is that bishops are in the state of " *perfectio exercenda*, " because " *ex munere omnes suas actiones impendere tenentur in exercitio virtutum propter aliorum salutem.* " (J. CHELODI - P. CIPROTTI, *op. cit.*, p. 381). — In Chelodi's view, Suarez says that, strictly speaking, it is enough for the bishop to do his best in the (necessary) exercise of his episcopal duty (*ibid.*, chap. xix, 9). Since the bishop takes the place of Christ among men, and since he must be the "*forma gregis*" and must adopt the apostolic rule of salvation by the Cross, there is no time when he is not completely bound by the demands of his charge. Certainly he is in no way obligated to take vows which are a means of perfection particular to the religious Life.

[3] *Minus securus et pluribus periculis expositus* (Suarez, *op. cit.*, chap. xviii, 13).

[4] Suarez says : *Opera quae exercet quo perfectiora sunt eo sunt ad crescendum in virtute aptiora. . . Licet episcopatus ad aliorum commoda per se primo institutus sit, quia vero commoda spiritualia sunt et per actiones valde perfectas proferuntur, non possunt in magnum spirituale bonum ipsiusmet operantis non redundare* (*op. cit.*, chap. xiv, 9, chap. xv, 9).

Martyrs stated : " It is absolutely false, as some maintain, that the exercise of the pastoral ministry hinders one from maintaining one's fervor and devotion. Is not this precisely the notion against which St. Bonaventure and many others reacted? " [1] Despite the definite dangers involved, the episcopal state contains in itself the means of sanctification which, to a great extent, make up for the dangers involved. As we have said, grace is abundantly given to those who humbly, generously and sincerely exercise their pastoral vocation. For this reason, Father Creusen maintains that the bishop is in the state of acquired perfection, since as soon as he freely assumes his tasks and fulfills them as he ought, this state objectively results in the exercise of perfect charity, [2] even though he himself may not yet have attained perfect charity. This last distinction is quite necessary since there are some bishops who are not good bishops just as there are some religious who are not good religious. It is true, nevertheless, that in regard to the personal life of the bishop, the episcopacy is a highly endowed way of perfection. [3] We may conclude by quoting Father Bouëssé : " The bishop's mission, consecrated as it is to the Church and so strongly linked to it that he can only achieve his own salvation by saving his flock, is the basis for the theology of the state of acquired perfection. " [4]

$$* \quad * \quad *$$

According to St. Thomas, the perfection of charity " consists essentially in following the precepts, " [5] thereby compelling us to follow Christ, in *sequela Christi*, by observing all the command-

---

[1] BARTHOLOMEW OF THE MARTYRS, *op. cit.*, p. 146.

[2] A. VERMEERSCH — J. CREUSEN, *op. cit.*, p. 437.

[3] According to Suarez (*op. cit.*, chap. V, 3), the episcopal state exists for the purpose of helping others, but it is a recognized state of perfection because of the personal benefit that the bishop can derive from it. For St. Thomas, the proper task of the bishop is that of *Perfector;* and he is sanctified precisely by his fulfilling this mission well.

[4] H. BOUËSSÉ, " *Le sacerdoce chrétien,* " *op. cit.*, p. 129.

[5] St. THOMAS, *Summa Theol.*, II-II, q. 184, a. 3.

ments.   Charity includes all of the other virtues in its sway.
It cannot cause us to love God as we ought without also requiring
us to observe all the precepts. [1]   It may also be maintained that
Christian perfection *simpliciter* (absolutely) consists of charity and
secundum quid (relatively) consists of the other virtues. [2]

Let us also consider that charity, of its very nature, tends
to the highest degree.   Thus we must love God with our whole
heart and strength.   This is not merely a matter of a counsel,
but concerns the law itself.   There is also in charity such a variety
of spiritual treasures that the fruits which are derived therefrom
are also conducive to perfection. [3]   Charity, then, is certainly the
mother of the virtues not only since it cannot fail to result in the
practice of the other virtues, but since its superabundance, *super-
abundantia charitatis*, as St. Thomas says, compels us to accomplish
our tasks perfectly in all circumstances. [4]   This is particularly
true since one of the best effects of charity is that pastoral zeal
increases through an abundance of the love of God. [5]

Those souls whose lives are consecrated to the exercise of
perfect charity, which is zeal for souls, are truly blessed.   This
is eminently true of the episcopal state of life in which the
commitment is so absolute that it constitutes a real state of
perfection.   We should also realize that such a total commitment
to the duties of the episcopal state of life, if it is to be truly
effective, must stem from perfect love of God.

To love Christ : that is everything.   *Si diligis, pasce*.   Father
Louis of Granada, speaking on the occasion of a bishop's
consecration, explained these words of Jesus to Peter : " In this
first choice of a shepherd for the Church, Christ wished to give
a criterion by which all subsequent shepherds would be chosen.

[1] St. Thomas, *Summa Theol.*, II-II, q. 188, a. 7.

[2] *Ibid.*, q. 184, a. 1, ad 2; q. 189, a. 1, ad 5.

[3] *Ibid.*, q. 186, a. 2.   *Consequuntur ex perfectione charitatis, pertinent ad perfectionem consequenter.*

[4] *Ibid.*, q. 186, a. 2; a. 7 ad 1.   We must not distinguish between an area of precepts
and an area of counsels, the latter being the domain wherein charity flourishes.   See
Msgr. E. Ranwez, *Morale et Perfection, op. cit.*, pp. 56 ff., 66-69, 103-4.

[5] St. Thomas, *Summa Theol.*, II-II, q. 184, a. 7, ad 2; q. 185, a. 1, ad 2.   See also the
text of St. Hilary of Poitiers repeated by Pius XII : see above p. 121.

Christ was not merely content with demanding whether or not Peter loved Him, but whether or not he loved Him more than the other apostles did. By this, Christ meant to indicate that in order to fulfill this great dignity, it is not enough to have a degree of charity equal to that of the others; rather, it is necessary to have a degree of charity surpassing theirs. " [1] The bishop should also be mindful that " the active life must be nourished by contemplation. " [2] He must be a man of prayer since, through prayer, he will obtain the refreshment of perfect charity, *spiritus gratiae . . . perfectae charitatis dulcedine abundanter reficiat.* Likewise, through prayer, he will maintain the fervor of his priestly ordination and his episcopal consecration. We read in the beautiful prayer to obtain charity : " O God, who turnest all things to the advantage of those who love You, implant in our hearts an undying love of You so that no temptation may have power to alter desires born of Thy inspiration. " [3]

* * *

Now, a problem arises. The episcopacy demands perfection *per se;* but as we have said, even though it procures the exercise of perfection, it does not directly confer the perfection of charity. Must the bishop then have recourse to the taking of vows? Must he take them at least privately? A negative answer must be given since vows are only instruments — assuredly valuable instruments, but instruments nevertheless — which are not necessary for the attainment of perfection. [4] What is demanded of the bishop, as of every Christian who wishes to be perfect, is that he deny himself according to the spirit of the evangelical

---

[1] LUIS OF GRENADA, *Traité du devoir et de la vie des évêques* (Fr. trans., Paris 1670), p. 16.

[2] O. LOTTIN, *La doctrine de saint Thomas, loc. cit.*, p. 391.

[3] " Orationes " *ad lib.*, n. 29.

[4] SUAREZ, *op. cit.*, Vol. I, chap. XIV, 8; XV, 11. Thus, the episcopacy is not recognized as a ' status perfectionis acquirendae.' F. WERNZ - P. VIDAL, *Jus Canonicum*, Vol. III (Rome 1933), *De Religiosis*, p. 6.

counsels. By a life of self-abnegation he will achieve the full flowering of charity. [1]

To observe the evangelical counsels means to deny oneself those things which are good in themselves, not only in order to remove any obstacles to the practice of charity, but also to permit charity to achieve its effects " with diligence, frequency and readiness, " which, according to St. Francis de Sales, are qualities of true devotion. [2] Of course, the counsels are particularly efficacious when they are vowed. This is why the expression the *evangelical counsels*, or simply the *counsels*, is frequently used as a synonym for vows. [3] It is quite important, however, to remember that the counsels can be observed without professing any vows, even private ones. St. Francis de Sales stated : " Certainly if they are vowed, and especially if solemnly vowed, they place a man in the state of perfection. Yet, to arrive at perfection itself, it suffices that they be observed.... Let us endeavor to practice well these virtues, each according to his vocation. Although they do not place us in the state of perfection, yet they will make us perfect. " [4]

Even if the counsels are vowed, perfection is not in them essentially, or *per se*, but only secondarily, instrumentally, dispositively. [5] They mark out and clear the way to perfection. The religious state is a state of tending to perfection, *status perfectionis acquirendae,* [6] somewhat like a school and a discipline, *exercitium et disciplina.* [7] Pope Pius XII constantly pointed out that, " When it is said that the religious state is a state of perfection, it is necessary to understand the expression in its

---

[1] On episcopal spirituality see especially, J. BORGONOVO, *Memoriale vitae et sanctimoniae episcopalis, Regole di perfezione, di vita, di governo* (Tipografia poliglotta Vaticana 1950).

[2] St FRANCIS de SALES, *Introduction to the Devout Life*, Part I, chap. I.

[3] See St. THOMAS, *Summa Theol.*, II-II, q. 184, a. 3; SUAREZ, *op. cit.*, chap. XI, 16; XIII, 8, 21.

[4] St. FRANCIS de SALES, *Introduction to the Devout Life*, Part III, chap. XI.

[5] St. THOMAS, *Summa Theol.*, II-II, q. 184, a. 3, q. 186, a. 2.

[6] *Codex Juris Canonici*, can. 488, § 1.

[7] St. THOMAS, *Summa Theol.*, II-II, q. 186, a. 3.

juridical sense. This would be better expressed by saying *state of tending to perfection.* " [1]

It is therefore necessary for each person, according to his vocation, to practice the virtues of poverty, chastity and obedience. On the one hand, the first principle is that fidelity to the precepts rules out any need of having recourse to the counsels since the duty of one's state greatly excels in these. [2] It is legitimate on the other hand, for many reasons, especially for the purpose of following a definite pastoral vocation, not to bind oneself by vows while, nevertheless, living in the spirit of the evangelical counsels. When we asked Pius XII what he felt about the insistence of some who presented the religious life as a life necessary for anyone who wished to obtain perfection, the Holy Father gave a very firm and direct answer to this question. The Pope stated : " This is true, but only for those who have a religious vocation. " Shortly after this, we received the *Note* which we published and which resolved the entire problem.

This is also the teaching, not only of St. Francis de Sales, but also of St. Thomas who found this same doctrine in the writings of such great bishops of the early centuries as St. Athanasius, St. Ambrose and St. Augustine. In considering the evangelical counsel of poverty, St. Thomas' *Summa* cites these Doctors of the Church.

How are we to regard the perfection of the bishops when the Church seems to conceive perfection in terms of a complete renunciation of the goods of this world? " If thou wilt be perfect, go, sell what thou hast and give to the poor, and come follow me. " [3] Are not the apostles the models of those who follow the Master? In fact, when they were going to preach in Galilee, He commanded them not to take along gold, silver or money. [4] They were aware that they had given up everything

---

[1] Pope Pius XII, " Note " (1952), Appendix I, pp. 301-303. See also the *Allocution to the Second Congress on the States of Perfection, loc. cit.*, pp. 35-36.

[2] Suarez, *op. cit.*, chap. xi, 1-3; St. Thomas, *Summa Theol.*, II-II, q. 185, a. 8. Thus, religious who become bishops are dispensed from the observance of the duties of their religious life in order that they may be able to accomplish their mission.

[3] Mt 19, 21.

[4] Mt 10, 9.

in order to be faithful to their vocation. [1]   Considering this
exegetical problem, St. Thomas questioned the universal application and the seeming absoluteness of this injunction.   He
argued that these great bishops could not have disregarded the
Gospel!   " It seems foolish to say that so many holy bishops as
Athanasius, Ambrose and Augustine would have disobeyed these
commandments if they felt themselves bound to observe them. " [2]

   *Perfectio non consistit essentialiter in paupertate, sed in Christi
sequela.*   Perfection does not essentially consist in poverty, but in
fidelity to the following of Christ.   Certainly, the possession and
administration of goods may very often be accompanied by
great cares and can therefore constitute an obstacle to the
attainment of perfection.   There is nothing wrong with material
goods serving as instruments of the active ministry.   Concern
for these material goods, moreover, can play a part in the service
of charity.   This was the understanding had by St. Thomas :
he did not understand why bishops should be required to give
away their goods since these goods could be used by them as
effective means of accomplishing their mission and of following
Christ in the way that He had devised for them. [3]

   Is this not also the view of Pius XII, expressed in one of his
last exhortations?   At the Second General Council of the States
of Perfection he stated, as we have seen, that a person can be
entirely consecrated to God and " never cease to offer to the
Lord an unreserved oblation of himself, " even in the midst of
material goods.   Giving further explanation, he declared, " There
are some who are compelled to surround themselves with a
certain wealthy apparel, take part in official functions and utilize
costly means of transportation, all things that would seem to be
hard to reconcile with the constant preoccupation with mortification of one who wishes to follow and imitate the poor and
humble Christ. " [4]

   [1] Mt 19, 27.
   [2] St. THOMAS, *Summa Theol.*, II-II, q. 185, a. 6, ad 2; compare q. 186, a. 2; SUAREZ,
op. cit., chap. X, 6.
   [3] *Ibid.*, ad 1; q. 186, a. 3, ad 5; q. 188, a. 7.
   [4] Pope PIUS XII, *Allocution to the 2nd Congress on the States of Perfection, loc. cit.*, p. 36.

Bishops are expected, however, to be careful not to become attached to riches so that they may be ready to give up everything in order to obey the Lord. [1] They are also expected to guard against ease and excessive comfort. [2] Although there have been, down through the course of centuries, many abuses, protests against these abuses were not lacking. Father Louis of Granada expressed the Church's feeling when he declared that extravagance and pomp could not be tolerated in the lives of those who profess to be living an apostolic and evangelical life.

Can we countenance a bishop's setting a magnificent table each day and drinking from vessels of silver and gold and retaining scores of brightly liveried lackeys, when we recall that he is the vicar on earth of the poor and humble Christ, who commands us to despise the goods of this earth? [3]

For those who object that times have changed, Louis of Granada answers :

Such ostentation, extravagance, wealth and pleasure are not overcome by more ostentation, extravagance, avarice and ease. Rather, ostentation is destroyed by humility, extravagance by sobriety, avarice by poverty, and ease and pleasure by austerity of life. If you still protest that times have changed, I will agree with you completely, provided that you agree that they have changed for the worse. Let no one doubt this. Since the malady is even greater now, a better remedy must therefore be devised. Since the corruption of our age is even greater than before, we need a greater degree of holiness due to the principle that grace must surpass sin. [4]

Concerning the counsel of obedience, allow us to quote from a recent work of Father Bouëssé :

The holiness of bishops is the greatest illustration in the

---

[1] St. Thomas says : *Hoc pertinet directe ad perfectionem... ad hoc maxime tenentur episcopi.* (*Summa Theol.*, II-II, q. 184, a. 7, ad 1 ; q. 185, a. 6).

[2] St. THOMAS, *Summa Theol.*, II-II, q. 188, a. 7.

[3] LOUIS OF GRANADA, *op. cit.*, p. 174.

[4] *Ibid.*, p. 184.

Church of sanctification through the fulfillment of the
duties of one's state of life. By not seeking even his own
interests, but by concentrating on the salvation of the
greatest number of souls (1 Cor 10, 33), the bishop, out
of love of God, renounces himself even more than the
religious. His external goods comprise what he must give
to others. For a long period of time, Church discipline
has demanded absolute chastity of a bishop. His obedience
is more extensive and more demanding than that of a
religious who obeys only one superior, because the bishop
becomes the servant of all those whom he seeks to direct.
He is the slave of all and not their master. The ministerial
activity of the Savior is summed up in the motto of the
Popes : *Servus servorum Dei.* [1]

It cannot be denied that the conduct of bishops was not
always exemplary, just as the conduct of other priests and even
monks was not always what it should have been. [2] It is quite
certain, however, that the Councils never ceased to remind them
of their mission to represent Christ among men. We would not
have enough space to enumerate all of the Fathers and the
spiritual writers who throughout the centuries have treated
priestly holiness. Canon Bardy, who made these observations,
adds : " History is more liable to record the bad examples than
the good ones. " [3]

*   *
*

In summing up, we can say that episcopal spirituality is
eminently a spirituality derived from the highly sanctifying duties
of the episcopal state of life. The bishop's total and irrevocable

---

[1] H. Bouëssé, *op. cit.*, p. 149.

[2] See, for example, the complaints of St. Augustine cited by G. Bardy, *Saint Augustin,
l'homme et l'œuvre, op. cit.*, p. 141. On the Middle Ages see L. Genicot, *Les lignes de faîte du
moyen âge, op. cit.*, esp. pp. 178-79. On modern times see above pp. 36-38.

[3] G. Bardy, " Le sacerdoce chrétien du 1er au ve siècle, " *Prêtres d'hier et d'aujourd'hui*
(Paris 1954), p. 42.

commitment to his pastoral mission is a perfect holocaust which places him in a state of perfection. Since this state of perfection is directly ordered to the spiritual good of his flock, it will guarantee to the bishop a continual exercise of perfect charity which, in itself, is sanctifying.

Bound more than anyone else to sanctity, the bishop draws his inspiration from the spirit of the evangelical counsels and is sustained by the sentiments of humility, detachment and generosity which they inspire. The love of Christ is also accompanied by the realization that he has been entrusted with serious responsibilities for which he will have to render account before God. " You have no idea what it means to be a bishop, " St. Pius X told his mother, " I stand to lose my soul if I do not perform my duty. " [1] The Servant of God, Bishop Scallabrini, once said that his blood grew cold whenever he considered the great responsibilities which a bishop possesses. [2] Another Servant of God, Bishop Moreau, Bishop of Saint-Hyacinthe in Canada, stated : " It is a serious business being a bishop, and I never cease to be struck with fear whenever I remind myself that I am a bishop and that I am responsible for thousands of souls. " [3]

---

[1] J. DAL-GAL, *Pius X*, Eng. trans. Thomas Murray (Westminster : Newman Press, 1954), p. 53.

[2] I. FELICI, *Il Padre degli Emigrati, Gi. B. Scalabrini* (Monza 1954), p. 295.

[3] F. LANGEVIN, *Monseigneur Louis-Zéphirin Moreau* (Québec 1937), p. 110.

Chapter 11

The Secular Priest and the
States of Perfection

There is no doubt, as we have said, [1] that the priest, because of his priestly state and the important tasks given him to perform, is called to practice charity to perfection even more than other members of the faithful and even more than simple religious. There can be no doubt either that the reverent exercise of his sacred ministry is highly sanctifying. It is precisely by living according to the spirit, at least, of the evangelical counsels that he will be assured of a ministry which will be reverently exercised and which will therefore be sanctifying.

The question that now arises is this : Is the priest in a state of perfection by virtue of his ordination, or is he introduced into it by his caring for souls? This was a much discussed question during the Middle Ages; and it has, within recent times, produced a vast amount of writing. We believe that it can be considered dispassionately and that some moderate conclusions can be reached which will be extremely reassuring to the diocesan clergy.

It is first of all necessary to ascertain whether the priestly state is being compared with the episcopal state or the religious state. When the priestly state is treated, it is also necessary to ascertain whether Holy Orders, or the pastoral ministry, or the various situations confronting the modern secular priest are directly under consideration.

* * *

[1] See above, p. 117.

From the time of St. Thomas, it has been generally agreed
that the priest who is neither a bishop nor a religious is not,
strictly speaking, in a canonical state of perfection. [1] Nevertheless, the best authors qualify their statements. "We cannot
deny," Suarez states, "that priests in some way enjoy at least
a rudimentary or inchoative state of perfection, *aliquo modo statum
perfectionis saltem inchoatum.*" [2] Is not the priest bound by virtue
of his priestly character, *ex vi sui ordinis*, to lead a highly virtuous
life? [3] Is not every priest required to accomplish many varied
works of perfection? [4] The first reason does not seem pertinent
enough to us because the obligation to be perfect is not sufficient
to constitute a state of perfection. [5] The second reason may
possibly show a connection between the episcopal state and the
priestly state, especially, as we shall see in the case of a pastor,
but not a connection with the religious state of tending to
perfection. The priestly state *in itself* does not include the
specific means of the religious life, which principally consist in
the perpetual obligation of practicing the evangelical counsels. [6]
The problem is quite different when account is taken of the
historical evolution in the circumstances of clerical life. History
shows more and more similitaries between the status of clerics
and religious. Especially when texts of the Middle Ages are
cited to compare religious and seculars, sufficient account is usually not taken of the historical evolution in institutions. We
have, on the one hand, the Tridentine organization of seminaries
for the secular clergy, along with the great number of recommendations concerning the spiritual life of priests as set down in
common law and diocesan statutes. We have seen, on the other
hand, that the law regulating religious underwent quite a few

---

[1] St. THOMAS, *Summa Theol.*, II-II, q. 184, a. 6, 8.   Pope Pius XII says this clearly in his
Allocution to the 1st Congress of Religious (1950), *loc. cit.,* p. 29.

[2] SUAREZ, *op. cit.*, Vol. I, chap. XVII, 4.   See also T. SCHAEFER, *De Religiosis* (Rome 1947)
pp. 49-50.

   SUAREZ, *ibid.;* T. SCHAEFER, *loc. cit.*, considers canon 124 of the Code of Canon Law,

[3] SUAREZ, *ibid*.

[5] See above p. 118.

[6] St. THOMAS, *Summa Theol.*, II-II, q. 184, a. 6; A. VERMEERSCH, *De Religiosis, op. cit*
Vol. II, p. 53.

transformations, or if you prefer, adaptations during, the course of centuries. [1]

St. Thomas, nevertheless, pointed out that in the Latin Church the reception of Major Orders includes the obligation to observe perfect chastity in much the same way as this is included in the profession of religious vows. [2] Father Vermeersch, in considering the present-day clergy, writes : " In the Latin Church, all priests must practice perfect chastity. The majority of priests devote themselves to the tasks of their ministry with the obligation, also, of practicing obedience to their bishops in many different ways. In this way they approximate the type of life proper to religious, although only partially and imperfectly, *imperfecte et diminutive.* " [3]

It should also be noted that the small amount of personal resources and the many demands on their charity very often result in our priests living a very simple type of life.

As in the time of Suarez, the danger still exists that some may enter into a life of ease and comfort; [4] but this danger is not always absent in the cloister, where, as some have said, poverty is sometimes " compatible with a certain amount of ease, which does not necessarily exclude the superfluous. " [5] In any case, the usual economic condition of our pastors and curates is not conducive to the acquiring of a fortune, and our youth are well aware of this and freely accept it when they join the ranks of the diocesan clergy.

---

[1] See above pp. 121-28.

[2] St. THOMAS, *Summa theol.*, II-II, q. 184, a. 6. It seems that papal documents do not use the word *vow* for the reception of sub-diaconate, whereas it is found in (e.g.) St. Thomas. It is rather an obligation imposed by authority on those who aspire to the priesthood in the Latin Church. To appreciate more fully how much this obligation is in keeping with the consecration and mission of the priest as well as why this obligation will always remain extremely fitting, confer : A. SIMONET, " Aspects de la chasteté sacerdotale, " *Revue diocésaine de Namur* Vol. X (1955-56), pp. 20-33. See *Célibat et Sacerdoce* by Le Centre d'Étude doctrinale de Lille (Paris 1961).

[3] A. VERMEERSCH, *De Religiosis, op. cit.*, Vol. II, p. 53.

[4] SUAREZ, *op. cit.*, Vol. I, chap. XXI, 4.

[5] Msgr. A. ANCEL, " Essai sur la spiritualité du P. Chevrier, " extract from *La Vie spirituelle* (July-Aug., 1935), p. 19.

Thus the vow of chastity, canonical and synodal prescriptions, as well as the precepts and directives of diocesan authorities which are freely and generously accepted, situate priests in a state which is itself conducive to an increase of their fervor.

We can attest that on the day of their ordination our priests intend to offer themselves unreservedly to Christ and His Church. This total giving of self is similar to that made by religious on the day of their profession. Our priests are aware that they have not been asked to make the same special commitments as religious, but they realize, nevertheless, that they are bound to achieve personal sanctification and that the priesthood demands a greater degree of holiness than the religious life. [1] Does their choice to enter the diocesan priesthood indicate a greater or lesser love of Christ than if they had entered religion? Pope Pius XII answers :

> It may be that the decision of a young man to follow the vocation of a secular priest is a determination to a lower personal perfection than if he had chosen the priesthood in the religious state. It is equally possible that one person's choice of a state other than the state of perfection may spring from a greater love of God and a greater spirit of sacrifice than another person's choice of the religious state. [2]

Many of our priests are precisely like those described by Pius XII, who, " in the midst of material goods, do not depart in any manner from the entire dedication of themselves to God and never cease to offer to the Lord an unreserved oblation of themselves. " [3]

We do not deny that there does exist, on the canonical plane, an hiatus between the type of life in which a secular priest is engaged and the type of life demanded by a state of perfection

[1] *Note* (1952), *loc. cit.*, Appendix I, pp. 301-303.

[2] *Ibid.*

[3] Pope Pius XII, *Allocution to the 2nd Congress on the States of Perfection* (1957), *loc. cit.*, pp. 36-37.

officially recognized by the Church. As we have seen, this hiatus can be eliminated by the taking of the three vows in a secular institute. [1] It can also be eliminated in the sight of God by the taking of private and secret vows, and perhaps the time will soon come when the Church will offer us the means by which these private commitments will be accorded canonical standing. [2]

We should recall at this time the exceptional and long-standing example of the Oblates of St. Charles who were founded by the great Milanese reformer, St. Charles Borromeo. Originally known as the Oblates of St. Ambrose, these secular priests dedicate themselves, by a vow of obedience, to St. Ambrose, who lives on, as they say, in the person of the current archbishop. They pledge themselves to serve the bishop of their diocese and take a vow whose obligations are similar to those arising from religious vows. Besides the vow of obedience, this vow also partially includes a vow of poverty. There have always been at least a few hundred Oblates in the diocese of Milan, and their institute has been imitated in other dioceses. [3]

* * *

Since the priest of second rank serves in a definite place and is a cooperator of the bishop, is there any reason why he should not be in a state of perfection comparable to the episcopal state of perfection, *status perfectionis exercendae et applicandae?*

The question can only be stated in terms of the diocesan priests' participation in the pastoral mission, which properly belongs to the bishop. The most typical case of such participation is that enjoyed by the pastor, but a case can likewise be made for any type of participation in the care of souls. [4] The

---

[1] See above, p. 120.

[2] See above, pp. 128-32.

[3] See above, pp. 21-25.

[4] It is interesting to consult the Code of Canon Law on this point. The Church no longer wishes to have any of her clergy functioning outside of an hierarchical framework (*Vagi*, Can. 111, § 1). Every priest must belong either to a diocese or to a society

pastoral mission of bishops is perpetual and of divine right, for, as Pope Pius XII states, the bishops, successors of the apostles, possess, under the supreme authority of the Roman Pontiff, the triple mission of teaching, ruling and sanctifying. [1] The bishops' pastoral charge, which is solemnly professed at consecration, is complete and so demanding that it imposes upon them the obligation of complete devotion to their flock even to the point of laying down their lives.

According to St. Thomas, the pastor's situation is different since his obligation to care for souls proceeds not from his priestly ordination, but from a definite appointment which he receives. St. Thomas therefore believes that the pastor's mandate is not perpetual but merely limited and administrative, and hence it is a lower degree of participation, *in quantum participant de cura*. According to St. Thomas, the office of pastor lacks sufficient stability to be considered a definite state. [2]

Suarez, however, is less categorical. There is, he nevertheless maintains, a certain amount of stability in the pastor's office since he cannot be freed of his charge without the authorization of his superior, the bishop.

This entails, moreover, a consecration of his life to the flock entrusted to his care as well as an ever increasing necessity to achieve perfection and the obligation of engaging in his parochial ministry, which is an exercise of perfect charity. St. Pius X wrote : " Those who possess the title and the authority of parish priests have the obligation to care for souls by virtue of their

that is canonically erected; even a secular priest cannot be ordained unless his bishop judges that he is necessary, or at least useful, to the diocese (Can. 969, § 1). Since the secular priest is of necessity attached to a residential bishop, he can be considered as being solely at the disposal of his superiors only for the purpose of accomplishing that mission which is the very purpose of Holy Orders, i.e., the governing of the faithful and the conducting of divine worship (Canon 948). Since the bishops rule their dioceses by divine right and by their own power, it follows that the secular priest is completely at the disposal of the bishop as regards the performance of those duties which the bishop assigns him, and that his role in the Church is closely associated with that of the bishop. This state is common to all diocesan priests. However, a pastor is entrusted with the care of a parish *by title* and in a stable way, *potestate ordinaria*, in order to direct it under the authority of the local ordinary (Can. 451, § 1). The view that we have set forth here is, therefore, in perfect accord with this legislation.

[1] Pope Pius XII, *Discourse to the Bishops* (May 31, 1954), *loc. cit.*, p. 314. See above, p. 96.

[2] St. Thomas, *Summa Theol.*, II-II, q. 184, a. 8; Suarez, *op. cit.*, Vol. I, chap. xxi, 3.

rank and in a sense by virtue of a contract, *quodam quasi pacto inito*, and are, to a certain extent, the pastors and teachers appointed by Christ. " Consequently, they possess the obligations of the pastoral ministry. [1]

The pastoral ministry, in addition to the effects of ordination, is an added reason why we can attribute to secular priests a state of perfection comparable to that of the bishop, *aliqualis status perfectionis, licet in gradu inferiori.*

St. Thomas recognized that when pastors engage in their pastoral ministry, [2] they are operating in the realm of perfection, *habent quoddam officium ad perfectionem pertinens.* [3] The same can be said, to some extent, of any type of participation in the multifaceted apostolate of the bishop — even if the part that some play is not specifically pastoral. [4] The various aspects of the life of a diocese are complex, and thus if the various programs of the diocese are to be accomplished, different tasks of the administrative and material order must necessarily be allotted. [5] We can apply to all the faithful collaborators of the bishop what Father Bouëssé says regarding the " zealous priest, " namely that " he must regard the episcopal state as the typical example of his own priesthood, " and that " by ecclesiastical delegation he participates in the bishop's mission and, consequently, also in the latter's state of life. " [6]

* * *

[1] Pope Pius X, Enc. *Acerbo nimis* (April 15, 1906), *AAS*, Vol. XXXVII (1904-5), pp. 618-19.

[2] Suarez, *op. cit.*, chap. xvii, 18, 19. See also T. Schaefer, *op. cit.*, p. 50. J. De Guibert (*Revue d'ascétique et de mystique*, [1920], Vol. I, p. 286) remarks that in practice the Church tends " not to allow a priest's life to be divorced from the exercise of the ministry on behalf of souls. " Recall Pius X's instruction to bishops urging them not to ordain priests beyond the needs of their dioceses. See above, p. 155 footnote 4.

[3] St. Thomas, *Summa Theol.*, II-II, q. 184, a. 8.

[4] If the religious state resembles the episcopal state in that both are canonical states of perfection, the pastor is closer to the bishop by his participation in the pastoral charge. St. Thomas, *Summa Theol.*, II-II, q. 188, a. 8, ad 5. When St. Thomas contrasts the work of different religious orders, he follows the principle that those which share more intimately in the episcopal charge are the more perfect : *Summum gradum in religionibus tenet, quae ordinantur ad docendum et praedicandum, quae et propinquissimae sunt perfectioni episcoporum* (II-II, q. 188, a. 6).

[5] See G. Thils, *Nature et spiritualité du clergé diocésain* (Bruges 1948), pp. 222 ff.

[6] H. Bouëssé, *op. cit.*, pp. 146-52. See also R. Carpentier in Msgr. S. Delacroix, *Pour le clergé diocésain* (Paris 1947), pp. 87-88.

Each person must attain sanctification according to his own vocation. St. Thomas warns us, as we have seen, that there are bad religious and bad bishops just as there are saints outside the states of perfection. [1] A person may, in the external forum, be established in a state of perfection while still remaining entangled in the world through his dispositions and affections. [2] Regardless of how excellent the means may be, what is most important is the end, which is perfect charity. [3] It is much more valuable to live according to the spirit of the counsels outside of these states of perfection than to belong to one of these states without profiting from them as one ought. [4]

The spirituality of the diocesan priest is a spirituality of the priestly and diocesan state of life. Because of his priestly character, and because of the important tasks entrusted to him, the priest is bound to practice charity to perfection. " The necessity of the diocesan priest's being a saint, " states Dom Paleari, priest of Turin, " does not need to be demonstrated. It is as evident as the fact that fire is hot. Heroic sanctity is expected of the priest. Ordinary sanctity is not enough. Priests are expected to have an amount of sanctity which far exceeds the ordinary sanctity of the faithful. " [5] Since he is the bishop's cooperator, the diocesan priest must be aware of the duties of the bishop's state and must realize that he shares in his responsibility to care for the flock and also in his obligation to sanctify himself and to be outstanding before God and men for his virtue.

The spirituality of the diocesan priest is sustained by confidence. Father Bouëssé states that " the bishop and *his priests* engaged in the apostolic ministry must develop a tremendous amount of confidence regarding the sanctifying power of their ministry. " [6] They must also, we may observe, have confidence in the tremendous graces bestowed upon them

---

[1] St. THOMAS, *Summa Theol.*, II-II, q. 184, a. 4.
[2] *Ibid.*, q. 188, a. 2, ad 3.
[3] *Ibid.*, q. 184, a. 1.
[4] *Ibid.*, q. 186, a. 3.
[5] E. BECHIS, *Il canonico Francesco Paleari* (Alba 1945), p. 209.
[6] H. BOUËSSÉ, *op. cit.*, p. 153.

at ordination. Through the imposition of hands, as we shall see shortly, a new supernatural power is conferred. This is the power which inspires and accompanies the priest in his efforts at sanctification and which results in the proper fulfillment of his vocation. The secular priest should likewise be animated by a sense of friendly rivalry in attempting to achieve a degree of perfection which is at least equal to that of religious. We stress that it should at least be equal to that of religious since the secular priest has a greater obligation to tend to perfection than those religious who are not priests. Venerable Chevrier stated quite clearly that secular priests, the most direct witnesses of Christ in the world, must surpass all religious without exception, and that since they are so obligated they can best achieve this by corresponding with God's graces and by properly exercising their priesthood. [1] The very same view is found in the accounts of what the Servant of God, Joseph Allamano, frequently told the seminarians of Turin : " The secular priest must be more virtuous and holier than the religious. Whereas the latter is protected by his cell, the former sets out into the world without much experience and he must know how to maintain the high purpose of his vocation. " [2]

The way to perfection is mapped out in the Gospel through the observance of the counsels of poverty, chastity and obedience. It is not necessary to take vows, but we cannot forget that their spirit is imposed on all who earnestly desire to advance towards perfection. Certainly the priestly ministry, especially the parochial ministry, is sanctifying in itself; but it will only be so if the priest enters upon a life of constant prayer and if he generously lives according to the spirit, at least, of the evangelical counsels. His Holiness Pope John XXIII, when he was Patriarch of Venice, told his priests at a diocesan synod that they must be good and holy collaborators of their bishop. [3] The

---

[1] Msgr. A. ANCEL, " L'apostolat sacerdotal d'après le P. Chevrier, " extract from *La Vie spirituelle* (June-July, 1944), p. 6.

[2] P. L. SALES, *Giuseppe Allamano* (Turin 1944), 3rd ed., p. 70.

[3] Pope JOHN XXIII, *Father and Pastor of Souls* (Nov. 1957), discourse to the diocesan synod of Venice, translated in *La Documentation catholique*, Vol. XL (1958), p. 1620.

view of St. Charles Borromeo, as well as the constant teaching
on priestly spirituality proposed during the period following the
Council of Trent, may be summed up as follows : " Obedience
to the bishop is the only true basis of clerical perfection. " [1]

Two approaches regarding priestly spirituality may be
discerned. Venerable Chevrier believed that it was only fitting
that the secular priest, while remaining a secular, should imitate
the life of religious in all matters compatible with his ministry
in the world. [2] Others, however, believed that the attempts of
some to force the ways of religious upon diocesan priests were
completely out of order. They argued that this would be an
unfortunate complication of their lives which would only result
in discouraging them. In the nineteenth century, especially
during the time of the *French School*, the ideal proposed by most
spiritual writers was " to live as priests and only as priests. "
The Berullian Oratory, therefore, can be described as having
" no spirit except that of the Church, no rules except those found
in her canons, no bonds except those of charity, no vows except
those of baptism and the priesthood. " [3]

In determining the different circumstances, inclinations and
inspirations of the Spirit, there is a great need for tact and
moderation.

In any case, whether a priest is a religious or a secular, what
is most important is that he avail himself of the tremendous
spiritual treasures inherent in the priesthood. This has special
relevance for the secular clergy who will find therein all their
inspiration, strength and holiness.

Bérulle stated :

The priestly state, which is a holy and sacred state of life
and which boasts the Son of God as its founder, requires and
contains in itself perfection, even though it is not the type

---

[1] J. B. Noulleau, " Oraison funèbre de Mgr de Vilazel, " cited by P. Broutin, *La
Réforme pastorale en France au XVIIe siècle, op. cit.*, Vol. I, p. 186.

[2] Msgr. A. Ancel, *L'apostolat sacerdotal, op. cit.*, p. 6.

[3] M. H. Vicaire, " Le clergé catholique du xve au xxe siècle, " *Prêtres d'hier et
d'aujourd'hui, op. cit.*, p. 192.

of religious perfection which is attained by observing the three solemn vows. We nevertheless are attempting to steep ourselves in devotion to Jesus Christ, Our Lord, the Institutor of the Priesthood, to whom this congregation (the Oratory) is pledged and dedicated. We contemplate Christ precisely in His role as Institutor of the Priesthood and offer to Him all the affections of our soul and daily engage in the contemplation and imitation of His most holy life. We likewise have special devotion to the Most Blessed Virgin and to all the saints who associated themselves with her and her Son on earth. We have no special rules. *Vivimus moribus, non legibus.* [1]

The priestly state is not a state of perfection recognized by the Church. However, it obliges us to seek the way of holiness; and if we practice prayer and penance, it will lead us to holiness. It is truly a highly endowed way of perfection — as is evidenced by the tremendous number of saintly priests that it has produced. Cardinal Van Roey once stated : " There is no reason to believe that the life of perfection is impossible for a secular priest. Fortunately, we have many priests of great virtue who are living wonderful priestly lives and who are closely united to God. " [2] We shall soon see that many saintly priests have been inscribed in the catalogue of the Church's saints, and that there are also many others whose cause for beatification or canonization has been introduced at Rome. The saintly Curé of Ars is not, as many seem to believe, an isolated case. He serves as a peerless model and a splendid example for our clergy. His Holiness, Pope John XXIII, speaking to a group of Roman seminarians, observed, " The figure of this heroic priest provides us with much reflection on his generosity in God's service, his great humility and his renunciation of earthly honors and ambitions. " [3]

[1] *Correspondance du Cardinal de Bérulle*, Vol. I, pp. 235 ff, cited by P. BROUTIN, *La Réforme pastorale in France au XVIIe siècle, op. cit.*, Vol. II, p. 427.

[2] Card. J. E. VAN ROEY, " Exhortations aux prêtres " (Aug.-Sept. 1928), *Au service de l'Église* (1939), Vol. I, p. 173.

[3] Pope JOHN XXIII, *Homily to the Students of the Minor Seminary of Rome* (Jan. 8, 1959), *L'Osservatore Romano* (Jan. 7-8, 1959).

4

Spirituality of the Diocesan Clergy

Chapter 12

Priestly Spirituality
in General

Cardinal Van Roey wrote :

> We know from experience that young men who are freely
> aspiring to, and generously preparing themselves for the
> diocesan priesthood are offering themselves unreservedly
> to God for the service of Christ and His Church. We
> cannot consider their receiving the imposition of hands
> and the sacred anointing, with all the dispositions required
> by this act, as anything less than a total dedication of their
> lives equivalent to that made by religious on the day of their
> profession. It is unfortunately quite possible that the
> manner of their former lives may reassert itself in the future.
> However, does the state of perfection preserve a religious
> from the danger of such a relapse? [1]

This quotation reiterates the thought of St. Francis de
Sales : " Bishops, priests and religious have a special obligation
to achieve sanctity; and they must strive after it in a more perfect
way than those living in the world because they are more specially
dedicated to the service of Our Lord. " [2]

Bishops and priests are the first to be listed among those
consecrated to God. When he gave his famous conferences to
the Visitandines, the Bishop of Geneva used to number himself
among those called to perfect devotion : " We who are conse-

---

[1] Card. J. E. VAN ROEY, " Le prêtre diocésain d'après les encycliques pontificales, "
Au service de l'Église, Vol. VIII (1955), p. 234.

[2] St. FRANCIS de SALES " Sermon for the Feast of the Circumcision " (Jan. 1, 1622),
Annecy ed., Vol. X, p. 151.

crated to God's service. " [1] We may rightly conclude, therefore, that the special call to higher sanctity is not the sole monopoly of religious, and that priests are especially called to tend to perfection by living according to the spirit, at least, of the evangelical counsels to the extent that the demands of their vocation allow.   This is the whole meaning of consecration.

This is exactly the idea set forth by Cardinal Suhard in his famous pastoral on *The Priest in the World*.   " It is important, " he stated, " to base one's entire effort at priestly sanctification on the doctrine of consecration, which is had from an understanding of the sacrament of Holy Orders, not only in regard to the tremendous powers that it confers, but also in regard to the great obligation and graces which the priestly state imposes. " [2]   This is the very heart of the problem of priestly sanctification, and therefore it is important to consider the mystery of the priesthood from the aspect of the consecratory and sanctifying character that it impresses upon our souls.

At the very beginning of a person's religious life, he is presented with a choice which gives full meaning and value to his life.   On the day of his profession, the religious chooses a state of perfection or, better still, *a state of tending to perfection* [3] and enters into a stable way of life which motivates and sustains him in his quest for personal sanctification and union with God. On the level of supernatural ontology, there has been no change from what Baptism and Confirmation wrought in him.   The special feature of the religious state is on the *moral plane* and is expressed in the professed's pledging himself to the practice of perfection.

The oblation or, if you prefer, the generous consecration of the levite in assuming the priesthood, is on a different plane.

---

[1] St. FRANCIS de SALES, *Les vrais entretiens*, entr. IV, Annecy ed., Vol. VI, pp. 64-65. Not long afterwards, Jacques Marchant spoke out as the Bishop of Annecy.   Referring to the teaching of the Fathers, he compared the laity to the sacrifices of the Old Law, of which only a part went to God, and the priests to the holocausts in which God claimed the entire victim : *Sacerdotes vero holocausti rationem habere debent, cuius nulla pars erat quae Deo non offerabatur* (*op. cit.*, p. 36).

[2] Card. E. SUHARD, " Le Prêtre dans la Cité, " *La Documentation catholique*, Vol. XLVI (1949), p. 798.

[3] See above, pp. 115 ff.

Priestly spirituality as such is only understood in relation to the sacrament of Holy Orders which effects a change in the supernatural existence of the Christian. Whatever the precise nature of the sacramental character may be, it is certain that the sacrament of Holy Orders confers on the recipient a conformation to Christ the Priest and therefore entails a consecration to God for the priestly ministry. [1] This consecration, which by itself demands *activity*, *digne agere*, is the very source of *supernatural activity : operari sequitur esse*. This is the constant teaching of the earliest sacramentaries. [2] There can be no doubt regarding the fact that priestly consecration gives rise to a new supernatural power and an entire complex of special graces. As long as the priest corresponds with these graces and generously lives out his life of commitment and consecration to Christ the Priest, he will be enabled to fulfill his vocation effectively. Father Roguet wrote : " The purpose of the sacrament of Holy Orders is not to create priests but to create good and holy priests. " [3]

This consecration must *first* develop in the area of our *priestly existence*, our conformation and consecration to Christ the High Priest. There is nothing wrong with making use of the special helps of religious life, such as life in common and the taking of vows, but it should be clearly understood that these elements of religious life are extrinsic to the tremendous spiritual power inherent in priestly consecration, which in itself and without these special helps, is fully capable of producing all its effects. " Strictly speaking, " Cardinal Richaud writes, " it cannot be said that the priest consecrates himself to the Lord. Rather, it seems that it is *much more* precise to say that *it is the Lord who has consecrated him for Himself.*

[1] Although there are a number of varying theological opinions on this matter, it is certain, nevertheless, that the *sacramental character* is a consecration necessary for conducting divine worship and governing the Church. See, e.g., A. M. ROGUET, " La théologie du caractère et l'incorporation à l'Église, " *La Maison-Dieu*, 32 (1952), pp. 74-89.

[2] B. BOTTE, *L'Ordre d'après les prières d'ordination*, loc. cit., p. 177; A. BERAUDY, " Les effets de l'Ordre dans les Préfaces d'ordination du sacramentaire léonien, " *La tradition sacerdotale*, *op. cit.*, pp. 86-87.

[3] A. M. ROGUET, " La théologie du caractère... " *loc. cit.* p. 87.

His perfection therefore derives more from the duties entrusted to him than from special practices which he himself chooses — although these latter are demanded as a necessary condition for the exercise of the great powers conferred upon him. " [1]   This type of perfection must go beyond the mere exercise of powers and the performance of duties; it must result in a substantial configuration to Christ the Priest. [2]   St. Paul's motto, " I live now, not I, but Christ lives in me, " [3] has special meaning for the priest, and it also provides an excellent insight into the nature of the priesthood.   Besides the state of spiritual childhood, dating from our baptism, the priesthood demands another state, namely that of *victim* with Jesus Christ. [4]

We feel no hesitation in concluding that consecration to God through ordination is greater both in dignity and merit than the consecration resulting from the profession of religious vows, and hence this consecration results in inestimable graces for priests. Of all vocations that of the priesthood is unique.   The priest is the only one whose person is consecrated to God for a special vocation by a sacramental character.   How truly regrettable it is when some maintain that the priesthood is greater in dignity than the religious life but that this is its only advantage.

* * *

The circumstances giving rise to a vocation to the priesthood are personal to each and differ from individual to individual. Who can gauge the part played by such influences as the home,

---

[1] Card. P. M. RICHAUD, *Y a-t-il une spiritualité du clergé diocésain?* (Paris 1944), pp. 8-9. See also A. BÉRAUDY, cited on p. 167, footnote 2.   He says that the grace of ordination " helps the minister to live according to the duties of his office, " and adds (p. 92) that the Christian life of a minister consists in his assuming the responsibilities of his state of life.

[2] Card. P. M. RICHAUD, " Configuration au Christ, " *Prêtres diocésains* (1955), pp. 245-51, 293-97, 342-48.

[3] Gal 2, 20.

[4] This is the doctrine of J. J. OLIER and of the Berullian School in general.   See H. BREMOND, *op. cit.*, Vol. III, pp. 18-192.   According to this French School, in the priest's relationship to Christ, the priest corresponds to the *consecration* which God works in him so that he may freely respond to God's gift.

the parish, the school, societies and friends? How many actually find their attraction to the priesthood in some of the more human aspects of clerical life such as the prestige enjoyed by priests and the splendor of the liturgical functions in which they engage? At most these are merely enticements, the importance of which has yet to be clearly determined. Nevertheless, they often give a child an acquaintanceship with things divine in much the same way as the parables serve as an introduction to the meaning of the Gospels.

Some of the best types of vocations come from young people and even adults who only slowly come to realize that they are being called by God. Since they have been constant in the practice of virtue, self-denial and humility, they are more readily disposed to heed a call to a higher state of life. This call can come to them through prayer, the advice of a friend or a superior or a confessor. Indeed, there is no reason why it should not come through an invitation from their bishop. This was the practice in the early days of the Church; and certainly such a practice as this eliminates an idea which is altogether too prevalent, namely that the question of vocations should rarely be discussed. [1] When the call from God is authentic, the important criteria of a vocation become evident. These consist of an attraction to the person of Christ, an attraction to the various phases of the ministry in which this life consists, an awareness of the efforts that must be made to secure sanctification and the means that it offers to obtain this. All of these elements also include a tremendous realization of the sacred and eternal nature of a vocation to the priesthood. Such invitations are constantly being made in the Gospels : " Come, follow Me. Come and see.... They came and saw and stayed with Him. Do you also wish to go away? Lord, where shall we go?... Do you love Me more than these?... Lord, You know that I love You. " [2]

---

[1] Regarding the necessity of being attentive to the divine call, see the thought-provoking pages of H. M. Féret, " Vocations, " *La Vie spirituelle*, Vol. L (1959), pp. 64-72. However, his views are a little too strict in our opinion.

[2] Mt 4, 19; Jn 1, 38-39; 6, 67-68; 21, 15-17.

At every step along the road leading up to priestly ordination, there shines forth the star of Mary, Mother and Queen
of the clergy. The young levite, more than anyone else, should
identify himself with the beloved apostle to whom Jesus entrusted
His Mother and he should realize that Jesus is entrusting her
once again to his care. The Scriptures give us the key to how
we should act : " And the disciple took her into his home...
I am thy servant and the son of thy handmaid. " [1]

It would be quite valuable to describe how Scripture and
Christian literature from the earliest times endeavored to
construct a program of life for those called to the sacred ministry.
To do this we need only examine a few pages of the New
Testament, such as the Gospel of Matthew, wherein we find the
excellent missionary discourse [2] and the parables on the
Kingdom. [3] The Acts of the Apostles describes the election of
Matthias, Paul and Barnabas and the beginnings of the first
apostolic mission bands. The Pastoral Epistles explicitly treat
of the call to Orders, [4] and the Apocalypse provides us with
an excellent description of clerical life in the early days of the
Church through its letters to the angels of the churches. [5]
The attention of the future priest must gradually be focused on
what is essential to the priesthood — otherwise a true understanding of what Christ's priesthood entails will not be had.
When papal documents treat of the sublimity of the priesthood,
they always " stress the basic similarity between Christ and His
priest : the priest is endowed by Christ, the Eternal Priest, with
divine powers. The priest represents Christ. We can even say
that as a priest he is another Christ. " [6] How simple and yet

[1] Jn 19, 27; Ps 116, 16.
[2] Mt 9, 35; 10, 42. On this discourse of Christ, this " road-map for His present and
future missionaries, " see Msgr. L. CERFAUX, *Apostle and Apostolate*, Eng. trans. D. Duggan
(New York : Desclée, 1959).
[3] Mt 13, 53; 18, 35.
[4] See our study, " L'appel aux ordres dans les épîtres pastorales, " *Collationes Namurcenses*,
Vol. XXXIII (1939), pp. 323-34.
[5] Ap 2-3; and commentaries such as J. BONSIRVEN, *L'Apocalypse de saint Jean* (Paris 1951),
pp. 102-27.
[6] Card. J. E. VAN ROEY, " Le prêtre diocésain d'après les encycliques, " *loc. cit.*, p. 22.
For the correct meaning of the expression, *alter Christus*, see J. LÉCUYER, " Le sacerdoce dans
le mystère du Christ, " *op. cit.*, pp. 297-99.

profound this observation is. Yet how truly momentous and sublime the consequences are. It is not our purpose here to present a treatise regarding the French School's teaching on the States of the Word Incarnate, the conformation of the priest to Christ the Priest and his share in His priestly ministry. We will be content merely with making a few general observations.

* * *

We must have a *priestly* devotion to Christ, and this must be one which does not exclude in any way the other aspects of His divine and human nature but one which, nevertheless, has special reference to His Priestly Existence and Ministry. Let us not forget that our priesthood is only a share in the Priesthood of the Son of God, and that therefore, in our priestly ministry, we are only the ministers of the Lord, the sole mediator and the principal dispenser of grace. Whether it is Peter or Paul or anyone else who visibly ministers, it is Jesus who baptizes, absolves, blesses, consecrates and sanctifies. There can be no genuine filial devotion to our Divine Master if we do not endeavor to live in union with Him under the guidance of the Holy Spirit.

Jesus is our example. We must be able to say with St. Paul : " Be imitators of me, as I am of Christ. " [1] The earliest ordination prayers attest that the grace derived from the imposition of hands demands " the acquisition of a degree of sanctity which will serve as a model for the Christian people. " [2] We must therefore come to know Jesus and to meditate, contemplate and conform ourselves to Him. We must come to know Him not only in the manner of theologians, but in the manner of the saints. Thus, such knowledge must not only be speculative, but it must also be affective and assimilative, through admiration, adoration, love and imitation. We should familiarize

---

[1] 1 Cor 11, 1.
[2] B. Botte, " L'Ordre d'après les prières d'ordination, " *loc. cit.*, p. 178.

ourselves with the entire Gospel and particularly those texts which treat of the Good Shepherd who took pity on His flock. We will come to realize that we know Jesus as a priest ought to, only when we can apply these words of St. Paul to ourselves : " For I determined not to know anything among you except Jesus Christ and Him crucified. " [1]

Regarding this text of the Apostle, it is important to point out that the priesthood of Christ was not solely bound up with His great act of reparation on the Cross. Besides the Passion, we must also consider the events of the Resurrection, Ascension and Pentecost. The paschal mystery culminates in the glorification of the Redeemer and in His universal lordship, as well as in the sending of His Spirit upon the Church, His Mystical Body. The priesthood therefore demands of those who are Christ's priests not only the necessity of making reparation but also a burning faith in the complete triumph of Christ, faith and confidence in His grace and complete devotion to the ministry. In all of our activity, and especially in our daily Mass and Divine Office, we commemorate Christ's " Passion, Resurrection and glorious Ascension " and thus prepare for the coming of the Holy Spirit among men. [2]

We should recognize that the celebration of Mass is the highpoint of our day and the most valuable of all priestly spiritual exercises. What St. Francis de Sales once wrote to Philothea has special importance also for priests : " The sun of all spiritual exercises is the most holy, sacred, and most sovereign Sacrament and Sacrifice of the Mass, the center of the Christian religion, the heart of devotion, and the soul of piety, an ineffable mystery that comprises within itself the abyss of divine charity,

[1] 1 Cor 2, 2.

[2] [As Archbishop of Milan, Pope Paul VI declared : " To understand the Paschal mystery is to understand Christianity. To be ignorant of the Paschal mystery is to be ignorant of Christianity, " *La Nostra Pasqua* (Milan, 1959)]. Of all the current books on this subject, the following are particularly noteworthy : F. X. DURRWELL, *The Resurrection*, Eng. trans. Rosemary Sheed (New York : Sheed and Ward, 1960); L. CERFAUX, *Christ in the Theology of St. Paul*, Eng. trans. Webb-Walker (New York : Herder and Herder, 1959). For the application of these notions to the Mass, see A. M. ROGUET, *The Mass, Approaches to the Mystery* (Collegeville : Liturgical Press, 1957), pp. 85-95.

and by which God really communicates Himself to us and in a special manner replenishes our souls with His graces and favors. " [1] The same description of the Mass as the sun of all spiritual exercises also appears in the writings of Father Garrigou-Lagrange :

> For every interior soul, the Mass ought each morning to be the eminent source from which spring the graces we need in the course of the day, the source of light and of warmth — similar, in the spiritual order, to the sunrise in the order of nature. After the night and sleep, which are an image of death, the sun, reappearing each morning, restores life, so to speak, to all that awakens on the surface of the earth. If we had a profound understanding of the value of daily Mass, we would see that it is like a spiritual sunrise that renews, preserves and increases in our souls the life of grace, which is eternal life begun. [2]

This is especially true in the case of the priest, the minister of the central sacrifice of Christianity, who must, because of his special vocation, dedicate himself to the divine work of redemption. Father Garrigou-Lagrange continues :

> The high point of the apostle's day must obviously be the time during which Holy Mass is celebrated. Since the apostle must appear to men as another Christ, at what period is he more united to His Master than when, at the consecration, he must become one with Him, as His conscious and free instrument, in order to pronounce the words of Transubstantiation? Personal devotion and pastoral zeal are likewise fostered by this great liturgical action. Even more than his regular devotions and his work of study, his liturgical prayer, and especially the celebration of Mass, provided it is celebrated recollectedly and prayerfully, is the high point of the priest's life since union to God is inherent in it. The priest's enthusiastic

---

[1] St. Francis de Sales, *Introduction to the Devout Life*, Part II, chap. xiv.

[2] R. Garrigou-Lagrange, *The Three Ages of the Interior Life*, Eng. trans. (London: B. Herder, 1947-8), Vol. I p. 406.

proclamation of the Word of God must descend like a stream
from this great mountain peak. [1]

This holds true not merely for preaching but also for all one's
pastoral activity, with all the liturgical, sacramental and apostolic
means that it uses to gather the Lord's flock around the altar
in the unity of the people of God.

Indeed, we cannot sufficiently stress the point that there is
no need to separate spirituality and pastoral activity in the life
of the priest.   Must not a priest who is desirous of attaining
sanctity base his vocation, as another Christ, on the fact of his
priestly consecration and his individual mission?   Since the first
principle of perfection is perfect conformity to the holy will of
God, it follows that the priest will never sufficiently realize God's
design for his priesthood.   His daily Mass, more than any other
practice, will remind him that he is dedicated to souls for the
glory of God and that his priestly state of life consists in
performing reverently and with dignity those activities which
have to do with the salvation of souls.   It is in this way that the
priest will appreciate the many valuable opportunities for sanctification which are offered to him. [2]

* * *

If we are to be faithful to our vocation, Jesus should be,
especially in the Eucharist, the object of our virile love.   It was
this type of love which prompted our choosing the priestly life,
and it is such a love that will continue to motivate it.   Jacques
Marchant states that Jesus must be for us the *pondus cordis et
amoris*, [3] the center around which our hearts, filled with love,
must gravitate.

---

[1] R. GARRIGOU-LAGRANGE, *L'amour de Dieu et la Croix de Jésus*, Vol. II (Paris 1929),
pp. 745-46.   On this matter see the recent study of O. MELANCON, " La Sainte Messe, fonction
principale du prêtre, " *Revue eucharistique du clergé*, Vol. LXI (1958), pp. 84-91.

[2] A. SIMONET, " Au service du peuple de Dieu, " *Revue diocésaine de Namur*, Vol. XI
(1957), pp. 14-36.

[3] J. MARCHANT, *op. cit.*, p. 446.

We should consider ourselves united to the Lord Jesus by a union more intimate and exacting than that existing between a husband and wife. Indeed, we may consider ourselves as close friends of Jesus, such as John the Baptist for example, whose happiness came from seeing the work of the Master prosper even at the expense of his own popularity : " This my joy, therefore, is made full. He must increase, but I must decrease. " [1]

Such priestly devotion to Christ may take different forms and suit different temperaments. It must be nourished by Holy Scripture, liturgy and theology. For some it will be more contemplative, for others it will be more active. It may even borrow here and there from the various schools of spirituality. It may place special emphasis on such doctrines as the Eucharist, the Sacred Heart, or any of the states of the Incarnate Word. It may also include special devotion to the saints, such as St. Joseph, the Precursor, the apostles, saintly priests and bishops, the patrons of the diocese and the parish, etc. The old adage, " Devotions easily become an obstacle to true devotion, " should always be kept in mind.

* * *

There is one devotion which is inseparable from devotion to Christ and which, like the latter, is presented to priests in a specifically priestly form. This is devotion to the Most Blessed Mother of God. Since we are the collaborators of Christ, the Redeemer, we are likewise the collaborators of the Coredemptrix, the Mother of the Redeemer. Since we are priests, other Christs, we are therefore by special title the children of Mary. These lofty considerations are filled with practical consequences. [2] In every activity in which he engages throughout his life, the

---

[1] Jn 3, 29-30.

[2] Card. L. J. SUENENS, *Théologie de l'apostolat de la Légion de Marie*, 7th ed. (Bruges 1957). Priests will also find great value in reading the excellent meditations and sermon outlines written by Msgr. J. LEBON in 1954 for the Marian Year: *Schémas de prédication pour l'année mariale* and *Réflexions mariales pour l'année sacerdotale* (Gembloux 1954).

priest should recall these words from the Gospel of St. John :
" And the Mother of Jesus was there. " [1] If our ministry is to be
completely effective, this must be our watchword.   Anyone can
see how closely our vocation parallels that of Mary.   By making
an adaptation of the words of St. Paul, we can even say that our
ministry makes up for what is wanting in Mary's work among
men.   Each time that we celebrate Mass, we *re-present* Christ
and His passion and effect a sacramental application of it and
thereby bestow upon souls the Emmanuel of the prophecy and
the abundance of His grace.   By our ministry, we beget Christ
in souls and also broaden and deepen in them the spiritual
maternity of our Lady until the time that her Divine Son,
according to the degree of their election, is formed in them,
when they attain the life of glory, the *dies natalis*, their birth in
heaven.   " My dear children, with whom I am in labor again
until Christ is formed in you. " [2]   Mary's universal mediation
makes the priest's life fruitful.   It is therefore important for him
to live closely united to her and to depend upon her.

Since Christ is a Priest, the Mediator, He presents Himself
for our contemplation as the Adorer of His Father, the Perfect
Religious, to borrow an expression of Bérulle, and also as the
Source of Life for men, the Apostle, the Ambassador of the
Father, the Source of every effective apostolate.   Thus there are
two important applications for priestly spirituality, fervor at the
altar and zeal for souls.   Fervor, Ardor, Flame.   These are all
expressions which evoke the notion of fire and recall the words
of Jesus : " I have come to cast fire upon the earth, and what
will I but that it be kindled. " [3]   The Book of Leviticus prescribes
that priests of the Old Law must each day tend the fire which
burns perpetually before the Ark of the Covenant.   The priests
of the New Law must likewise keep the flame of adoration and
love burning before God, the Father of Our Lord Jesus Christ.
This is done during the official praise rendered to God through

[1] Jn 2, 1.
[2] Gal 4, 19.
[3] Lk 12, 49.

our Mass and Divine Office. It must also be done in conjunction with our fervent quest for perfection. Thus, reacting against any lukewarmness, we must strive to rekindle the grace which we received through the imposition of hands at Ordination. [1]

Jesus said : " I have come to cast fire on the earth. " He also said to His apostles and therefore to all priests : " Behold, I am sending you forth. Go, therefore, and make disciples of all nations. " [2] *Ignem mittere... Mitto vos!* It is our task to spread this fire and to kindle it in souls and to fan the flames so that it may burn bright and thus purify and become a Pentecostal fire. Clearly this means that religious fervor must result in apostolic zeal. The apostolate! St. Hilary, and later on Pope Pius XII, [3] would frequently state that there was nothing greater nor anything more excellent. Richard of St. Victor wrote : " I do not know of any greater gift given to man by God than that, because of a man's obedience and submissiveness to God out of charity, others are able to achieve salvation. " [4] What better way is there of responding to Jesus' love for his priests? Jacques Marchant wrote : " If we love Jesus with all our heart, we must love Him in souls. He does not wish merely to be loved in Himself but in them. Let us love His love for souls. Let us love those souls which are as precious as children to Him. Let us love the price of blood with which they were redeemed. By loving them, we will obtain their conversion, their pardon and sanctification. There is no task more noble, meritorious and pleasing to God. " [5] We are reminded of those titles of nobility which St. Paul applied to himself : " Paul, servant of Jesus Christ, set apart for the Gospel. " [6] We have quoted at different times from the writings of Jacques Marchant. The following quotation is another valuable piece of advice for priests :

> In all that you do, center all of your efforts on the chief reason for your zeal, the glory of God. Do not become

[1] 2 Tim 1, 6.
[2] Mt 10, 16; 28, 19.
[3] See the text cited above, p. 121.
[4] Cited by J. MARCHANT, *op. cit.*, p. 439.
[5] J. MARCHANT, *op. cit.*, p. 446.
[6] Rom 1, 1.

entangled in secondary purposes such as the success of
your apostolic activities. We indeed plant and cultivate,
but it is God who gives the increase if He so decides. [1]
If our undertakings are not as successful as we would have
hoped them to be, what matters most is that the will of
God is done and that the kingdom of God will come.
It is therefore most important that we continue to work
even though we may not succeed. [2]

To accomplish this we must purify our motives and have Christ
constantly before our minds in all of our undertakings. Such is
the sentiment expressed by the beautiful prayer of Jacques
Marchant : " Father of Shepherds, do not allow your fellow
shepherds to be puffed up by fame and popularity. Instead, let
the solid food of Your truth nourish them so that they may be
able to feed their sheep not for their own sake, but for Your sake
and not only their own sheep but Yours as well, for Your honor
and not their own. " [3]   Such devotion to Christ directed, at the
same time, both to the Father and to men is an excellent example
of that " ardent, zealous and active charity " to which Pope
Pius XII refers in his apostolic exhortation to the Catholic
clergy, *Menti Nostrae.* [4]   This important document is frequently
referred to in order to describe the program of priestly sanctification which is inherent in the practice of the various virtues.
We need only recall how insistently the Pope recommends the
practice of such virtues as humility, " the foundation of Christian
perfection, " [5] obedience, " which the priest considers the foundation of his own personal sanctification, " [6] detachment from
worldly possessions and a love for evangelical poverty, " which
should manifest itself in the simplicity and modesty of their
manner of life, in their living quarters and in their generosity

[1] 1 Cor 3, 6-7.

[2] J. MARCHANT, *op. cit.*, p. 222.

[3] J. MARCHANT, *op. cit.*, p. 216.

[4] Pope PIUS XII, *Exhortatio apostolica Menti nostrae, loc. cit.*, pp. 660-61.

[5] *Ibid.*, p. 662.

[6] *Ibid.*, p. 662.   Compare *Codex Juris Canonici*, can. 132, § 1, 2.

to the poor. " [1]   Besides these virtues, there is also the law of celibacy, that perfect chastity so beautifully described in the Encyclical *Sacra Virginitas*. [2]   As we can readily see, the Holy Father is inviting priests because of their priesthood to follow the three evangelical counsels of poverty, chastity and obedience. When the Pope stated in his Discourse to Religious in 1950 that the clerical state, since it proceeds from divine law, does not impose, " by reason of its very nature or at least by reason of a postulate of that same nature, " the practice of the evangelical counsels, he was describing the type of profession of these counsels made by members of religious communities. [3]

If there are some who doubt this, they need only consider the recent statement of His Holiness, Pope John XXIII. After having recalled these words of Pius XII to religious, he continues :

> Yet the man who would presume to infer from this that clerics are less bound than the members of religious communities by the obligation of tending toward evangelical perfection is certainly misrepresenting the true meaning of the same Sovereign Pontiff who was so concerned with the holiness of the clergy, and is contradicting the constant teaching of the Church on this subject.   The truth is completely opposed to this unwise inference.   For the proper performance of the priestly duties there is required a greater interior holiness than even the state of religious requires.

[1] Pope Pius XII, *Exhortatio apostolica Menti nostrae, loc cit.,* pp. 663-64.   Compare *Codex Juris Canonici,* can. 124-142.

[2] Pope Pius XII, Enc. *Sacra Virginitas* (March 25, 1954), *AAS,* Vol. XLVI (1954), pp. 161 ff.   We cannot resist quoting here a prayer of J. Marchant : " Jesus, most pure exemplar for priests, source of all purity and chastity, imprint on their hearts Your zeal, Your love, Your solicitous concern.   Every day they must handle Your virgin body, consecrate and consume the wine which itself makes them virgins.   Let them share this grace that inwardly they may sincerely seek and cultivate that chastity which is so necessary, and show outwardly its pleasant fragrance.   Grant that they may remember in whatever they think, do and say that they are anointed and consecrated to God in soul and body, so that they may praise Christ in their heart and glorify God in their body (*op. cit.,* pp. 504-5). "   Here we again find the idea of consecration.   A little further on, Marchant takes up this idea and applies it to detachment from material goods : " Priest, remember that you are a man of God, remember that you are Christ's; behold Him whom you serve, the one to whom you are consecrated.   Consider the proper spirit which should guide you. "   Applying this, he continues, " Dispose of your possessions while they are still your own; after death, they are no longer yours " (*op. cit.,* p. 512) .

[3] Pope Pius XII, *Allocution to the Congress of Religious* (1950), *loc. cit.,* p. 28.

Even though the evangelical counsels are not more mandatory by the force of the clerical state itself for ecclesiastics
so that they may be able to attain the sanctity of life,
nevertheless for ecclesiastics as for all the faithful these
same counsels constitute the surest way to attain the desired
goal of Christian perfection. [1]

It is therefore quite clear that what is demanded is not the
profession of the evangelical counsels but rather their spirit.

* * *

Ubi Petrus, ibi Ecclesia; *Ubi Ecclesia, ibi Christus*.   The priest,
more than anyone else, is aware of the importance of the sacred
Hierarchy.   He realizes that his union to Christ must necessarily
function within an hierarchical Church.   His heart is loyally
dedicated to the common Father of the Church, the Vicar of
Jesus Christ, the center of unity and the pledge of security.   Not
only must he be completely submissive to the Pope, but he must
also share in all of his cares and anxieties for the Church.   Like
the Holy Father, he must combine both fidelity to the message
of Christ and presence in the world.   In other words, he must
serve truth and diffuse charity.

* * *

All priests of second rank, *secundi ordinis*, have received the
priesthood in order to be the helpers " of the Catholic bishop, "
as we read in the Rite of Ordination.   Since the bishop gives to
them certain powers of Orders, and since he qualifies them for
all forms of the ministry, he does this nevertheless with all the
reservations implied in the very notion of collaboration.   Thus,
when they preach, govern, dispense the sacred mysteries, they
do so only under the bishop's authority; and should they also

---

[1] Pope John XXIII, Enc. *Sacerdotii Nostri primordia, loc. cit.*, p. 550.

have the care of souls, they enjoy this only through an extension of the fatherhood of the bishop. In the diocese, the Hierarchy is principally personified in the local bishop. According to Canon Law and the directives of the Sovereign Pontiffs, his priests are his collaborators. Pope Pius XII stressed that collaboration with one's bishop is required of all priests, including religious, [1] by divine law and that every aspect of the apostolate must be under the bishop's direction. [2] The late Holy Father also emphasized that obedience to the bishop is the first principle of priestly obedience and apostolic activity [3] and that the union of priests to their bishops is precisely that bond of unity desired by Christ, and therefore " unprecedented and extravagant activities " contrary to this unity cannot be blessed and cannot, despite their appearances, " cooperate effectively in spreading the kingdom of Christ. " [4] The Apostolic Exhortation *Menti Nostrae* refers to the text of St. Ignatius of Antioch on the necessary unity in thought and action that must exist between the bishop and his priests. [5] Applying this same principle, the Pope reminded the parish directors of Catholic Action of the necessity to be submissive to the bishop and his delegates. [6] This submission to the bishop is necessarily implied in submission to the Supreme Pontiff, the chief guardian of the Church's divinely established laws. [7] We have already quoted the words of Pius XII to the Bishop of Lourdes : " Without submission to and respect for the bishops, there can be no Church. The type of submission that is demanded is that of love. Whoever does not love his bishop cannot obey him as he ought. " [8] In one of his last documents Pius XII declared that

---

[1] Pope Pius XII, *Allocution to Religious, loc. cit.*, p. 28.

[2] *Ibid.*, p. 29; *Allocution to the General Chapter of the Society of Jesus* (Sept. 10, 1957), *AAS*, Vol. XLIX (1957), p. 812.

[3] Pope Pius XII, *Exhortatio apostolica menti nostrae, loc. cit.*, pp. 662-63, 690, 695-96.

[4] *Ibid.*, pp. 690, 695-96.

[5] *Ibid., Letter to Cardinal V. Valeri* (Sept. 20, 1956), *loc. cit.* See St. Ignatius of Antioch, *ad Eph.* 4, 1; *ad Magnes.* 13, 1; *ad Trall.* 12, 2.

[6] Pope Pius XII, *Discourse to the Directors of Catholic Action and to the Members of the Marian Congregations* (May 3, 1951), *AAS*, Vol. XLIII (1951), pp. 788-89.

[7] Pope Pius XII, *Allocution to Religious, loc. cit.*, p. 29.

[8] Msgr. P. M. Théas, *L'évêque dans l'Église;* already cited above, p. 54.

it is important "to emphasize this truth and to stress the unchanging principle that the holiness of a priest's personal life is firmly based and supported on constant and unswerving obedience to the Hierarchy. "[1]

For those who cite the case of the exemption of religious, the Pope points out that the latter are dependent upon the bishop to the extent that his mission and pastoral ministry demand. [2] The Code, in fact, imposes the obligation upon religious superiors, regardless of whether or not they are exempt, to collaborate willingly with the local ordinary and the pastors of the diocese in which they reside. [3] The majority of religious do comply, but there are some regrettable exceptions. Can certain religious communities be said to be faithful to the principles just described when, after having sought from the bishop a special assignment in the diocese or even his approval, they then no longer pay any attention to the directives that he enacts for his diocese and even act contrary to them? Certainly the dignity of the priesthood does not formally consist in the priest's participation in the pastoral ministry of the bishop. Nevertheless, every priesthood of the second rank is one of collaboration. The priest's relation to and dependence upon the Hierarchy and particularly upon the Pope and the local bishop is essential to the priestly ministry of all priests, since their ministry is the Church's ministry and the Church was divinely founded upon the apostles and bishops. Dom Gréa wrote : " The priesthood of the diocesan priest, since it is the same priesthood as that of the bishop, is a shared priesthood, which is derived from the episcopacy and which places the priest in a necessary and essential dependence upon the bishop. "[4] In a letter which Pope Pius XII, toward the end of his life, wrote to Cardinal Feltin, we read :

---

[1] Pope Pius XII, *Letter to Cardinal Feltin on the Third Centenary of the Death of Venerable Olier* (March 25, 1957), *AAS*, Vol. XLIX (1957), p. 275.

[2] Pope Pius XII, *Allocution to Religious, loc. cit.*, pp. 28-29. Compare this with the *Codex Juris Canonici*, can. 1338, § 2 which does not distinguish between those who are exempt and those who are not.

[3] *Codex Juris Canonici*, can. 608, § 1.

[4] Cited by Msgr. F. Vernet, *Dom Gréa* (Paris 1937), p. 186.

At the present time, the union existing among priests, their dependence upon the Hierarchy and their fidelity to the teachings and directives of the Holy See are such important factors for the Church's progress that we cannot sufficiently insist upon the virtues required for this testimony of unity and charity. All efforts must be centered solely around the bishop, since he alone in the diocese is responsible for the apostolate and the doctrine taught therein. If a priest is not deeply involved in the common task of the Church, in whatever area and sphere it exists, his own particular ministry runs the risk of losing its supernatural effectiveness in much the same manner as a river cut off from its source soon runs dry. [1]

The promise of obedience and reverence which is made toward the end of the ordination ceremony only makes explicit the nature of the ministry of cooperation. The obedience of priests to their immediate or mediate ecclesiastical superiors is different from the vow of obedience made by religious. It is a help to the priest's personal sanctification since it does not add any obligations to the already existing means of perfection. Rather, it makes the priest aware of what the obligations of his priestly and apostolic life can do for his sanctification. It also gives him confidence in the graces which accompany the obligations of this state.

We will end these considerations by quoting two conclusions which Father Broutin reached through his studies on the pastoral ministry in the sixteenth and seventeenth centuries : " Commited as they are to a ministry of sacrifice, prayer and preaching, they (priests engaged in the parochial ministry) must join their interior life to their public ministry. Their whole spirituality consists in joining the graces of their state of life with the duties of their state. " [2] In the area of the obligations of the state of life, " obedience to the bishop is the real basis of clerical perfection. " [3]

* * *

[1] Pope Pius XII, *Letter to Cardinal Feltin*, *loc. cit.*, p. 275.
[2] P. Broutin, *Le Pasteur d'Église au cours de l'histoire*, *loc. cit.*, No. 51, p. 2.
[3] P. Broutin, *La Réforme pastorale en France au XVIIe siècle*, *op. cit.*, Vol. I, p. 186.

As priests of the Church, those who have received the grace
of the priesthood should open their minds and hearts to all the
inspirations of the Holy Spirit, and they should be receptive to
the appeals which arise from the people of God.   There is much
to be said on this subject.   It is sufficient to note here, however,
that priests definitely have the duty of making adequate provision
in their ministry and spirituality for the ever increasing collaboration of the laity through Catholic Action. [1]

[1] See Msgr. G. Philips, *Le rôle du laïcat dans l'Église* (Tournai 1954); Y. M. J. Congar,
Lay People in the Church (London : Chapman 1959).   Regarding what is termed the " priesthood
of the faithful " see Msgr. L. Cerfaux, " Regale Sacerdotium, " *Revue des sciences philosophiques
et théologiques*, Vol. XXVIII (1939), pp. 5-39 and *Recueil Lucien Cerfaux* (Gembloux 1954),
pp. 288-315; E. Boularand, " Sacerdoce de l'Église, sacerdoce du baptisé, " *Revue d'ascétique
et mystique*, Vol. XXXII (1956), pp. 361-96.

Chapter 13

Priestly Spirituality and
the Diocesan Clergy

There is no reason to consider the diocesan clergy as second rate. Such a notion, prevalent during the Middle Ages, [1] still exists in certain quarters today. [2] Nor is there any reason to consider the apostolic origin of the diocesan clergy the exclusive claim of the secular clergy, as though the regular clergy, with respect to the priesthood, were only a " subordinate and auxiliary clergy. " [3] The unicity of the priesthood must be unequivocally affirmed. All priests enjoy the same priesthood; they are the legitimate heirs of the same apostolic ministry and have the same essential relation to the Hierarchy. Divine Law gives no preference either to seculars or regulars on the basis of the reception of Holy Orders. The differences between the two clergies are matters of ecclesiastical law, and the Church might some time in the future modify their statutes and reciprocal relations. Many differences exist among the various religious societies with respect to their way of life. As far as the secular clergy are concerned, we are aware that their way of life is not the same in the Latin Church as it is in the Eastern Churches, despite the fact that their powers are the same and they have the same obligations to seek sanctification. [4]

Now that we have made these distinctions, can we speak of a spirituality of the diocesan clergy? [5] First of all, what are

---

[1] L. GENICOT, *La spiritualité médiévale* (Paris 1958), pp. 47-48.

[2] Card. D. J. MERCIER, *La vie intérieure* (Brussels 1919), pp. 160 ff; Pope PIUS XII, " Note " (July 13, 1952), Appendix I, pp. 301-303.

[3] Pope PIUS XII, *Allocution to the First Congress of Religious, loc. cit.*, p. 28.

[4] Pope PIUS XII, " Note " (July 13, 1952), Appendix I, pp.301-303.

[5] On the advantages and disadvantages of various types of spirituality, see G. THILS, *Christian Holiness, op. cit.*, pp. 36-38.

we to think of such expressions as *diocesan priest* and *diocesan clergy*? Certainly, the expression " *secular* " is in great use at this time. It is this expression which is employed by the Code of Canon Law. Long ago when priests were distinguished from monks by the fact that they lived in the world, the term secular might well recall the following prayer of Christ : " I do not pray that thou take them out of the world. " [1] Today, this term really does not express the same idea since most religious also function in society. Thus, according to current usage, this term is liable to be understood in the pejorative sense of a worldly life and mediocrity in one's devotion to the ministry. [2] A greater preference is shown for the use of the term "*diocesan,*" as is evident in many official documents. [3] Neither should the term " *diocesan* " be understood in an exclusive and polemical sense, nor is it to be understood as a description of a new type of spirituality, the principles of which have been gleaned from different schools of spirituality. It conveys no more of a sense of opposition than the term " *religious,* " which is used to describe those living in the religious state, the canonical state of tending toward perfection. Seculars are also adequately endowed with the means of living a religious life by observing the evangelical counsels.

If secular priests prefer to be called diocesan, it is only because their function and canonical status derive from their collaboration with their bishop in his pastoral ministry in the diocese. Thus, they consider their relation and service to the bishop as the means of their sanctification. We will consider this in more detail in another section. [4] It has been sufficient for our purposes to show here how the term *diocesan priest* is best explained in terms of a spirituality based on collaboration in the bishop's pastoral ministry through service in his diocese. Bishop Guerry states, " The diocesan priest's spirituality consists in living the life of the local church, which, by divine law, resides

[1] Jn 17, 15.

[2] Card. D. J. MERCIER, *La Vie intérieure, op. cit.*, p. 198.

[3] This is the term used by the *Annuario Pontificio* (1959), p. 4. See especially the Apostolic Constitution of PIUS XII, *Sedes Sapientiae* (May 31, 1956), *AAS*, Vol. XLVIII (1956), p. 355.

[4] Msgr. S. DELACROIX, " Pour le clergé diocésain, " *op. cit.*, pp. 124-25.

in the person of the bishop, the successor of the apostles. " [1]
Cardinal Richaud, describing the work of the diocesan priest,
likewise wrote : " The diocesan priest is unique in that he has no
specialty. His holiness consists in his not being restricted to
any special form of spirituality and in his not having to choose
his field of endeavor. Instead, he is all things to all men and is
completely at the disposal of souls wherever and whenever there
is a need. He is directly subject to his bishop, the chief who
gives the commands and to whom he has said, " *Promitto
obedientiam.* " [2] We have already observed that collaboration in
the work of the Hierarchy forms an integral part of priestly
spirituality. The secular or diocesan priest is completely subject
to the bishop of the diocese since, unlike the religious, he has no
restrictions arising from canonical exemption and also because
no longer is there any interference by any canonical authority in
the relationship existing between the bishop and his priests.
Quite simply, diocesan priests follow the directions of their
bishops in much the same way as the first priests were subject to
the directions of the apostles and their successors. [3] Such an
attitude describes the ideal of the diocesan priesthood in much
the same way as the love of poverty and devotion to truth
describe the ideal of the Franciscan and Dominican Orders
respectively. It must be emphasized, however, that this element
is not exclusively proper to diocesan priests. Who can deny
that such an important principle of diocesan spirituality
aptly describes the basic ingredient in every priesthood of
collaboration?

* * *

[1] Msgr. E. GUERRY, " Le clergé diocésain, " *op. cit.*, p. 50.

[2] Card. P. M. RICHAUD, *Y a-t-il une spiritualité du clergé diocésain? op. cit.*, p. 15.

[3] We realize that certain canons regular, such as those of Prémontré, are *implanted*
in the diocese, and by intention and vocation are committed to the active ministry in the diocese
in which their abbey is located. (See especially Y. BOSSIÈRE, *Les chanoines réguliers de Prémontré,*
Mondaye 1944, especially pp. 123 ff.) They could be called diocesan in a certain sense,
but the fact remains that they are not as fully diocesan as secular priests. This restriction
did not hold for the primitive canons who professed the evangelical counsels while remaining
completely under the authority of the bishop, e.g., the clergy of St. Augustine. — Moreover,
in a broader sense, all those priests who work in collaboration with the bishop of the diocese
are diocesan; see p. 223, footnote 2.

The Church is in great need of more and more diocesan priests who will fully realize the great importance of their ministry. We cannot stress sufficiently enough the necessity of considering the apostolate in terms of the problems facing the modern world. It is primarily the priest, collaborating with his bishop on the diocesan level, who is contributing to the Universal Church.

It is indeed quite remarkable that Pope Pius XII, who was always most careful not to restrict the apostolate to the limited area of dioceses and parishes, strongly emphasized that the organization of the Church is diocesan and that the parish's strength and vitality are " irreplaceable and essential " to Christian life. [1] This conviction of the late Holy Father is particularly apparent in the discourse that he made, as Bishop of Rome, to the pastors of his own diocese. " The direct and immediate care of souls in the life of the parish, " he stated, " has been, and continues to be, everywhere and always, the fundamental factor, and, as it were, the solid framework which ensures the Church's perennial vitality. " How else does the Church form and prepare a man for Christian living, " if not above all by the day-to-day ministry of souls, *la quotidiana cura delle anime?* " [2]

On a number of occasions Pius XII again considered this question. He reminded the pastors of Rome that a part of his own flock had been entrusted to them and that under his direction they too are shepherds. He invited all Christians to fashion their parishes into fervent and effective communities similar to the family-like communities of the early Jerusalem Church. Total uniformity, by the very fact that it destroys variety, would be a strategic error; and there must be the greatest respect accorded the various associations approved and blessed

---

[1] Pope Pius XII, *To the Directors of Catholic Action, loc. cit.*, p. 788. On the necessity of the parish, see above, pp. 17-18, 154-55; R. SNOEKS, " De significatione paroeciae in vita Ecclesiae, " *Collectanea Mechliniensia*, Vol. XLIV (1959), pp. 40-41; D. GRASSO, " Osservazioni sulla teologia della parrocchia, " *Gregorianum*, XL (1959), 297-314; J. HAMER, " Vocation catholique de la paroisse, " *Evangéliser*, Vol. XIV (1960), 361-72.

[2] Pope Pius XII, *Discourse to the Pastors of Rome* (March 16, 1946), *AAS*, Vol. XXXVIII (1946), p. 184.

by the Church, but " an uncontrollable variety without unified control at the summit would have harmful consequences in the conduct of the peaceful campaign for the conquest of the world for Christ. " Not only must unity in the diocese be centered around the bishop, but it must also be centered around the pastor on the parish level. [1]

St. Francis de Sales also stressed the importance of having a good parochial organization, and he emphasized the need of having good pastors. He stated :

> Good pastors are needed just as much as good bishops; and bishops actually labor in vain if they do not provide their parishes with priests who are pious, learned and exemplary in their lives. These are the shepherds who must walk ahead of their flocks in order to show them the way to heaven and to give them good example. I have learned from experience that people easily become devout when the clergy stimulate the practice of virtue in them through preaching and good example, and that they quickly stray when their priests are ignorant, when they lack zeal for the salvation of souls and when they do not give good example. [2]

Some may contend, however, that there is an urgent need to adapt one's time and efforts to the modern forms of the apostolate. Pope Pius replies to this as follows :

> Without any doubt, the extraordinary efforts in their many and various forms of zeal are useful and even indispensable. Particularly today, in the face of religious indifference and atheism, a vast field is opened to their overflowing ardor. There is no danger that this extraordinary apostolate will be estimated at less than its value. Not infrequently, one has the impression that this appreciation can go too far, and

---

[1] Pope PIUS XII, *Discourse to the Representatives of the Parish of Santa Sabina* (Jan. 11, 1953) *L'Osservatore Romano* (Jan. 21, 1953); *Discourse to the Pastors of Rome* (March 27, 1953), *AAS* Vol. XLV (1953), pp. 238 ff.

[2] St. Francis de Sales, a conversion reported by P. Philibert de Bonneville : see Dom H. B. MACKEY, " Saint François de Sales et la formation du clergé français, " *Revue du Clergé français*, Vol. XXV (1901), pp. 520-21.

not without harm to the ordinary care of souls. In fact, the ordinary care of souls always remains the principal and fundamental element of the apostolate, at least where the ecclesiastical institutions have taken firm root and religious conditions are in some degree normal.

The Holy Father treated at length the various elements of the parish apostolate such as catechetical instructions, care for the sick, administration of the sacraments and the direction of souls. In short, this is what is ordinarily called the traditional ministry; and it demands a constant adaptation and cannot be allowed to become merely a routine. [1]

* * *

Certainly, persistent and anxious demands for self-sacrifice come from all quarters. Nonetheless, there can be no sacrifice made at the expense of the diocese and particularly at the expense of service in parishes. The drain exerted by such demands must not result in the slightest decrease in other vocations and apostolic endeavors in the future. Pope Pius XII reminded pastors that their primary concern must be with those sheep who are not yet in the fold, although in particular circumstances, it may be necessary to leave the ninety-nine sheep to go in search of the one that has strayed. It is always important, however, to make certain that the good sheep are " in the safety of the fold, " to preserve life in those who possess it. *Haec oportet facere et illa non omittere.* [2]

In all of the varied and necessary forms of the apostolate, prime importance must be accorded the pastoral ministry.

---

[1] Pope Pius XII, *Discourse to the Pastors of Rome* (March 23, 1949), *AAS*, Vol. XLI (1949), pp. 182-83. Adaptation is necessary, but it must be done with prudence and caution. See " Problèmes de pastorale, " in our *Lettres pastorales*, Vol. I (1948), pp. 357-404. Recently, two excellent studies appeared in the *Lettres pastorales*, Vol. V (Tournai 1958), pp. 372-90; Msgr. Charles M. HIMMER, " La paroisse, communauté missionnaire "; Fr. HOUTART, " Aspects nouveaux de la paroisse. " See also J. LALOUX, *Problèmes actuels du monde rural* (Brussels 1956); Msgr. E. J. DE SMEDT, *Le Christ dans le quartier* (Bruges 1960).

[2] Pope Pius XII, *Discourse to the Pastors of Rome* (March 27, 1953), *loc. cit.*, p. 243.

Although in the eyes of the world there may be other more outstanding vocations, it is, nevertheless, greatly desired that young men who aspire to the care of souls in the parochial ministry will come to share, as far as possible, the way of life of their flocks. This is done, as Pius XII says, by living in their midst and sharing " their anxieties, emotions, hopes and fears. " [1] It is earnestly hoped that young men and their families will come to understand the sublime dignity of such a vocation.

When Cardinal Pacelli was Secretary of State to Pius XI, he delivered an extremely fine discourse which, when he became Pope, was widely publicized. Addressing his remarks to the noble families of Rome, he stated :

Alas! For many young people, for many minds tortured by doubt, and for many tormented souls and hearts yearning for greater virtue as well as for many unfortunates in the grip of the most agonizing material and spiritual misery, the healing balm of resignation cannot be given because there are not sufficient priests. I am not speaking only of pagan lands such as Asia and Africa. I am speaking of our Christian lands, for here also the harvest is abundant and the laborers few.

Yes, the harvest is great even in the Holy City of Rome, the See of the Vicar of Jesus Christ. On the shores of the Tiber there are to be found two ecclesiastical Romes : the universal Rome and the Diocese of Rome.

The former is the Rome of Peter, the Head of the Catholic Church, the Rome of the Sacred Congregations, and the headquarters for the Religious Orders and Congregations; the Rome of seminaries and national colleges, the Rome of the schools of higher learning; the Rome of the different rites. The great number of priests and clerics who gather here and who work in the various congregations, seminaries and religious houses accounts for the faithful not being aware of the tremendous need for clergy to serve the Diocese of Rome, whose Head is also the Sovereign Pontiff, despite the fact that the direction of the diocese is entrusted to

[1] *Ibid.*, p. 238.

a Cardinal Vicar. In the midst of the present–day upheaval, where then are the first flowerings of a priestly vocation to be nurtured? What protection will be given to those young men who love Jesus and who wish to associate themselves with Him through serving Him at the Altar? I would like to see such vocations coming from among the sons of the great families of Rome. In their homes are preserved the memory of such illustrious ancestors as bishops, cardinals and popes. These great houses would experience a new sense of glory if from them there came priests who, after realizing the vanity of human success, would devote themselves to the poor and abandoned by imparting to them the message of salvation and the bread of life. Bending over the dying, they will open to them, by means of the absolution and blessings that they impart, the way to heaven. [1]

Such language on the part of the Bishop of Rome is completely in line with the hopes of every bishop who is faced with the great need for vocations and disturbed by the prospects of so few vocations, and who is particularly grieved at the very slight attraction that the diocesan clergy holds for members of the wealthier classes. Certainly, no one questions the necessity that exists for vocations to the Foreign Missions and the various other fields of the Church's universal apostolate. However, there is also a great need for vocations to the diocesan clergy. For the most part the countries in which Catholicism has existed for the longest time continue to be the best organized and the most fertile reserves of the Church. Should our parishes be deserted, Christian life itself would soon languish, and thus the real source of all vocations would be destroyed. Concerning his priests and particularly his pastors, Cardinal Van Roey wrote :

If the number of brave soldiers of Jesus Christ should become insufficient, or should their ranks no longer be able to be filled because of a lack of vocations — a danger which

---

[1] Card. E. PACELLI (Pius XII), *Comme les anges, Sermon à la Trinité des Monts* (January 31, 1932), French trans. (Rome : Polyglotta Vaticana 1944), pp. 20-22.

is not merely imaginary — we would be faced with an extremely critical situation. Our daily experience clearly attests to the fact that the vitality of a parish depends upon the presence and constant activity of one or several priests. It is therefore evident that the ministry of the diocesan clergy is, at this time, of prime importance and more necessary than ever before. It must be respected and its value appreciated and, to use a good expression, it must be reappraised. [1]

The conclusion, therefore, is that in the discerning of vocations a balanced and truly Christian attitude is at all times necessary. Unfortunately, at times, this is not practiced by some vocation directors.

When young men, attentive to the call of their bishop, seriously wonder if they are making the right decision in choosing to study for the diocese in which the bonds linking them to Christ and His Church were first tied, they are in no way to be dissuaded from doing so. As far as the bishop is concerned, he should be aware of the needs of the Universal Church and willingly consent to the desires of any of his subjects who feel called to labor in the mission fields. I am deeply convinced that if such an attitude is taken all causes will be better served.

* * *

As important as the diocesan ministry is for the Church, it is also perfectly suited to promoting priestly sanctification. We have constantly said that, because of the type of graces guaranteed by Holy Orders, every priest is to achieve his individual sanctification by the proper fulfillment of the duties of his priestly state of life. The spirituality of the diocesan clergy is based on the strong conviction that in a priest's generous dedi-

---

[1] Card. J. E. VAN ROEY, Preface to the book of P. Fécherolle, *Le clergé diocésain aux avant-postes* (Tournai-Paris 1948). This text appears in the collection, *Au service de l'Église*, Vol. VI (1948), pp. 491-93.

cation of himself to the diocesan state of life the necessary means for sanctification are to be found. With the exception of the priest who feels that he is being called to the religious life, there is no need for a priest to resort to the special practices of religious life. We have already referred to the following principle that Father Broutin often repeated to members of the diocesan clergy to remind them that " their entire spirituality consists in joining the grace of their state with the duties of their state. " [1]

In order to be sanctified by the duties of one's state, the virtues necessary for their fulfillment must be effectively practiced. Love of Christ and love of souls, constantly stimulated by the graces of the priesthood, can result in the most earnest practice of the spirit of the evangelical counsels. It should also be remembered that according to St. Francis de Sales each person is called to practice the evangelical counsels according to his particular vocation. The diocesan priest is, therefore, expected to practice the evangelical counsels according to the circumstances of his priestly and diocesan ministry. [2] The *canonical* way of life with its religious vows, particularly as it exists in institutes of common life, assures the necessary means by which the personal sanctification of many can be attained. Pius XII, as we have seen, formally declared that the clerical state does not require the profession of the evangelical counsels *either by its nature or by virtue of a postulate of that nature*. [3] Not even a postulate of that nature! The priest can, therefore, with the help of God and without too much difficulty, attain priestly perfection by the ordinary means inherent in his Christian life as well as by his clerical and apostolic mission. Father Edward Poppe stated that the motto of secular priests is " to sanctify ourselves for and by our apostolate. " [4] By this he meant that the apostolate was naturally to be exercised in accordance with the canons and

---

[1] P. BROUTIN, " Le Pasteur d'Église au cours de l'histoire, " *loc. cit.*, p. 2.

[2] St. FRANCIS de SALES, *Treatise on the Love of God*, I, VIII, ch. VI-IX : " We are all bound to practice these three virtues although not in the same way. "

[3] Pope PIUS XII, *Allocution to the First Congress of Religious, loc. cit.*, pp. 29-35. Compare the " Note " (July 13, 1952), Appendix I, pp. 301-303.

[4] E. POPPE, *Entretiens sacerdotaux* (Paris-Averbode 1933), p. 49.

directives of the Church. This, therefore, demands fidelity to prayer and study. Otherwise, mediocrity and moral laxity would easily result in making the pastoral ministry a constant source of danger for priests and the souls entrusted to them.

The duties of a diocesan state of life are closely related to those of the bishop. Is not the diocesan priest's ideal to share in, as far as possible, the bishop's mission and to live with him and for his diocese the entire program of this priestly ordination — *cooperatores ordinis nostri?* This is important since the episcopal Order causes the bishop to be, by mission and grace — although at times not sufficiently enough — the *perfector animarum*, the one who by his apostolic life is the source of perfection for the Christian people. " In the eyes of the Church, the bishop has committed himself to devote all of his efforts to caring for his flock and to live in the perfection of charity in order to sanctify his subjects. " [1] It is the bishop alone who, because of his consecration and his relation to the apostolic hierarchy, is constituted in a state of perfection, *status perfectionis acquisitae et communicandae.* Nevertheless, there is no reason why this state may not be imitated and serve as a source of sanctification for those who share as collaborators in the work of the bishop. [2] If the bishop is regarded as being in a special way a perfector for his priests, this is so only because he allows them to be so closely associated with him in the exercise of his mission. It is in this way that he can lead them to the perfection of the priestly state. Thus, the bishop is pre–eminently the father of his priests.

Through his priests the bishop extends his fatherhood to his flock. Bishop Guyot states :

> When a priest is raised to the episcopal dignity, he may be inclined to think of himself as *less of a father* than before. It most often happens that his obligations no longer permit his exercising certain basic priestly ministrations such as

---

[1] F. Van Steenberghen, " Le prêtre diocésain d'après le Cardinal Mercier, " *loc. cit.*, pp. 66-67. See above, pp. 133-35.

[2] Our present-day *Auxiliaires de l'Apostolat* live a similar type of spirituality, but as lay people. See A. Simonet, " Une nouvelle forme de vie apostolique : Les Auxiliaires de l'Apostolat, " *Revue diocésaine de Namur*, Vol. XI (1957), pp. 585-87.

hearing confessions and giving spiritual direction. His contact with souls may seem remote, less direct and somewhat impersonal. Actually, he is more of a father than ever before; and his fatherhood is even more evident and fruitful since it is exercised through the many and varied activities of his priests. Through them it is greatly enlarged and broadened. [1]

Canon Fécherolle, in an excellent work on the diocesan clergy, wrote : " The bishop is aware that in the person of his pastors he is at the very center of his mission. Through them the bishop is, so to speak, right up at the front lines, among his people and engaged in the important duties of the apostolate. " [2]

It is also necessary to consider how the diocesan priest ought to regard the function of the pastor. Canon Fécherolle wrote :

The pastor's duties are specifically those of the diocesan ministry. Thus, every priest engaged in the service of a diocese must look ahead to his fulfilling the office of pastor. This must not be an earthly type of ambition, an example of which would be a desire for a parish which would be considered ideal either because of the excellent area in which it is located or because of its fine rectory and the excellent monetary benefits to be derived. It must rather be an ambition stemming from the purest motives and a perfect understanding of the obligations of the pastor. Such an aspiration must not destroy the virtue of holy indifference. This can easily happen when a priest is concerned with seeking favors and making requests. Rather, the priest should maintain a healthy balance and by a baptism of desire experience some of the joys of being a pastor. This aspiration must also impel the priest who is not engaged in the direct care of souls to fulfill himself by engaging in the pastoral ministry and by adding to his professional life, to the extent that the circumstances of this life allow, activities of a pastoral nature. Such a share in the pastoral ministry is an activity of the whole diocesan community,

---

[1] Msgr. J. GUYOT, " La paternité du prêtre dans le monde d'aujourd'hui, " conferences reproduced in *Prêtre et Apôtre*, Vol. XLI (1959), p. 6.

[2] P. FÉCHEROLLE, " Le clergé diocésain aux avant-postes, " *op. cit.*, pp. 41-43.

which arises as much from the spirit of union that it presupposes among all members of the clergy as from an actual share in the direction of part of the flock entrusted to the bishop. There will not be too much difficulty in understanding the answer to the following question if what has just been considered has been properly understood. What is a diocesan priest? A diocesan priest is a pastor of souls : actually, potentially and even by desire. [1]

It is in this manner that the concept of the diocese acquires all its grandeur. For the diocesan priest especially, the local church " is not an administrative framework, or a territorial division. It is instead a real unit in which there is to be found, in the union of its bishop to the Sovereign Pontiff, the entire mystery of the Church Universal. " [2] As we stated on one occasion, " A diocese is somewhat like a family, since the bishop, the center of the diocese, is not only an administrator, but, more importantly, he is also the highpriest of the community, the shepherd and father of souls. The priest, his collaborator, also participates in this pastoral and paternal mission. " [3] Even in parishes, the cells of the diocese, the diocesan family is organized like a family. If the bishop is the father of the diocesan family, he exercises his paternity through his collaborators and, as the Belgian Catechism declares, primarily through the pastors in charge of souls in parishes. In other words, the pastors exercise their fatherhood because they share in the bishop's fatherhood. [4] According to St. Anthony Maria Gianelli, " A pastor is nothing else than the the father of a large family entrusted to his care by God and the Church. " [5]

The common life and the holding of goods in common may have some advantages, but the strong bonds existing among the diocesan clergy arise from a spiritual community among priests

[1] P. Fécherolle, *op. cit.*, pp. 49-50.

[2] Msgr. E. Guerry, *Le clergé diocésain, op. cit.*, p. 84.

[3] " Mandement de carême de 1959, " in our *Lettres pastorales*, Vol. II (1959), pp. 533-34.

[4] *Catéchisme à l'usage de tous les diocèses de Belgique*, p. 113.

[5] *St. Antonio-Maria Gianelli*, by a Daughter of Mary dell'Orto (Rome 1951), p. 54.

who are completely dedicated to the pastoral ministry under the direction of their bishop for the welfare of his flock. What impels diocesan priests to devote themselves generously to their diocese is their love of Christ and the people from whom, for the most part, they have descended and to whom they are related by the strongest bonds. Is it not necessary to " preserve one's heritage? " [1] Is it not necessary to enrich it and to make it even more fruitful and profitable for the entire Church of Christ? This, then, is the reason why the diocesan clergy are directly attached by law to the diocese. [2] This is the very notion of the *presbyterium*, the essence of which is not to be found in cohabitation but in collaboration. Union through obedience and charity is the ideal. Very rare indeed are the occasions when the activities of priests require the special intervention of the bishop in order to be valid. However, there are a number of situations in which the priest is obliged to act in accordance with the wishes of the bishop. The whole idea of collaboration, springing as it does from the very notion of the episcopacy and of parish life, demands a share in the anxieties and cares of the bishop and a filial regard for his views and decisions. This ideal attitude was admirably summed up by the early bishops. For St. Cyprian, the Church is a people united to its High Priest and gathered around its Shepherd, *Ecclesia plebs Sacerdoti adunata et Pastori suo adhaerens*. [3] At the beginning of the second century, St. Ignatius said :

> It is proper for you to act in agreement with the mind of the bishop, and this you do. Certain it is that your presbytery is a credit to God, for it harmonizes with the bishop as completely as the strings with a harp. This is why in the symphony of your concord and love the praises of Jesus Christ are sung. But you, the rank and file, should also form a choir so that joining the symphony by your concord, and by your unity taking your keynote from God, you may

---

[1] P. FÉCHEROLLE, *op. cit.*, p. 53.

[2] Y. BOSSIÈRE, *op. cit.*, p. 140.

[3] St. CYPRIAN, " Epistle LXIX, " *PL*, Vol. IV, col. 406.

with one voice through Jesus Christ sing a song to the Father, who will listen to you. [1]

It should be observed that this attitude is quite different from the notion of some who believe that ecclesiastical obedience only exists, as they say, when a formal command is given by one in authority.

* * *

Let us consider once again the question of perfection and the means to attain it. Too many Christians think that only those in convents and religious houses must strive to attain perfection, instead of realizing that every baptized person is called, as Pope Pius XII says, " to the personal perfection of his state. " [2] Even when the excellent attributes of one of their pastors are singled out for praise, too many people are prone to think that these qualities are ordinarily not expected of secular priests. This unfortunate error is certainly not new and is even sometimes used by vocation directors in their attempts to influence young men who are considering the choice of a state of life. We must, as Pius XII directs us, react against such an attitude and against such distressing misrepresentations which reduce the choice between the secular and religious clergy to a question of generosity and which, as a general rule, prescribe that young men, desirous of devoting themselves entirely to God, must be advised against entering a diocesan seminary. The text of the papal document on this matter is most explicit :

It follows that it would not be correct to say that the secular priest, in regard to his own personal sanctification, is any less called to perfection than the regular priest, or to say that the decision of a young man to follow the vocation of a secular priest is a determination to a lower personal

---

[1] St. IGNATIUS OF ANTIOCH, *ad. Eph.* IV.

[2] Pope PIUS XII, " Note " (July 13, 1953), Appendix I, pp. 301-303.

perfection than if he had chosen the priesthood in the religious state. It is possible that it might be so; it is equally possible that one person's choice of a state other than the state of perfection may spring from a greater love of God and a greater spirit of sacrifice than another person's choice of the religious state.

The late Holy Father declared that this type of propaganda, employed by recruiters for the religious life, has theoretical foundations that are inexact and liable to lead to error and, in practice, is, to say the least, lacking in loyalty. Moreover, " bishops are within their rights if they place proper and definite limits to such propaganda by an administrative decision. " [1]

As we have already stated, the clerical state demands perfection more than any other vocation. In an address on the priesthood published after his death, Pius XII stated this once again : " The sacramental character of Holy Orders seals, on the part of God, an eternal pact of His love and predilection, which in exchange demands sanctification, the sanctification of the one chosen. " [2] This address was to have been delivered to the professors and students of the regional seminary of Puglie, and it develops many of the points treated in the Apostolic Exhortation *Menti nostrae* of 1950. The Pontiff, like St. Paul in his Pastoral Epistles, places great stress on the natural virtues and human qualities of the priest : " One does not become a perfect priest unless, in some way, one is a perfect man. " [3] Of necessity, this will lead to true holiness :

> Also, the so-called natural virtues are required of priests by the apostolate, because without them a priest would offend or drive others away. Added to this perfection, already acquired in the best possible way, is the perfection which is proper to the priestly state, that is to say sanctity. In the exhortation which we have already referred to,

[1] Pope Pius XII, "Note " (July 13, 1953), Appendix I, pp. 301-303.
[2] Pope Pius XII, *Allocution to the Students of the Regional Seminary of Pouglie* (posthumous), *AAS*, Vol. L (1958), p. 966.
[3] *Ibid.*, p. 969.

we illustrated at length the equivalence and virtual identity of the priesthood with sanctity.   This is the primary element that makes of the priest a perfect instrument of Christ, because the instrument is the more perfect and effective the more strongly it is bound to the principal cause which is Christ. [1]

In order to cultivate a priestly soul and to prepare to become fitting instrument of Christ, one must attend a good seminary and profit sufficiently from the formation that it affords those aspiring to the priesthood.   If a priest is to persevere throughout his life, despite the difficulties that he will experience and which, if they are not attended to immediately, may easily lead to serious and dangerous pitfalls, it is necessary for him to prepare himself for these trials by being aware of their existence and by taking the necessary steps, when still young, to safeguard himself against them.   Pope Pius XII declares :

> Above all, treasure your strength, reckoning together into one sum total the strength that God shall give you. However, do the utmost to preserve your strength intact, to increase it by adopting the caution and resources that the Church offers to you.   In the exercise of perseverance, you may expect much from the wise guidance of spiritual directors and furthermore from the uninterrupted uprightness of your behavior, from your orderly schedule and from moderation in undertaking and carrying out external activities.   Sublime is the dignity to which God has called you ; numerous and easy to attain are the aids to be used with great profit by you.   All, however, could turn into a painful disappointment unless you do not, like prudent virgins, take care to remain watchful and to persevere. [2]

In short, the life of the secular priest is very demanding and certainly exposed to many dangers which should not be underestimated.   Young priests have quite a few excellent means by

---

[1] Pope Pius XII, *Allocution to the Students of the Regional Seminary of Pouglie* (posthumous), *AAS*, Vol. L (1958), p. 969.

[2] *Ibid.*, p. 971.

which to persevere as long as they loyally and generously follow
the directives given to them by the Church.   Once again, the
Pope is not speaking of vows, which, presumably, he would
have done, had this matter been at least a postulate in the nature
of the priesthood. [1]   What attitude are we to take toward those
young men who are at the point of choosing their vocation?
As with any other decision concerning a vocation, the personal
leanings, attractions and attitudes will be the deciding factors in
an individual's choosing either the secular clergy or the religious
life.   Treating the religious life specifically, Pius XII, in
December, 1950, stated that it is important to encourage those
who manifest a certain attraction for the religious life. [2]   This
is the ordinary and supreme rule of perfect submission to the
Holy Spirit.   It is most important to respect Divine Providence
and not to sin by excess in either way.   It is also important to
realize that what is not true cannot be beneficial — even if the
end pursued is one of the best.   However, as Bishop Ancel has
remarked, " direct calls from God are relatively rare. " [3]   Apart
from such cases where God clearly imposes His choice, those
who counsel young men are ordinarily faced with the problem
of discerning vocations.   " Young men need to be assisted in
discerning God's will for them. " [4]   Such guidance should be
given prudently and discreetly and should be devoid of prejudice
and sectarianism.   It should attempt to correct any misconcep-
tions that there may be about a particular type of life and should
objectively evaluate the various features of the life.   In the course
of this direction, the important place of the diocese and the
parish, as well as the obligation to be concerned with the future
of one's diocese and the valuable means of sanctification inherent
in the parochial ministry should be emphasized.

* * *

[1] Pope Pius XII, *Allocution to the 1st Congress of Religious, loc. cit.*, pp. 29-35.

[2] *Ibid.*, p. 31.   Compare the *Codex Juris Canonici*, can. 487, and Pope Pius XI, Enc. *Rerum Ecclesiae, loc. cit.*, p. 152.

[3] Msgr. A. ANCEL, *Plaidoyer pour le clergé diocésain* (Paris 1947), p. 4.

[4] *Ibid.*, p. 5.

Members of the secular clergy may be attracted to the religious life. Because a person is already canonically engaged in a definite way of life and, through an attraction to the religious life, is endeavoring to give to his life an entirely new orientation, the signs indicating this must of necessity be quite definite. It should be recalled that according to a decree of July 25, 1941, the Sacred Congregation of Seminaries and Religious demands that when someone leaves a seminary to enter a novitiate or leaves the religious life to enter a seminary, recourse must be had to Rome to permit such a change. [1]

By the eleventh century, St. Gregory VII reacted against the ease with which priests abandoned the active ministry to enter a monastery. [2] We have already seen what St. Robert Bellarmine thought of a bishop's desire to enter a monastery. [3] It is not only a bishop's right, but also his duty, to test the desire manifested by one of his clerics and *a fortiori* by one of his priests to enter religious life whenever the bishop is uncertain about the authenticity of such a call from God. The individual who is desirous of entering religion also has the obligation to be certain of his own decision. If this procedure were not employed, hesitant souls would always be uneasy about the choice that they had made. How reassuring are the following words of St. Francis de Sales :

> Do not attempt to be what you are not; instead, work hard to be yourself. Set your mind to perfecting yourself by bearing up under whatever crosses are sent your way. Believe me, this is the best and, unfortunately, the least understood piece of advice that could be given on the spiritual life. Let each one strive to love in his own way. Few people love as they should and as God wishes them to love. What use is there in building castles in Spain when we have to live in France? This is the advice that

---

[1] *Decree of the Sacred Congregation of Religious and Seminaries* (July 25, 1941), *AAS*, Vol. XXXIII (1941), p. 371.

[2] " Letter of St. Gregory VII to the Abbot of Cluny, " cited by L. GENICOT, *La spiritualité médiévale, op. cit.*, p. 47.

[3] See above, p. 138-39.

I wish to give to you and ponder it well. Let me know, my daughter, how well you are putting it into practice. [1]

St. Vincent de Paul gave the same advice. He reminded his Daughters of Charity : " Your convent is the house of the sick, your cell is the room you rent, your chapel is the parish church, your cloisters are the streets of the town, your seclusion is obedience, your grill is the fear of God, your veil is holy modesty. " This was an almost revolutionary innovation, and not a few of the good women were somewhat disturbed by it. The founder informed them : " If there are any discontented souls among you who might say it would be far better to live as religious, then, my sisters, the society would be in need of the last rites since, when we speak about nuns, we speak about seclusion, whereas the Daughters of Charity must go everywhere. " [2] This was the first non-cloistered religious society of women, and the principle set forth here has an even wider application today.

* * *

Certainly, priests, without leaving the diocesan clergy, may understandably turn to the cloisters to learn how to conform themselves more closely to the evangelical counsels. This is also the case with those who wish to strengthen their priestly lives by pronouncing the three vows or by adding to the implicit vow of subdeaconate the other two vows of poverty and obedience. Pope Pius XII discussed this matter on several occasions. In 1950 he stated that it has always been possible to bind oneself freely and privately to the practice of the evangelical counsels. [3] More recently, in December 1957, he was even more explicit.

---

[1] St. FRANCIS DE SALES, " Letter to President Brûlart, " Annecy ed., Vol. XIII, p. 291. Notice the similar recommendations made to Religious, Vol. XIX, pp. 390-409.

[2] See these texts in *Vies des Saints et des Bienheureux;* under St. Louise de Marillac (March 15) and St.Vincent de Paul (July 19), Vol. III (Paris 1941), p. 327; Vol. VII (1949), p. 473.

[3] Pope PIUS XII, *Allocution to the First Congress of Religious, loc. cit.,* p. 29.

There is no need to be situated canonically and juridically in a state of perfection recognized by the Church, since private or secret vows are known to God alone and accord to those who take them the constitutive elements necessary for the attainment of evangelical perfection. [1] The introduction of the secular institutes took place in 1947. Their form of perfection is adapted to life in the world, and thus they offer secular priests the opportunity to strive after evangelical perfection without changing their status. [2] Finally, as we have observed, it may come to pass that the Church will recognize one or another of the forms of the state of perfection in which vows are taken individually, without any need to become a member of a particular society or group. [3] This would be a great help to secular priests, whose only organizational attachment is to the diocese.

Up until now, however, most priests have elected not to take vows. They realize, on the one hand, that the priesthood in no way obliges them to do so, and that perfection is principally to be pursued according to the state proper to each person. On the other hand, they are equally aware that it is not always advisable to assume such definite obligations. Msgr. Brunhes observes :

> It should be pointed out that although the Church does not impose this vow (obedience) on all priests, she in no way means to dispense them from the obligations of tending toward a higher degree of perfection through the practice of obedience. Rather, she wishes them to have a greater freedom to exercise the sovereign virtue of charity, which essentially constitutes perfection, in all the situations that arise in their parochial ministry.

Once again we must return to the advice of St. Francis de Sales :

[1] Pope Pius XII, *Allocution to the Second Congress on the States of Perfection, loc. cit.*, pp. 35-37. See above, pp. 128-29.

[2] J. Dermine, *La dévotion au Sacré-Cœur de Jésus* (Tournai 1952).

[3] See above, pp. 128-32.

God does not want each one to observe all the counsels, but only those which are suitable, according to the differences of persons, time, occasions and strength, as charity requires. For it is charity that is queen of all the virtues, all the commandments and all the counsels and, as the summation of all the laws and all Christian activity, determines the rank, the order, the time and value for all. [1]

These words of wisdom are certainly in keeping with the sentiments expressed in the *Note* which we received from Rome in July 1952 and which we have printed in the appendix of this volume.

A propos of St. Francis de Sales, the following quotation from his *Introduction to the Devout Life* is particularly enlightening :

Charity alone can place us in perfection, but poverty, chastity and obedience are the three principal means to attain it. Although a vow gives many graces and merits to all the virtues, to make us perfect it is not necessary that they should be vowed, provided they be observed. If they are vowed, and especially if solemnly vowed, they place a man in the state of perfection. Yet, to arrive at perfection itself, it suffices that they be observed. There is indeed a difference between the state of perfection and perfection itself. All bishops and religious are in the state of perfection, and yet all have not arrived at perfection itself, as is too plainly to be seen. Let us endeavor, then, Philothea, to practice well these virtues, each one according to his vocation. Although they do not place us in the state of perfection, yet they will make us perfect. Indeed, we are all obliged to practice them, though not all in the same manner. [2]

Fanfani states :

In principle, the religious state is more perfect than any

---

[1] Msgr. G. BRUNHES, " L'obéissance sacerdotale, " *Notes salésiennes* (1930), First Series, No. 3, p. 60.

[2] St. FRANCIS de SALES, *Introduction to the Devout Life*, Part III, ch. XI; see also his *Treatise on the Love of God*, Bk. VIII, ch. VI.

other state of life which simply requires the obligation
of fidelity to the precepts of God and the Church... but,
in practice, each will find perfection not in what objectively
is more perfect, but in that which subjectively is more in
keeping with his capabilities sustained by God's grace.
Thus each person must embrace the type of life to which
he feels called by God. [1]

Certainly this is what really matters. A priest abuses his prestige
and the influence that he has upon youth when, in responding
to their desire to seek perfection, he employs a type of vocational
propaganda which does not make these basic distinctions.

$$* \quad * \quad *$$

The type of training for the priesthood afforded by our
seminaries, the Church's legislation governing the life of the
clergy as expressed in the Code, diocesan statutes and provincial
councils, the constant concern of bishops for their priests, as
well as their own mutual concern for one another are all
important factors enabling them to remain faithful and zealous
laborers of Christ. The Hierarchy should be well disposed
toward those associations which provide priests with added
helps. [2] In Belgium, for example, the Fourth Provincial Council
of Malines included these associations among the means by
which priests can persevere and make progress in virtue.
However, it does not seem proper for diocesan authorities to
impose these associations upon their priests. Yet they should
encourage and even foster the establishment of those associations
which seem best suited to the needs of their priests.

---

[1] L. FANFANI, *De Jure religiosorum ad normam Codicis juris canonici*, 3rd ed. (Rovigo 1949),
pp. 3-4. Cardinal P. M. Richaud says : " 'Higher state' does not mean the most preferable
state for each and every one. The preferable state for each one is that state marked out by
divine providence which will best bring him to perfection. " *Dans les chaînes du Christ, op.
cit.*, p. 174.

[2] *Acta et Decreta Concilii Provincialis Mechliniensis quarti, anno* 1920 *Mechliniae habiti*
(Malines 1923), d. 246.

In the first section of this book we considered the principal associations or societies for priests. Some of these, as we saw, provide for the taking of vows and a limited degree of life in common. Others, without requiring this, insure priests a greater control of their spiritual life and provide the added incentives to this life which are to be derived from a particular school of spirituality. These groups also afford priests the great consolation of fraternal cooperation. There are certainly a sufficient number of these associations from which to choose. It is up to each priest to decide which one is best suited to his needs. *Spiritus ubi vult, spirat.* [1] We must, however, point out one danger to be avoided. The diocesan priest, whether he is a member of a secular institute, or has made private vows, or has made no vows other than that of subdeaconate, should realize that his sanctification is to be sought mainly through the performance of the duties of his state of life as these are set forth in the Code and in the statutes of his diocese. There is a real danger that the hierarchy of values may be reversed in this area. However, this danger can be avoided. This is especially to be feared among seminarians who might tend to underestimate their seminary formation and might pay more attention to the directives of some other authority instead of heeding those of their superiors. They might even band together into exclusive cliques, and as a result their own humility and their relations with other seminarians would no doubt be impaired. Abuses of this type were not always avoided in the more or less exclusive and secret societies of the past. [2] It is for this reason that the seminarians of our own diocese, prior to their ordination, are not allowed, except by special permission, to join any associations which have not been officially established at the seminary by diocesan authorities.

---

[1] Jn 3, 8.

[2] Msgr. C. TOURNIER, *Le chanoine Maurice Garrigou, op. cit.*, pp. 205-7.

Chapter 14

Mutual Cooperation
Between Priests

The Church is a mystery of unity. " That all may be one even as Thou, Father in me and I in Thee, that they also may be one in us. " [1] This prayer and the law implied in it have meaning for all Christians, but particularly for those who, through their priesthood, must supervise and animate the community of the faithful. The principle of unity is the Holy Spirit, the Spirit of Pentecost, who came to each one of the apostles and who comes to each Christian to perform in all the same work in unity and love. Father Congar states : " The role of the Holy Spirit is to make the gifts that He bestows upon each person function together as one. " His law is the " interior law of communion and unity. " [2]

This is apparent when we read the Gospel accounts of the formation of the apostles. Jesus gathered them around Him for two or three years, and after He had formed them to His own image, [3] He sent them to their respective missions. He created fraternal bonds among them through a common life of prayer, preaching and mutual concern for one another. He accustomed them to traveling two by two and promised that He would be in their midst whenever two or three were gathered together in His name. [4] He established the Hierarchy with Peter at the head and confided to him the direction of the Kingdom of God.

[1] Jn 17, 22.

[2] Y. M. J. CONGAR, " Saint-Esprit et esprit de liberté, " *La Revue nouvelle*, Vol. XXIX (1959), p. 14.

[3] Mk 3, 13-14; 6, 7; Lk 10, 1.

[4] Mt 18, 20.

These fraternal bonds are also sealed for all those who share in the priesthood of Christ. The law of the priesthood is one of cohesion and mutual assistance, unity and charity. Any deviation from this through individualism is a crime against the entire priesthood. The statutes of our diocese remind our priests of their obligation to live together in fellowship, mutual understanding and collaboration. [1] These statutes reiterate the constant recommendations of the apostles : " Love one another heartily and intensely. Bear one another's burdens. Love one another with fraternal charity. Be careful to preserve the unity in the bond of peace. Fill up my joy by thinking alike, having the same charity, with one soul and one mind, and let us also continue in the same rule. " [2] The application of these principles on the diocesan level is clear. Since the bishop is the head and the father of his diocese, priests, his most intimate collaborators, must engage in common and fraternal work in the diocese. The fraternity of the priesthood derives from the fatherhood of the bishop. Although they are many in number and oftentimes far removed from their bishop, thereby rendering their collaboration with him less apparent than in the early Christian communities, the ancient concept of the *presbyterium* centered around the bishop should nevertheless be maintained by diocesan priests. Just as there is a diocesan spirituality, so also must there be a diocesan plan for the pastoral ministry.

This holds true for all priests, but even more so for diocesan priests. On the day of their ordination, Abbé Poppe states, they are united " to the bishop as their shepherd and father and also to the other priests of their diocese as their spiritual brothers, *confratres.* " [3] This is particularly apparent when the sacrament of Holy Orders is conferred upon a number of levites who trained together at the same seminary and who together lie prostrate on the floor of the cathedral sanctuary, the Mother Church of the

---

[1] *Statuta Diœcesis Namurcensis*, st. 39.

[2] 1 Pt 1, 22; Gal 6, 2; Rom 12, 10; Eph 4, 3; Phil 2, 2; 3, 16. All these texts are cited by the *Statuta Diœcesis Mechliniensis*, st. 6.

[3] E. POPPE, *Entretiens sacerdotaux, op. cit.*, p. 76.

diocese! The Code of Canon Law refers to the immediate entourage of the bishop as the episcopal family, [1] but this expression can also properly be applied to all the clergy of a diocese.

* * *

The basis of this fraternity and the necessity for mutual cooperation are not exactly the same in the priesthood and in the religious life. For religious, this fraternity arises from the fact that they belong to the same state of perfection and follow the same method of spirituality. It is the fraternity of the baptized in which those who have set out together upon the road of religious life, under the direction of the same superiors, share a common life and are expected to help one another along the road to perfection.

Participation in the same priesthood also requires us to regard this form of cooperation from another viewpoint. This type of cooperation is primarily one of joining together in a united effort to fulfill the common mission of the priesthood. We should not forget that this mission definitely demands holiness in one's personal life, and therefore priests can no longer be disinterested in the sanctification of their colleagues. If the faithful are expected to ask God to give holy priests to the Church, how much more the clergy ought to place this intention uppermost in their prayers. They should make every effort to contribute to the sanctification of their fellow priests.

It is not our intention to consider here all the different areas in which this mutual cooperation among priests can be practiced. It is sufficient merely to indicate the important areas of prayer, study, work and fraternal relations. We are dealing primarily with a question of *esprit de corps*. Thus, the priest who is aware of the bonds uniting him to his confreres will have many opportunities to show them understanding and sympathy and to cooperate with them in pastoral activities.

[1] *Codex juris canonici*, can. 1359, § 2.

Prayer

We should get into the habit of reserving a part of our Breviary and rosary for our fellow priests. We should enjoy praying in common during such occasion as conferences and retreats. Together with the faithful, we should pray for the sanctification of the clergy, for seminarians and vocations to the priesthood, as well as for the diocese, the deanery, the parishes which are conducting missions and the various special apostolates in our area. When we celebrate the *Missa pro Populo*, we should include in the *Memento of the Dead* those departed priests who exercised their ministry in our parish.

Study

Although the circumstances of our particular ministry, especially in the country, may result in our not being close to one another and consequently may not permit us to collaborate as freely with one another as we would like, it is always possible for us to think alike, to pool our experiences and to study the various problems facing the apostolate. There are very few parishes which are immune to social change, which can afford to ignore current opinions and trends and which are not experiencing a constant shift in population. These problems exist today on such a vast scale that parish priests should realize that it is very important for them to cooperate with other priests in the area as well as with the directors of schools and social organizations. The local clergy must take proper steps to adapt their apostolate to the specific needs of their area. Very often they know more about these needs than even the local and federal governmental agencies do. Thus it is important that they meet with one another to determine the particular problems of the area and to see whether or not there is any relation between these problems and the attitudes, leanings and policies of the past. What a tremendous amount of practical knowledge will be derived from such meetings between pastors who are desirous of working closely with one another! Naturally, holy priests are very necessary; but holiness of life also demands devotion to the duties of one's state and consequently the need for study is evident.

Activity is only beneficial when it is adapted to concrete situations. To do this, it is necessary that the area in which it is going to be exercised be known as thoroughly as possible.

Work

Cooperation between priests is traditional and comparatively easy in such matters as hearing confessions, preaching sermons and conducting services. Even greater strides may be made in what has been termed the traditional ministry : giving retreats, assuring greater liberty to the sick during the period of the Easter duty by providing two or three priests for confession, etc. Much also remains to be done in such areas as youth activities, campaigns for decent entertainment and various other projects in particular locales. If collaboration in such projects is to be successful, it will only be so through a sustained effort at being sympathetic, trusting and kind.

We must now consider the subject of fraternal relations between priests. Are we seriously and generously striving to promote this among ourselves? Thank God, the clergy are for the most part hospitable and fraternal. We must fully realize that such constant fraternal relations among priests will serve not only as a guarantee of their moral preservation, but will also do much to insure their pastoral zeal. We should experience deep regret when it is not possible for us to attend priestly gatherings. At any rate, we should attend these gatherings not only for our own benefit but also, and more importantly, because of our concern and regard for others. A priest who isolates himself is guilty of an injustice against the entire priestly community.

We should visit our sick confreres, those who are being tried in some way and those who seem to be depressed. Retired priests especially should be visited, since oftentimes they suffer from inactivity and from a feeling of loneliness and abandonment. Conference meetings would do well to include, as part of their program, the extending of comfort and companionship to retired priests living in the area.

* * *

Would not this type of cooperation between priests be better assured through community life? We know that in principle the Hierarchy strongly recommends this, but it is a very difficult thing to impose. It is not always feasible; and the Council of Trent, in its strict regulations on residence, all but confirmed the practice of having the diocesan clergy live apart from one another. In fact, is not the ministry in rural areas better served by having the clergy spread out from one another in different villages? Even though the means of travel today reduce distances to such a degree that one pastor can conveniently provide services in a distant area, experience proves that parish communities are less familial and very often less fervent when the pastor does not reside in the area. For this reason, some would like to see the old system maintained. However, there are more and more objections being brought against this practice. There must be a sufficient number of priests to permit this as there must also be a sufficient amount of work for a priest to perform. It can also happen that rural areas may become apathetic and dechristianized in certain countries to such an extent that the sustained heroism necessary for a priest to persevere, may be lacking. Finally, the sociological changes presently taking place may indeed warrant a regrouping of parishes into larger units which would of necessity have to be entrusted to several priests. [1] This last consideration should be heeded by bishops. The problem, however, is a complex one; and, naturally, the solutions that are offered are not the same for every situation.

As far as the type of life that should be lived by priests is concerned, we must point out that the common life is not a panacea. Cardinal Saliège observed :

The priest engaged in a teaching assignment may experience a sense of loneliness even though he is in the city and close to his fellow priests. In the country, on the other hand,

[1] See the article devoted to the community of priests of Lugny-lez-Mâcon in the diocese of Autun : " Communauté et pastorale diocésaine, " *La vie spirituelle*, supplement, 42 (1957), pp. 291-331.

a priest may not feel that he is alone. There can be loneliness when one is alone and even when one is in the company of others. How are we to overcome this feeling of loneliness and isolation? Through community life? Not necessarily. Community life sometimes separates more than it unites. A feeling of loneliness and isolation, with all its consequences, can only be overcome by team spirit on the part of priests engaged in the same work and striving after the same end. This spirit will create common interests and attitudes among priests and will result in their working together for the same purpose. Team work demands the pooling of experiences as well as the division of apostolic labor. If all priests function as a team, individualism and aloofness will be eliminated. [1]

This subject is so important today that we must also quote Cardinal Feltin. The following advice was given by him in 1958 on the occasion of the priest retreats in Paris.

For a long time in France, and particularly in Paris, the individualism of the priest, even the parish priest, has been quite noticeable. Every man for himself seemed to be the general rule. Nowadays, the necessity of working together for the success of the parochial ministry, in all its vast missionary dimensions, is quite evident. Young people dread isolation and loneliness and are fully aware of their dangers. They want to feel that they are being personally supported and guided. Generally, all of them are looking for a type of common life. Unfortunately, we do not always have the means to grant this, since all our existing parishes have not yet been able, for a number of good reasons, to establish this type of life for their priests. There are also many legitimate family considerations which prevent many from living a community life which they would certainly prefer to do. However, we should be realistic. A community spirit is not simply fostered by living together. There are many happy results which

[1] Card. J. G. SALIÈGE, " Conférence aux retraites ecclésiastiques " (August 1954), *La Documentation catholique*, Vol. LI (1954), cols. 1179-80.

can be achieved through a common effort at prayer and apostolic activity. I know of nothing better than to urge you to direct all your efforts towards the realization of this truly collective and fraternal apostolate. The demands of an ever more complex ministry and the emphasis that is today placed on social and community affairs compel us to make up for several decades of individualism in one of the most important areas of the Catholic priesthood.

After considering the traditional idea of the presbyterium united to the bishop, the Archbishop of Paris strongly recommended team work among priests through prayer and the study of the problems confronting the apostolate. [1]

* * *

The Presbyterium! A notion which refers more to the profound reality of a spiritual community of souls than to the existence of socially organized communities. Participating together, as they do, in the one priesthood of Christ, hierarchically united to the bishop, Christ's representative among them, priests should be conscious of the bonds uniting them. There is a radical, ontological relationship between them, which is centered in the person of Christ, the High-Priest " who joins them together on the level of His own nature. "

The consequences that this has for the life of the priest on the moral plane are very important. The priesthood establishes, to use an old Roman expression, a spiritual cognation between priests. This calls for their collaborating in mutual trust and friendship as they endeavor to comfort souls and reconcile sinners. The friendship existing between priests, Bishop Garrone declares,

[1] Card. M. FELTIN, " Pour un authentique esprit sacerdotal, " conference of Sept. 1958, *La Documentation catholique*, Vol. LVI (1959), col. 90. The problem of community life is present in Belgium also. See two recent episcopal documents : Msgr. C. M. HIMMER, " L'isolement et l'écartèlement du prêtre, " in his *Lettres pastorales*, Vol. VI (1960), pp. 184-89; Bishop J. B. MUSTY, " Vie commune travail en équipe, soutien sacerdotal, " *Revue diocésaine de Namur*, Vol. XIV (1960), pp 14-26.

does not take the same form as human friendships. Unlike human friendships, it does not develop out of a feeling of loneliness and isolation. Rather, it is a friendship arising from a sort of unlimited possibility for a type of lasting fellowship unheard of in the world. The many barriers that normally exist in ordinary living do not exist among priests, since they have a basic community of interests between them which allows for free exchange and facilitates the forming of lasting friendships. Bishop Garrone continues :

> There is no priest who would contest the evidence. Not even the inevitable human contradictions of meanness or weakness can undo this fellowship. Unfortunately, priests are capable of not loving other priests. Yet they know that they are capable of loving one another as no one else can. They are aware of the type of fellowship to which they are invited, and certainly no priest suffers as much as one to whom this common friendship is refused—often through his own fault. The priest who disregards this is certainly to be pitied since he must, as a result, look elsewhere for what he has refused from the hand of God, or choose to remain apart by himself. It is indeed regrettable that something as valuable as priestly fellowship can at times be disregarded by the very ones for whom it was intended. [1]

The bonds of priestly fellowship are important and necessary. This type of fellowship can exist without the presence of a common life or common activity. However, without it human plans and accomplishments would be uncertain and less meaningful. [2]

* * *

Community life, team work, fraternal cooperation. The importance of the function of the deans is immediately evident.

---

[1] Msgr. G. GARRONE, " Communauté et communautés sacerdotales, " *Prêtres diocésains* (1955), pp. 52-54.

[2] Msgr. S. DELACROIX, " Pour le clergé diocésain, " *op. cit.*, pp. 143-50.

In the Code of Canon Law the deans are referred to as the *vicarii foranei*, [1] those who take the place of the bishop in the various areas of the diocese. It is their task to " watch " the progress of the ministry; [2] but, as Bishop Dubois writes :

> There are various ways of watching. One can watch merely with his eyes, ears and mind. One can also watch *with his heart* in much the same manner as a father watches over his children. Such sincere vigilance, or better yet, such total dedication as is exercised by a father, is the chief function of the dean. It is this which will guarantee his fulfilling his duties perfectly. Let him love as a father loves, and he will come to regard his responsibilities as a labor of love. [3]

He should also get to know his priests and encourage them to do likewise. In this way, the spirit of working together in common and of functioning as a family unit will be developed. The importance of the dean's function in extending, through his priests, the bishop's pastoral and paternal mission is more important today than ever before. What we have said concerning the function of the deans also has application to the rectors of seminaries, colleges and other priestly communities.

* * *

Bishops should have special concern for the junior clergy working in their dioceses. A diocesan statute for the diocese of Namur, reiterating a sentiment expressed at the Provincial Council of Malines, makes this strong recommendation : *Juniores*

---

[1] *Codex juris canonici*, can. 445.

[2] *Ibid.*, can. 447.

[3] Msgr. M. M. Dubois, " Le clergé personnel de l'évêque, " *Semaine religieuse de Rodez* (1953), p. 193. If some day the Church raises to the altar the archpriest of Lanzo-Torinese, Frederick Albert, the deans will then have a patron such as Msgr. Dubois desires. J. Cottino, *Il venerabile Frederico Albert* (Turin 1954), pp. 207-15.

senioribus reverentiam praestent, seniores vero zelum juniorum intelligant et tutentur. [1] The following is a commentary by a young priest on this statute :

> A breach between the two generations need not exist. It would certainly be regrettable if the senior members of the clergy looked down their noses, so to speak, at the junior clergy and treated them as altar boys. It would be equally regrettable if the members of the junior clergy believed that they had nothing to learn from their elders and considered them behind the times. We simply ask the senior clergy to show themselves receptive, to break the ice and to recall the time when, as young curates, they arrived upon the diocesan scene. They should also realize that, except for a few rare exceptions, the junior clergy are not intent upon changing and revolutionizing everything. What they seek is merely to be guided *(tutentur)* and to be shown some understanding in the area to which their bishop has appointed them *(intelligant)*.

We sincerely believe that when our young priests leave the seminary they wish to do their best to serve the diocese and seek only to profit from the experience of their elders. Are they to be reproached for having a keener awareness of the problems of their own generation? Since the Church is expected to be of assistance to men in every age and to use the immutable wisdom of the Gospels in solving their problems and needs, she must combine, along with her fidelity to the eternal message, a constant concern for adaptation. Clerical formation does not end when one leaves the seminary. It still awaits the test of experience. Truly fortunate is the priest who, at the beginning of his ministry, finds a pastor or superior who welcomes and encourages him and cares enough to form him.

There is no more important task than preparing aspirants for the priesthood and initiating young priests into the ministry. We feel no hesitancy in concluding that every other apostolic endeavor must yield to this important duty. This notion was

---

[1] *Statuta Diœcesis Namurcensis,* st. 39.

certainly far better expressed in the posthumous exhortation of
Pius XII : " We should say to the senior clergy : Do not mislead
a young priest.   Undoubtedly, disappointments are unavoidable,
whether they spring from general human conditions or from
particular local motives.   However, such disappointments must
never occur from the fact that senior priests, who are perhaps
discouraged by the disillusionments of life, dull the lively energies
of young priests.   In those cases in which mature experience
does not require a determined " no, " let them make plans, let
them try; if they do not succeed, comfort and encourage them
toward new undertakings. " [1]

---

[1] Pope PIUS XII, *Allocution to the Students of the Regional Seminary of Pouglie, loc. cit.*, p. 271

Chapter 15

Religious
in the Diocese

Along with St. Francis de Sales, we are firmly convinced that
true devotion leading to sanctity is to be found in all states of
life. We also agree completely with Pius XII that whenever
the religious life is justifiably praised, no one should conclude
from this, as was done in the past, that the value of the diocesan
clergy is somewhat questionable. Likewise, no attempts should
be made to dissuade young men from joining the ranks of the
diocesan clergy. [1] Now that we have said this, we nevertheless
subscribe wholeheartedly to the advice given by the Code of
Canon Law : " *Status religiosus... ab omnibus in honore habendus
est.* " [2] We recognize the tremendous value of the offering made
to God through religious profession, as well as the great
importance of the evangelical counsels for the pursuit of
perfection, particularly when they are vowed and lived in a
community life. We are also convinced that when vocational
literature is neither indiscreet nor partisan, recruiting for both
clergies can be carried out harmoniously, according to the plan
of God, for the greater good of the Church. All priests, religious
and secular, on the day of their ordination, receive the same
priesthood in exactly the same way. The only ceremony that
is different is that of the *Promitto*. Every priesthood of second
rank is a participation in the episcopacy and a share in the
Episcopal Order. [3] All priests therefore are brothers and have

---

[1] See above, p. 185.

[2] *Codex Juris Canonici*, can. 487.

[3] Pius XII often reminded religious of the apostolic nature of every consecration to
God, even in a vocation to the contemplative life. See R. CARPENTIER, *La Vie religieuse,
Documents pontificaux du règne de Pie XII* (Rome 1959), pp. 179 ff.

the same claim to the title " other Christs. " They have the same essential powers and are equally dependent, as regards their ministry, on the Pope and the bishop of the diocese in which they function. All are obliged to celebrate Holy Mass and to exercise their ministry *cum Papa nostro et Antistite nostro.* [1]

Conditions in the life of the diocese vary. Although incardination and the *Promitto* attach the diocesan priest to his diocese and to his bishop in a stable manner, the ties that the religious have to the diocese and the bishop are not very strong. The religious, as regards his personal and community life, is dependent upon his superiors. The length of his stay in any diocese is indefinite, and his activities therein are necessarily dictated by the spirit and constitutions of his society. [2] Although the bishop may appoint him to a particular post or give him a special work to perform, such an appointment is not dependent solely upon the bishop. Thus, in the exercise of his priesthood, he is responsible to two superiors. Clearly then, the religious is not as much at the disposal of the local bishop as the secular priest who, according to the spirit of the Canons, is expected to be completely at his disposal. The bishop is totally committed to a fatherly concern for his diocesan priests, whereas this concern is only partial, although no less real and meaningful, for the religious working in his diocese.

Now that we have made these reservations, we must state, nevertheless, that religious should be made welcome in the diocese; and both clergies cannot too often be exhorted to live and cooperate in a spirit of mutual trust and respect. Since the Pope insistently stresses that the bishop must be the center of unity in the diocese, seculars and religious will only be perfectly faithful to his will when they foster this unity by living together as brothers. It is strongly hoped that the parochial clergy will continue their fine tradition of extending hospitality and courtesy

[1] On exempt religious, see above, p. 182. The Pope is the highest superior of all religious who must obey him by virtue of their vow of obedience : *Codex Juris Canonici*, can. 499, § 1. The ordinary universal power of the Pope extends to all the faithful and thus to all priests. The Catholic clergy, in short, are the Pope's clergy : *Codex Juris Canonici*, can. 218, § 2.

[2] On the canons regular, see above, p. 187, footnote 3.

to the religious staying in their rectories. What bishop is there who would not concur with the exhortation addressed by Bishop Dubois to the religious of his diocese. " Let each one, " he told them, " think diocesan. Let each one love the diocese in which he is invited to labor. In short, let each one do all that he can to be a member of the diocese and not a stranger. " The Archbishop of Besançon put it this way :

> The religious must refrain from being critical and partisan. Rather, he should enter wholeheartedly into the work of the diocese, not only by performing his duties, but also by sharing the hopes and anxieties for the diocese that are had by the one primarily responsible for the diocese, namely the bishop, whose representative he should sincerely wish to be considered. Since he has received from the local bishop both the authorization to work in his diocese and a share in his powers, he should endeavor to use these powers in a way that is entirely in keeping with the mind of the bishop. [1]

There is great hope that the Second Vatican Council will do much to bring about a closer collaboration between both clergies. The Synod of Rome has apparently cleared the way for this. [2]

* * *

An appeal for unity in thought and action must also be extended so as to include religious men and women. We should manifest toward them a profound sense of gratitude for their assistance, as well as a high regard for their vocation. With the exception of the priesthood, religious consecration is the finest

---

[1] Msgr. M. M. DUBOIS, " Le clergé personnel de l'évêque, " *loc. cit.*, p. 188.

[2] In connection with the synod of Rome, Msgr. A. GLORIEUX recently wrote that the Pope on several occasions has spoken of his " diocesan clergy, both secular and religious. " (" Perspectives et difficultés du renouveau pastoral dans le diocèse de Rome, " *La Croix* Feb. 6, 1960). Certainly this type of unity is more easily attainable at Rome where the situation of the bishop is unique, but the principle should hold true everywhere.

homage that a creature can render to God, and it is the surest guarantee of a fruitful apostolate. This understanding of the religious life should also be imparted to the faithful; but we priests must first make certain that we sincerely share this conviction. We feel no hesitation in stating that the fear of many parents to give their children to God, either for the priesthood or the religious life, is one of the surest signs of dechristianization.

5

The Models
and Patrons
of the Secular Clergy[1]

---

[1] For this section we have utilized, along with a number of individual biographies, several articles in dictionaries and encyclopedias — especially those in the *Enciclopedia cattolica*, published by the Vatican Press from 1948 to 1954. We have derived special benefit from the collection of the Benedictines of Paris entitled *Vies des Saints et des Bienheureux selon l'ordre du Calendrier, avec l'historique des fêtes*. This monumental undertaking originated with Dom J. Baudot, but the work was later taken up and continued by the monks of the Abbey of Sainte-Marie (de la Source), in Paris. The first five volumes are mainly the work of Dom Baudot, while the rest have been published under the direction of Dom J. Dubois. Volume 13 (1959) provides a supplement with articles pertaining to hagiography. As far as their critical value is concerned, the later volumes are undoubtedly far superior. The older work by Dom J. Baudot, *Dictionnaire d'hagiographie* (Paris 1925), must be used with caution.

Chapter 16

Are there Saints among the Diocesan Clergy ?

It is true that the priesthood does not, in itself, constitute a state of perfection in the official sense of the word. However, do not the activities in which priests engage and the type of life that they lead provide many excellent means for attaining sanctity? To answer this question we have more than theories, we have facts provided by the lives of truly saintly priests. Some of them have already been canonized, and others are presently awaiting beatification. There are also many other priests whose lives have been a source of great edification for the faithful. [1] One has only to read their lives to become quickly impressed by the high degree of sanctity, and even heroic sanctity, that flourished among diocesan priests. It is appropriate to recall here the following saying of St. Francis de Sales : " There is nothing as useful and worthwhile as reading the lives of the saints, which are to the Gospels what sung music is to sheet music. " [2]

This saint also declared on another occasion : " Read Church history and the lives of the saints and realize that in no other Order or vocation will you find as many saints as you do among bishops. There is no other state in the Church of God which furnishes as many opportunities for sanctification and perfection. The best way to make progress in perfection is by teaching it to

---

[1] The lives of many priests, other than those who are candidates for beatification, are also edifying. Thus, one of the early pioneers of Catholic Action, who died just recently, lived an extremely holy life in our own diocese. See G. Hoyois, *Monseigneur Picard, Aux origines de l'Action Catholique* (Brussels 1960).

[2] St. Francis de Sales, *Letter to Msgr. André Frémyot* (Oct .5, 1604), Annecy ed., Vol. XII, p. 306.

others through word and example, and it is to the fulfilling of this task that bishops are obliged by their state. "[1]   Such an assertion as this will undoubtedly astonish more than one reader. It must be understood, however, in the context of the sixteen-hundreds, the period prior to the numerous canonizations and beatifications of religious.   Since that time religious have come to occupy a greater place in the Sanctoral.

If the list of early canonizations and particularly the Martyrology are consulted, it will be readily seen that the largest group in each of these is comprised of bishops.   It is also evident that a great many of these bishops came from the secular clergy.

*   *
*

The history of the Sanctoral is a complex one.   Three periods, corresponding more or less to the three major periods of Church history, can be discerned.   It should also be stressed that the liturgical calendar, the principal witness of the Sanctoral, for a long time differed from place to place.   By the twelfth century attempts were being made to universalize it, but it is only during the pontificate of St. Pius V (1566-1572) that we can truly speak of a universal calendar.   Caution is even more necessary in considering the Martyrology.   In these documents we are afforded only a partial view of the Church's veneration of saints, particularly for the first eleven centuries. [2]   However it is interesting to compare the Church's present universal calendar with the Roman Martyrology.   Over the years both have undergone changes by way of suppressions and additions; yet they furnish an excellent insight into the early centuries.   The first saints to be venerated at Rome were martyrs; and as time

---

[1] Msgr. J. P. Camus, *L'Esprit de saint François de Sales*, Estienne ed. (Paris 1747), Part VII, chap. II, p. 207.   (Eng. trans. New York : P. O'Shea, 1867).

[2] On the problems relating to the Sanctoral, see the articles of G. Löw in the *Enciclopedia cattolica* : " Beatificazzione, " Vol. II, cols. 1090-1100; " Calendario della Chiesa Universale, " Vol. III, cols. 364-72; " Canonizzazione, " Vol. III, cols. 569-607.   On the Martyrology, see *ibid.*, A. Bugniori, " Martirologio, " Vol. VIII, cols. 244-58.

went on there were soon added apostles, confessors of the faith, the great Doctors of the Church, the monastic founders and the patrons of the more influential abbeys, as well as a few women saints and quite a number of Popes. The spread of devotion to Popes who were not martyrs is attributed to Gregory VII († 1085) whose pontificate seems to have marked the culmination of the early liturgical evolution.

By the twelfth century a number of new strides were made in this area. The first that should be noted is the case of St. Thomas à Becket, Archbishop of Canterbury, martyred in 1173.

> By inscribing Thomas à Becket in a calendar whose most recent saint was Gregory the Great († 603), the Roman Church introduced the veneration of contemporary saints. This heralded a practice which really developed in the following century with the flourishing of sanctity brought about by the Mendicant Orders. Thus, Anthony of Padua and Peter of Verona were inscribed in the Catalogue of Saints only one year after their death. Francis and Clare of Assisi were so honored after two years, while Elizabeth of Hungary and Dominic after four and thirteen years respectively. About the same time as the Roman Ferial was being brought up to date, it was also universalized. It became a record of the Church's life. A universal view of sanctity in the Church was substituted for the restricted notion of local cult. [1]

The above quotation mentions the canonization of Elisabeth of Hungary. This, however, is only one case in the whole series of canonizations of lay saints such as Henry II of Germany, Edward of England and Louis IX of France. Martyrs, bishops and monks therefore have no monopoly with regard to sanctity. The correction of the opposite view actually began in the eleventh century when Gregory VII chided the Abbott of Cluny for having admitted the Duke of Burgundy to the monastic way of life. The Pope believed that it would have been far better

---

[1] P. JOUNEL, " Le Sanctoral romain du VIᵉ au XIIᵉ siècle, " *La Maison-Dieu*, 52, pp. 87-88.

if the latter had continued to function as a prince and knight. Professor Genicot writes : " These almost revolutionary ideas grew slowly and really only applied to the upper classes and the nobility. They had a tremendous influence and resulted in enhancing the position of the secular clergy and the lay state. Interest in the active life was also rekindled. " [1]

These ideas fully caught on in the thirteenth century when St. Francis founded his Third Order in 1221 and put sanctity within the reach of the common man. In this same year, 1221, Blessed Davanzanato joined the Third Order. For seventy years he was the pastor of a small parish on the outskirts of Florence. He died in 1295. Two other priest tertiaries who lived during the Middle Ages have been accorded the honors of the altar, namely, Blessed Bartholomew Buenpedoni, pastor of Pichena in Etruria († 1300) and Blessed Oddo Barolli, pastor of Fossano in Piedmont († 1400). Mention should also be made of James Oldi († 1404), who was converted and died at the age of 40 as a result of the extreme penances that he performed. Rome has been petitioned to recognize his cult.

Meanwhile, various local churches began to devise their own calendar and sanctoral. The practice of venerating holy bishops and other high ranking persons of a particular area was followed, since this corresponded to what was done at Rome by the Popes and their entourage. It is often quite difficult to draw a proper line between history and legend in this matter. There are, moreover, many interesting cases of priests, particularly pastors, who were accorded the honors of the Altar and held in constant veneration despite their humble rank and station. In the sixth century, Gregory of Tours preserved from oblivion the names of several priests of the Diocese of Auvergne. The two Archdeacons of Clermont, Tigridus and Justus, who lived in the fourth century and whose feasts are celebrated on the 16th of February and the 21st of October respectively, as well as a pastor of Riom by the name of Amabilis, who lived during the fifth century and whose feast is celebrated on the 18th of October,

---

[1] L. GENICOT, *La spiritualité médiévale, op. cit.*, pp. 46-48.

are just a few examples of those cited by Gregory of Tours. It is a shame that the writers of local history were not all of the same caliber as Gregory of Tours!

The names of several priests passed from local martyrologies into the Roman Martyrology. There is the case, for example, of St. Severus, a humble priest of Abruzzo, who died about 530, after having led a life of prayer, work and charity at his little church dedicated to our Lady. His feast is celebrated on the 15th of February. It may happen during our lifetime that Rome will recognize a number of these ancient cults. Pius IX confirmed the cult of St. William of Leavol who was the humble pastor of Mogex during the seventh century. His feast, which falls on the 7th of February, is still very popular in the Diocese of Aosta.

* * *

The ninth century, the age of Charlemagne, inaugurates the period of greater intervention by Rome in matters pertaining to the Sanctoral. These interventions multiplied, as we shall observe; and by the twelfth century they became even more definite and formal. The early canonizations, however, did not have the same force and meaning in the beginning as they have today, and there are a number of them which are not really certain. [1] There are, besides, a number of cults dating back to the early centuries and to the Middle Ages which have been confirmed in recent times. This is what is referred to as the

---

[1] To date, the Sacred Congregation of Rites has not published an official list of beatifications and canonizations. A great amount of valuable information may be found in the article of G. Löw who was a member of the historical commission of this congregation, *loc. cit.*, Vol. II, cols. 1098-1100; Vol. IV, cols. 599-602. Lists are also presented by other authors, notably Msgr. A. Battandier, "Liste des béatifications et canonisations au xixe siècle," *Annuaire pontifical catholique*, Vol. IV (1901), pp. 528-55; also "Canonisations formelles," *ibid.*, Vol. VI (1903), pp. 409-19; J. Broderick, "A census of the Saints (993-1955)," *The American Ecclesiastical Review* (1956), pp 87-115. Much information is to be found also in the *Vies des Saints et des Bienheureux*, published by the Benedictines of Paris. We have marked with an asterisk the names of those saints whose canonization is not recorded by G. Löw.

confirmatio cultus, which has the juridic force of a beatification and which, since the thirteenth century, has known several different procedures. [1]

In the list that follows as in the lists that we have drawn up for modern times, we have italicized the names of those bishops and priests who entered religious life after having served as secular priests.

A) a) Canonized Bishops : Ulric of Augsburg († 973); Conrad of Constance († 976); *Rudesindus* of Compostella († 977); *Adalbert* of Prague, martyr († 977); Gerard of Toul († 994); Bernwald, Bishop of Hildesheim († 1022); [2] *Bruno of Würtzburg († 1045); *Pope Leo IX († 1054); *Annon of Cologne († 1075); Stanislaus of Cracow, martyr († 1079); Osmund of Salisbury († 1099); *Benno of Miessen († 1105); Gerard of Potenza († 1119); *Bruno* of Segni († 1123); *Bertrand of Comminges († 1125); Ubald of Gubbio († 1136); Otto of Bamberg († 1139); William of York († 1154); Thomas à Becket of Canterbury, martyr († 1170); Galdinus of Milan († 1176); *William* of Bourges († 1209); William of Saint-Brieuc († 1234); Edmund Rich of Canterbury († 1240); Richard of Chichester († 1253); Thomas of Hereford († 1282); *Bienvenuto Scotivoli* of Osimo who, prior to his consecration, took the Franciscan habit and was professed in the same Order († 1282).

Inscription in the universal calendar of the Church is presently considered equal to canonization; and therefore we are justified in adding the name of *St. Norbert*, priest of Cologne, founder of the Premonstratensians and Archbishop of Magdeburg († 1134). He was inscribed in the universal calendar of the Church in 1621.

— b) Bishops whose cult has been recognized by Rome since the reign of Urban VIII : Cecard of Luni († 815); Pope Adrian III († 885); Veremundus of Ivrea in Piedmont

---

[1] On the confirmation of a cult, confer G. Löw, " Santi, Conferma del culto, " *Enciclopedia cattolica*, Vol. X, cols. 1855-56. We are listing here only those names which appear in the index of the Sacred Congregation of Rites, which we have been able to consult.

[2] It was by mistake that Bernward of Hildesheim was designated as a Benedictine.

(† c. 1000); Thibaut of Vienne-en-Dauphiné († 1001); Guy of Acqui († 1070); *Pope Urban II* († 1099); Ismido of Die († *C.* 1115); *Hugh* of Grenoble († 1132); *Bogomil* of Gnesen, who became a monk at the age of 60 († 1182); *Vincent Kalubka* of Cracow, who became a Cistercian after serving ten years as a bishop († 1223); Pope Gregory X († 1276); Peter Paschasius of Grenoble, later Bishop of Jaën, martyr († 1300); [1] Renaldus of Ravenna († 1321); Bertrand d'Angoulême of Aquila, martyr († 1350); Stephen Pondinelli of Otrante, martyr († 1480). [2]

B) a) Priests and clerics who have been canonized. *Peter of Trevi, Deacon, famous for his preaching and penances († 1050); *Gilbert of Simpringham*, priest and pastor of Lincoln, founder of the Gilbertines († 1189); *Hyacinth Odravaz*, Canon of Cracow, who later became a Dominican († 1257); *Raymond of Peñafort*, archpriest of Barcelona, who also became a Dominican († 1276); Yves Hélory of Rennes, pastor of Trédrez and later of Lovannec († 1303); John Nepomucene, Canon and pastor in the Diocese of Prague, martyr († 1383); [3] John of Kenty, professor at the University of Cracow and for a time the pastor of Olkusz, a town close to Cracow († 1473); *John of San-Facondo*, priest of Burgos, who later joined the Hermits of St. Augustine († 1479).

As in the case of St. Norbert, there are two saints listed in the universal calendar of the Church whom we should also include here : *St. Bruno*, priest of Cologne, and later Canon of Rheims, founder of the Carthusians († 1101) and *St. Sylvester Guzzolini*, priest and Canon of Osimo, founder of the Silvestrians († 1267). Their feasts were extended to the Universal Church in 1623 and 1890 respectively.

— b) Priests whose cult has been officially recognized : Amalbert, pastor of Michaelsbuch in the Diocese of Ratisbon

---

[1] Peter Paschasius was not a religious of Mercy, as is sometimes alleged.

[2] Stephen Pondinelli, Bishop of Otrante, was a member of a group of martyrs from this town whose cult was confirmed in 1771. There were about 800 victims, most of whom were priests. See A. ANTONACI, *Otranto, testi e monumenti* (Galatine 1955), pp. 67-73; also, his " Il 'procesus canonizationis' dei Martiri d'Otranto, " *Studi Salentini*, Vol. I (1957), pp. 1-12.

[3] 1383 is given as the date of John Nepomucene's death. However, there are quite a few problems connected with this saint. It appears that the Martyr for the Confessional Seal is really John Sarkander, who was put to death in 1620 and was beatified in 1859.

(† c. 800); Ariald, deacon of Milan, martyr († 1066); *Ceslaus*, Canon of Cracow, who later became a Dominican († 1242); Thomas Hélye, preacher at the court of St. Louis and missionary in the Diocese of Coutances († 1257); Bartholomew Buenpedoni, pastor of Pichena in Tuscany († 1300); *John Ruysbroeck*, Canon of Sainte-Gudule in Brussels and later Canon regular of Groenendael († 1381); Oddo Barolli, pastor of Fossana in Piedmont († c. 1400); the martyred priests of Otrante († 1480). [1]

* * *

During the period extending from the year 800 up until the early decades of the sixteenth century, other members of the secular clergy had been and continued to be venerated locally as saints.   The list of saints found in the appendix of this book contains a few names that are also included in the Roman Martyrology.   Rome has given a certain amount of approbation to these saints and particularly to those who lived during and after the twelfth century.   We estimate that there are about 25 bishops, among them St. Albert of Louvain, Bishop of Liège, who are not mentioned in the lists dealing with canonizations and the recognition of cults.   There are also 13 priests similarly not mentioned, the eleven martyrs of Cordova (ninth century) as well as St. Lié, priest of Orleans († 875) and St. Grimoald, Archpriest of Montecorvo, near Aquinato in the Campagna († 1137).

As for other local cults, Rome has at least authorized the celebration of their feasts.   In the Diocese of Versailles, the feast of Blessed William, pastor of Pontoise († 1166), is celebrated on the 10th of May, that of St. Odulph, pastor of Oirschot († ninth century) is celebrated in the Dioceses of Utrecht and Bois-le-Duc on the 12th of June.   In the Diocese of Namur the feast of St. Walter, pastor of Onhaye, is celebrated on the 27th of June.   He paid with his life for his fidelity to the pastoral

[1] See p. 233, note 2.

office († thirteenth century). We have already mentioned the two Italian priests who were Franciscan tertiaries, namely Blessed Davanzanato († 1295) and Blessed James Oldi. It is hoped that their cults will be accorded recognition in the future.

To the best of our knowledge there exists neither a complete collection of the Propers of every diocese nor a list containing all the cults that were venerated in various local dioceses similar to those contained in the detailed calendars of religious orders.

* * *

In reference to this, we should realize that the secular clergy were in a less favorable position than the long established religious orders which, as a matter of course, handed down from monastery to monastery and from generation to generation, the extremely edifying accounts of the lives of their members. In 1942 Dom Schmitz published a calendar of the Benedictine Order which lists more than 800 names of religious men and women, priests and brothers. We should have nothing but respect and admiration for this list, but it should be pointed out that almost all the names mentioned in it belong to those periods when the Holy See ordinarily did not intervene in these matters. We find some fifteen religious men cited there who were beatified as martyrs by the decree of Urban VIII, which we shall discuss. These were the victims of the sixteenth and seventeenth century English persecutions and the eighteenth century French Revolution. [1]

* * *

Beginning with the twelfth century, the Popes began to intervene much more directly in matters pertaining to the Sanctoral. Canonization and recognition of cults came more and

---

[1] P. SCHMITZ, *Histoire de l'Ordre de Saint-Benoît, op. cit.*, Vol. II, pp. 396-421. Note that since then (1954), Pius XII beatified an Italian Benedictine, Placid Riccardi, who died in 1915. The causes of other Benedictines are now being examined, notably that of Dom Columba Marmion of Namur.

more to be considered reserved to the Holy See as is evidenced by a letter of Alexander III written in 1170. [1] Nevertheless, a firm and definite policy on this matter only dates from July 5, 1634 when Pope Urban VIII published his Apostolic Constitution, *Coelestis Hierusalem*. This pontifical document practically approved the Sanctoral for the period prior to the reign of Alexander III. For the period extending from the latter's pontificate up until the year 1534, that is to say 100 years before Urban VIII's Constitution, a tolerance was accorded those cults which were venerated from time immemorial. Moreover, the official confirmation of a well established cult, equivalent to a beatification, can always be attained if Rome judges this expedient. The causes of those who died after 1534 were strictly reserved to the judgment of the Holy See; and the first condition, required before any investigation would be undertaken, was to establish that no veneration had already taken place. This is what is meant by the expression *non-cultus*. Henceforth, a very thorough investigation would have to precede every beatification and canonization process. [2]

It is therefore quite understandable that the success or failure of a cause depends in large measure upon the lengthy, detailed and often painstaking labor that goes into its preparation. Each cause also needs a loyal and attentive group of individuals who are willing to introduce it, ready to follow it up and to promote it actively. This is why the great religious families as well as certain interdiocesan societies take great pains to delegate this function to *postulators* who are experienced in these matters. Many causes are abandoned because, as Bishop Fontenelle says, like the paralytic at the pool of Bethsaida, the candidate can say : " *Hominem non habeo.* " [3] Sometimes a cause that has been in eclipse for a long while attains success when it is taken up again by interested and active supporters. The cause of Blessed John

---

[1] G. Löw, " Canonizzazione, " *loc. cit.*, col. 580.

[2] See G. Löw, *ibid.*, col. 591. See also, e.g., A. Vermeersch — J. Creusen, *Epitôme Juris Canonici*, Vol. II, 5th ed. (Bruges 1940), pp. 421-22.

[3] Jn 5, 7.

of Avila, the patron of the Spanish clergy, who was only beatified in 1894, [1] is just such an example. We need not be discouraged or surprised by the fact that most of the causes that are introduced and which attain success are those sponsored by the major orders and societies. On this subject it is especially worthwhile to read the book written by Bishop Gannon, Archbishop-Bishop of Erie, Pennsylvania. North America has seen eight Jesuit martyrs canonized in 1930, Philippine Duchesne beatified in 1940, Frances Cabrini canonized in 1946, Margaret d'Youville beatified in 1959 and more recently Elisabeth Seton beatified in March 1963. There is also a movement under way to propose the names of 110 American martyrs for canonization. One of these is a Belgian priest, Bishop Charles Seghers who was born at Ghent and attended the American Seminary at Louvain. Called the Apostle of Alaska, he was brutally murdered there during an episcopal visitation. [2] America can certainly take its place alongside Italy, France and Spain, nations which have always had the most causes pending before Rome. This is certainly to their credit, but here also, God has need of men. Clearly then, the proclamation of the Church on the occasion of a beatification or a canonization is unquestionably a tremendous recommendation of the type of life led by the new saint or blessed. One must, however, be extremely prudent in citing the number of saints in a particular country, diocese or religious order as an argument of comparison with other less favored areas and religious communities. We have already stated that the Benedictine Sanctoral lists very few saints of recent times. The same can be said for the Sanctorals of the Cistercians, Premonstratensians and other orders. Are we to conclude from this that the contemplative or canonical way of life is less apt to lead to heroic sanctity?

Be that as it may, we will now examine the list of saints of the secular clergy. This list includes bishops and priests who

[1] On the problems involved in the process of John of Avila, see L. M. Fernandez de Bobadilla, " Situacion de la canonizacion del Beato Juan de Avila, " *El Beato Juan de Avila, Conferencias pronunciadas en la Semana Nacional Avilistica en Madrid, op. cit.*, pp. 193-209.

[2] Bishop J. M. Gannon, *The Martyrs of the United States of America* (Erie 1957).

died after 1534. It is recorded that St. John Vianney was
astonished by the fact that there were, as he said, no pastors
accorded the honors of the Altar! I have even heard it said that
the Curé of Ars was an exception! Let us see if this is so.

* * *

We will proceed by periods : first from 1534 to the end of
the seventeenth century, then each century thereafter. We will
first list the bishops and then list the other secular priests and
clerics. After presenting the list of canonized and beatified in
each category, we will also include, in small print, those who are
presently considered Servants of God and whose causes have not
yet reached the final stage. [1]

A. From 1534 to 1699.

1. Bishops : *Saints :* John Fisher, Cardinal, Bishop of
Rochester, martyr († 1535); Charles Borromeo, Cardinal, Arch-
bishop of Milan († 1584); Turibius, Bishop of Lima († 1606);
Francis de Sales, Bishop of Geneva and Doctor of the Church
(† 1622); Gregory Barbarigo, Bishop of Bergamo, and later of
Padua († 1697).

Blessed : John Juvenal Ancina, Bishop of Saluces († 1604);
John de Ribera, Bishop of Badajoz and later of Valencia († 1611);
Oliver Plunket, Archbishop of Armagh, martyr († 1681); Pope
Innocent XI († 1689).

> *Venerables :* Peter George Odescalchi, Bishop of Vigevano
> († 1620); John Baptist Grault, Oratorian, Bishop of Marseille
> († 1643); John de Palafox y Mendosa, Bishop of Osma
> († 1659).
> *Servants of God :* Francis Aguilar y Seixas, Bishop of
> Michoacan in Mexico († 1698); Nicholas Stenon, a brilliant
> university professor who came from Denmark, Vicar
> Apostolic of Hanover († 1686).

---

[1] Most of these names are cited in the official publication of the Sacred Congregation
of Rites, *Index ac status causarum beatificationis Servorum Dei et canonizationis Beatorum* (Vatican
City 1953).

2. Priests : *Saints :* Jerome Aemiliani, priest of Venice, founder of the Somaschi († 1537); Anthony Zaccaria, priest of Cremona, founder of the Barnabites († 1539); Cajetan of Thien, ordained a priest in Rome, founder of the Theatines († 1547); four of the martyrs of Gorkum put to death in 1572 (Andrew Wouters, a pastor, converted on seeing the suffering and defection of several of the condemned; Godfrey Van Duynen or Dune, a retired pastor; Leonard Vechel, pastor of Gorkum; Nicholas Janssen or Poppel, curate in Gorkum); Philip Neri, priest of Rome and founder of the Oratory († 1595); *Andrew Avellino*, priest of Naples, joined the Theatines († 1608); *John Leonardi*, priest of Luca, founder of the Clerics Regular of the Mother of God († 1609); *Joseph Calasanctuis*, priest of Urgel and founder of the Clerics Regular of the Mother of God of Pious Schools (Piarists) († 1648); Vincent de Paul, pastor of Châtillon in the Diocese of Bourg, founder of the Vincentians († 1660).

Blessed : John of Avila, priest of Cordova, Apostle of Andalusia († 1569); Mark Crisin, Canon of Gran in Hungary, and seminary professor, martyr († 1619); John Sarkander, Moravian pastor, martyr of the confessional secret († 1620); two Japanese martyrs, Leo of Satzuma, cleric in minor orders († 1622) and Jerome de Torres, priest († 1632); Anthony Grassi, an Oratorian of Ancona († 1671). Mention must also be made of the ninety-one English martyrs put to death between 1535 and 1680. [1]

> *Venerables :* Ferdinand de Contreras, priest of Seville († 1548); John Baptist Bertran, pastor of Alcora in the Diocese of Tortosa († 1601); Charles Carafa, priest of Naples († 1633); Michael Le Noblez, diocesan missionary of Quimper († 1652); Jean-Jacques Olier, Oratorian, pastor and founder of the Society of Saint-Sulpice († 1657); Bartholomew Holzhauser, pastor of Bingen in Austria, founder of the Apostolic Union († 1658); Bartholomew de Quental, founder of an Oratory in Portugal similar

[1] It is said that several English martyrs became religious during their incarceration. This is currently disputed. See R. A. HUTCHINSON, *Diocesan Priest Saints* (St. Louis and London, 1957), pp. 11-13. In Appendix II, however, we have listed them all as religious.

to that of St. Philip Neri († 1694); Benignus Joly, priest
of Dijon, called " The Father of the Poor " († 1694). There
are also sixty-seven Venerables among the secular clergy
who were martyred in England during the sixteenth and
seventeenth centuries.

Servants of God : Gellius Ghellini, pastor of the Church of
SS. Faustus and Jovita in Vicenza († 1615); Nicholas Rusca,
pastor of Sondrio, in Ticino, martyr († 1618); Liborio
Wagner, pastor of Altenmünster in the Diocese of
Würzburg, martyr († 1631); Balthasar-Bernard Rodriquez
de Cisneros, Canon of Palencia († 1677). [1] Finally, there
is a whole group of Irish Martyrs of the Reformation, among
whom there are several bishops and priests.

B. The Eighteenth Century.

1. Bishops : *Saints : Alphonsus Liguori,* priest of Naples,
founder of the Redemptorists, later Bishop of Santa-Agatha near
Naples, Doctor of the Church († 1787).

Blessed : Francis Joseph de la Rochefoucauld Maumont,
Bishop of Beauvais; John Mary du Lau d'Alleman, Archbishop
of Arles; Peter Louis de la Rochefoucauld Bayers, Bishop of
Saintes. All three were among the victims of the September
2, 1792 massacre at Paris.

Venerables : Francis de Laval-Montmorency, first bishop
of Quebec († 1709); John Francis Tanderini, Bishop of
Civitta-Castellana († 1739).

Servants of God : Anthony Barbarigo, Bishop of Monte-
fiascone († 1706); Charles Francis de Saint-Simon, Bishop
of Agde, martyr († 1794); Nicholas Bankovic, Bishop of
Macarsca in Yugoslavia († 1710).

2. Priests and Clerics : *Saints :* Joseph Oriol, priest of
Barcelona, engaged in the parochial ministry († 1702); *Louis Marie
Grignion de Montfort,* secular priest, later founder of the Montfort
Fathers († 1716); *John Baptist de la Salle,* Canon of Rheims,

---

[1] Balthasar Rodriguez is not well known.   He is listed in the *Index Causarum* of the
Sacred Congregation of Rites as a canon of Valencia.   He was, in fact, a canon of Palencia
where he was born in 1630 and died in the odor of sanctity Nov. 10, 1677.   These corrections
were provided to us by Don Jose San Martin, canon-archivist of the Cathedral of Palencia.

founder of the Brothers of the Christian Schools († 1719); John Baptist de Rossi, priest of Rome, popular preacher († 1764).

Blessed : Gomidas Keumrudjian, Armenian pastor, martyr for Reunion († 1705); Sebastian Valfre, Oratorian of Turin, " another Philip Neri " († 1710); 125 priests and seminarians among the September martyrs in Paris (1792); *John Martin Moyé*, pastor in the Diocese of Saint-Dié, who later joined the Paris Foreign Mission Society († 1793); Noël Pinot, pastor of Louroux-Béconnais in the Diocese of Angers, martyr († 1794); fourteen priests of the Diocese of Laval, martyrs († 1794); *Peter René Rogues*, priest of Vannes who later joined the Paris Foreign Mission Society, martyr († 1796); Emmanuel Tru, native priest of Cochin China, martyr, († 1798); John Dat, native priest of Tongking in Viet Nam, martyr († 1798).

> *Venerables :* Felix Testa, priest of Foligno († 1721); John Andrew Parisi, priest of Rome, attached to the Church of Saint-Gual, died at the age of thirty-five († 1735); Anthony Alonso Bermejo, priest of Valladolid († 1752); Bartholomew Dalmonte, priest of Bologna († 1778); Ignatius Capizzi, priest of Palermo († 1783); Marianus Arciero, the Apostle of Calabria († 1788).

> *Servants of God :* Anthony Moreau, pastor and dean in the Diocese of Blois, another Vincent de Paul († 1702); three Canadian priests martyred in the United States between the years 1702-1730; George Martinelli, priest of Milan, founder of the Missionary Society of Rho († 1727); Peter Vigne, priest of Valencia († 1740); John Baptist Trona, priest of Mondovi in Piedmont, Oratorian († 1750); Charles Taruggi, Vicar General of Albano († 1762); Francis Maria Imperioli Lercaro, preacher and missionary, originally from Genoa, died at Rome († 1770); Louis-Philip Alfaro, priest of Mexico († 1776); James Abbondo, pastor of Tranzano in the Diocese of Vercelli in Lombardy († 1788); Bernard Custos, deacon at the seminary of Palermo († 1792). There are also more than 200 priests who were put to death during the French Revolution and among them, there are seventeen Vicars

General, sixty Canons, fifty pastors and almost eighty curates, etc. [1]

C. The Nineteenth Century.

1. Bishops : *Saints : Vincent Maria Strombi*, priest of Viterbo who joined the Passionists and later became the Bishop of Macerata († 1824); Anthony Gianelli, Archpriest of Chiavari in the Diocese of Genoa and later Bishop of Bobbio († 1846); *Anthony Mary Claret*, priest of Catalonia in Spain, founder of the Claretians and later Archbishop of Santiago de Cuba († 1870).

Venerables : John Nepomucene de Tschiderer, Bishop of Trent († 1860); Francis Xavier Rudigier, Bishop of Linz († 1884).

Servants of God : George Michael Wittmann, Bishop of Regensburg († 1833); John Haam, Archbishop of Eger in Hungary († 1857); Matthias Loras, first Bishop of Dubuque, Iowa († 1858); *Charles Joseph Eugene de Mazenod*, Bishop of Marseille and founder of the Oblates of Mary Immaculate († 1861); Anthony Martin Slomsek, Bishop of Maribor in Slovenia and martyr for Reunion († 1862); *Simeon Berneux*, priest of Mans, and *Anthony Daveluy*, priest of Amiens, both of whom joined the Paris Foreign Mission Society and were martyred in Korea († 1866); Frederick Baraga, first Bishop of Marquette, Michigan († 1868); Georges Darbois, Archbishop of Paris, martyr of the Paris Commune († 1871); Xystus Riario Sforza, Archbishop of Naples and Cardinal († 1877); John Zwijsen, Archbishop of Utrecht († 1877); Pope Pius IX († 1878); *Daniel Comboni*, priest of Verona, founder of the African Missions of Verona, Apostolic Vicar († 1881); Hyacinth Vera, Bishop

---

[1] The causes connected with the French Revolution which are presently under consideration are — from Paris (Charles-François de Saint-Simon and companions, 1793-94); from Angers (Guillaume Repin and companions, 1794-95); from Rennes (Jean- Baptiste Besnard and companions, 1793-1800); from La Rochelle (Jean-Baptiste Souzi and companions, 1793-95); from Arras (Jean Poulin and companions 1793-96); from Besançon (P. Pachomius and companions, 1798); from Lyon (Thomas Merlé de Castillon and companions, 1794); from Cambrai (André Ignace Gousseau and companions, 1794); from Rouen (Tussien-Marie Gombault-Duval and companions, 1792-99); from Nantes (Louis-Joachim de la Roche and companions, 1793-95). Of the total, which is a little over 300 priests and religious, two-thirds are members of the secular clergy.

of Vancouver and Apostle of Alaska, murdered († 1886);
Peter Rota, Bishop of Mantua, where he was known as a
" second Athanasius, " and later Canon of St. Peter, at Rome
of Montevideo († 1822); Charles John Seghers, Bishop
(† 1890); Aloysius Sodo, Bishop of Telese-Cerreto († 1895);
Joseph Marello, Bishop of Acqui in Piedmont († 1895).

2. Priests and seminarians : *Saints* : Andrew Hubert Fournet,
priest of Poitiers, pastor of Maillé († 1834); *Gaspar del Buffalo*,
priest of Rome, founder of the Missionaries of the Precious Blood
(† 1837); *Peter Chanel*, priest and pastor in the Diocese of Belley,
who joined the Marist Fathers and was later martyred († 1841);
Joseph Cottolengo, priest of Turin, vicar, founder of the
Associations of Valdacco in Turin († 1842); John Vianney, priest
of Belley, pastor of Ars († 1859); Joseph Cafasso, priest of Turin,
professor at the major seminary and man of charity († 1860);
Michael Garricoïts, priest of Bayonne, founder of the Fathers of
the Betharam († 1863); *John Bosco*, priest of Turin, founder of
the Salesians († 1888); *Vincent Pallotti*, priest of Rome and
founder of the Pallottines († 1850); *Peter Julian Eymard*,
priest and pastor in Grenoble, who joined the Marist Fathers and
later founded the Blessed Sacrament Fathers († 1868).

Among the priests beatified during the nineteenth century,
there are three confessors and a number of martyrs. The
confessors are *Marcellinus Champagnat*, priest of Lyon, founder
of the Marist Brothers († 1840); *Innocent da Berzo*, priest of Brescia
and later a Capuchin († 1890); Louis-Marie Palazzolo, priest of
Bergamo († 1884). The last two were beatified by Pope
John XXIII.

The martyrs are *Peter Maubant*, priest of Bayeux and *James
Chastan*, priest of Digne; both of these men joined the Paris
Foreign Mission Society and were martyred in Korea in 1839;
Andrew Kim, the first native priest of Korea, was put to death
shortly after his ordination in 1846; *Augustus Chapdeleine*, priest
of Coutances, joined the Foreign Missions and was martyred in
China in 1856; four native Chinese priests and two seminarians
(† 1815-1861); twenty-four Indochinese priests and one semi-

narian († 1838-1861). These native priests and seminarians were beatified in 1900, 1909, 1925 and 1951.

Venerables : Anthony Sylvester Receveur, priest of Besançon († 1804); Ignatius Jennaco, professor at the seminary of Naples († 1828); Vincent Romano, pastor of Herculanum in the Diocese of Naples († 1831); Louis Baudoin, priest of La Rochelle († 1835); John Baptist Guarino, pastor of St. Peter's Church in Naples († 1847); Anthony Pennachi, chaplain at the Church of St. Andrew in Assisi († 1848); Placid Bacher, pastor of the Gesu Vecchio at Naples († 1851); *Gaspar Bertoni*, pastor in the Diocese of Verona and founder of a congregation of priests for the purpose of aiding bishops († 1853); Andrew Soulas, priest and preacher of the Diocese of Montpellier († 1857); John de la Mennais, priest of Vannes and founder of the Brothers of Christian Instruction of Ploërmel († 1860); Ignatius Falzon, a Maltese cleric in minor orders († 1865); John Claude Colin, priest of Lyon, founder of the Marist Fathers († 1875); Frederick Albert, pastor of Lanzo in the Diocese of Turin († 1876); Anthony Chevrier, priest of Lyon and founder of the Society of the Priests of Prado († 1879).

Servants of God : Francis Gaschon of the Diocese of Clermont († 1815); Bartholomew Ferri, Archpriest of Onano in the Diocese of Acquapendente in Piedmont († 1822); Seraphin Morozzone, for 49 years the pastor of Chiaso, a small town of 200 inhabitants in the Diocese of Milan († 1822); Peter Blanchard, pastor of Soyhière in the Bernese section of the Jura mountains († 1824); Dominic Lentini, priest of Policastro in the Campagna († 1828); *Pius Lanteri*, priest of Turin and founder of the Oblates of the Blessed Virgin Mary († 1830); John Joseph Allemand, priest of Marseille, considered the founder of youth organizations († 1836); *Peter Joseph Coudrin*, priest of Poitiers and founder of the Fathers of the Sacred Hearts, also known as the Picpus Fathers († 1837); Louis Lafosse, pastor of Echauffeur in the Diocese of Séez († 1849); Louis Pavoni, pastor in the Diocese of Brescia († 1849); *William Joseph Chaminade*, priest of Perigueux, founder of the Marianists († 1850); Joseph Chiron, priest of Viviers, Apostle of Roussillon († 1852);

Maurice Garrigou, priest of Toulouse, engaged in works of charity († 1852); James Bazin, priest exiled by the Revolution, pastor, and later on rector of the seminary and vicar general in the Diocese of Séez († 1855); Charles Steeb, converted from Protestantism, priest of Verona († 1856); Peter Monnereau, pastor of Brouzèle in the Diocese of Luçon († 1856); Peter Noailles, priest of Bordeaux, conducted missions († 1861); Peter Khang, native priest of Tongking, martyr († 1861); Peter Bonhomme, priest of Cahors, engaged in teaching († 1861); *James Laval*, priest of Evreux, who later joined the Holy Ghost Fathers († 1864); Adolph Kolping, priest of Cologne, pioneer in organizations for working men († 1865); Nicholas Mazza, priest of Verona, engaged in teaching and missionary work in Africa († 1865); four Korean secular priests and two seminarians († 1866); Joseph Frasinetti, pastor of Santa-Sabina in Genoa († 1868); Louis Edward Cestac, priest of Bayonne († 1868); *Basil Moreau*, priest of Mans, founder of the Society of the Holy Cross († 1873); Agnellus Coppola, priest of Naples, engaged in the parochial ministry and chaplain at the Church of San Gennaro; Victor Scheppers, priest of Malines, founder of the Brothers of Mercy († 1877); *Emmanuel d'Alzon*, priest of Nimes, founder of the Augustinians of the Assumption († 1880); Aloysius Balbiano, priest of Turin, who was a curate at Avigliano for forty-six years († 1884); Aloysius Scrosoppi, priest of Udine, a man of charity († 1884); Blaise Verri, priest of Milan, engaged in charitable works († 1884); Joseph Gras y Granollers, priest and Canon of Granada, writer and editor of the paper *El Bien* († 1886); Francis Frà di Bruno, university professor, ordained late in life as a priest of Turin, engaged in teaching and charitable works († 1888); James Cusmano, priest of Palermo, Rector of the Church of the XL Martyrs and a man of charity († 1890); Joseph Bedetti, priest of Bologna, the apostle of the poor († 1889); John Gailhac, priest of Montpellier, a man of charity († 1890); John Henry Newman, the famous convert and author, Cardinal († 1890); Pascal Attardi, priest of Naples, engaged in the parochial ministry and a man of charity († 1893); Henry Chaumont, priest of Paris, founder of the Priests of St. Francis de Sales († 1896); Henry Osso y Cervello, priest of Tortosa, preacher and spiritual director († 1896). Among the martyrs of the Paris Commune († 1871), there are, besides Bishop Darbois, six secular priests, one archdeacon of Notre Dame, two pastors, one curate, a military chaplain and a seminarian.

D. The Twentieth Century.

We have already witnessed the canonization of St. Pius X, Pope, former curate, pastor and spiritual director in the seminary of Treviso, and later Bishop of Mantua and Patriarch of Venice († 1914).

Among the Chinese martyrs († 1900) of the Boxer persecution, there were five secular seminarians, who were members of the Third Order of St. Francis. They were beatified in 1946.

1. Bishops : *Servants of God :* Louis Moreau, Bishop of Saint-Hyacinthe in Canada († 1901); Edward Rosaz, Bishop of Suze in Piedmont († 1903); John Baptist Scalabrini, Bishop of Placentia and founder of a society of priests to minister to Italian emigrants († 1905); Marcel Spinola, Cardinal and Archbishop of Seville († 1906); Francis Benjamin Richard, Cardinal and Archbishop of Paris († 1908); Joseph Torras y Bages, Bishop of Catalonia and noted author († 1916); Sylvan Carillo, Bishop of Sinaloa, in Mexico († 1921); Andrew James Ferrari, Cardinal Archbishop of Milan († 1921); Raphael Merry Del Val, Cardinal Secretary of State under St. Pius X († 1930); Guido Conforti, Archbishop-Bishop of Parma and founder of a Foreign Mission Society († 1931); John Volpi, Bishop of Arezzo († 1931); Raphael Guizar Valencia, Bishop of Veracruz in Mexico († 1938); Clement Von Galen, Cardinal and Bishop of Münster in Westphalia († 1946). We must also add the victims of recent persecutions : Florentio Assensio Barroso, Bishop of Barbastro and Salvio Huix Miralpeix, Bishop of Lerida († 1936) who were martyred during the Spanish Civil War.

2. Priests : *Servants of God : Leonard Murialdo*, priest of Turin, founder of the Oblates of St. Joseph († 1900);

Joseph Mañanet Vives, priest of Lerida and man of charity († 1901); Augustine Roscelli, assistant pastor in a suburb of Genoa and man of charity († 1902); Paul Taroni, spiritual director at the seminary of Faenza († 1902); *George Bellanger*, priest of Arras, military chaplain, who joined the Brothers of St. Vincent de Paul at the age of 35 († 1902); Clement Marchisio, pastor for 43 years of Rivalba in the Diocese of Suze in Piedmont († 1903); Gennaro di Rosa, pastor at Naples and penitentiary of the Cathedral († 1905); Peter Savelberg, priest of Roermond, engaged in teaching and founder of societies of Brothers and Sisters († 1907); Aloysius Brisson, Vicar General of Troyes and founder of the Oblates of St. Francis de Sales († 1908); Joachim Rossello Ferro, priest of Majorca, founder of a congregation of Missionaries of the Sacred Heart († 1909); Emmanuel Domingo y Sol, priest of Tortosa, pastor and later on professor of religion († 1909); *Arnold Janssen*, priest of Roermond, founder of the Fathers of the Divine Word († 1909); Alphonsus Maria Fusco, priest of Nocera, in the province of Salerno, preacher († 1910); John Costa de Beauregard, priest of Chambery, a man of charity († 1910); John Piamarta, priest of Brescia, engaged in charitable works and in teaching († 1913); Peter Joseph Dergent, priest of Malines, pastor of Gelrode, murdered out of hatred for the faith († 1914); Aloysius Ganella, priest of Como, " another Cottolengo " († 1915); Francis Spinelli, priest of Cremona, man of charity († 1916); Charles de Foucauld, priest of Viviers, who always had the intention of leading an austere and apostolic life such as he led in Africa († 1916); [1] Vincent Grossi, priest of Lodi, curate, and later pastor of a number of difficult parishes († 1917); Vincent Tarozzi, priest of Bologna, seminary professor, later summoned to Rome to become Leo XIII's secretary for Latin Letters († 1918); *Francis Jordan*, priest of Freibourg im Breisgau, founder of the Society of the Divine Savior († 1918); Edward Poppe, priest of Ghent,

[1] His intention to do so was clear from the time that he received the Major Orders: see J. S. SIX, *Itinéraire spirituel de Charles de Foucauld* (Paris 1958), pp. 258-59, 264. This does not prevent the *Index causarum* of the Sacred Congregation of Rites (*op. cit.*, p. 46) from listing Charles de Foucauld as a secular priest. His incardination into the Diocese of Viviers assured him a freedom (acceptable to his bishop) which permitted him to follow the course that God had devised for him.

curate, spiritual director and one of the early promoters of the Eucharistic Crusade († 1922); *Joseph (Dom Columba) Marmion*, priest of Dublin, curate, seminary professor, who later became a Benedictine and the Abbott of Maredsous in the Diocese of Namur, also well known for his works on the spiritual life († 1923); Andrew Manjon, priest of Granada, professor of Canon Law and man of charity († 1923); *Leon Dehon*, priest of Soissons, one of the pioneers of social work in France, founder of the Priests of the Sacred Heart († 1925); Joseph Allamano, priest of Turin, nephew of St. Joseph Cofasso, spiritual director at the seminary and founder of a diocesan missionary society († 1926); *Hannibal di Francia*, priest of Messina, founder of the Rogationists († 1927); Alphonsus Ariens, priest of Utrecht, pastor of Steenderen, and later of Maarsen, pioneered social work in Holland († 1928); Louis Tyssen, priest of Roermond, dean of Sittard († 1929); Peter Bonilli, priest of Spoleto († 1935); Peter Poveda Castroverde, priest of Oviedo, founder of the Academias Teresianas († 1936); Bruno Marchesini, minor seminarian at Bologna and student at the Lateran in Rome († 1938); Francis Paleari, priest of Turin, spiritual director in the seminary and Vicar General († 1945); *Francis da Cruz*, priest of Lisbon, preacher, and spiritual director who joined the Jesuits at the age of 80 († 1948). We should also add the victims of persecutions in Mexico, Spain and the Communist countries. In Mexico, Christofal Magallanes and his curate Augustine Calora and a renowned spiritual director, José-Maria Roblès, were put to death in 1927. In Spain, there are a number of outstanding causes, one example of which is that of Joseph Tapies Sirvant, curate in the Diocese of Urgel († 1936).

*   *   *

Let us conclude this section by giving some statistics. We can state that for the first eight centuries there are about 800 bishops, priests and other clerics of the diocesan clergy who are venerated as saints by the Universal Church. [1]

---

[1] In dealing with the cults of the first eight centuries, one must distinguish between

For the centuries following this period, we must limit ourselves and make mention only of those saints of the secular clergy whose cults have been accorded formal recognition by Rome through canonization, beatification or recognition of cult. We should also recall the reservations that we made concerning the early interventions of the Holy See.

It is only with these reservations in mind that we can respond to the following question : How many members of the secular clergy who died after the year 800 have been canonized, beatified or have had their cults officially recognized by Rome? The numbers in parentheses indicate those who founded religious societies of men and took vows in their own societies as well as those who entered already existing religious communities.

Bishops	Canonized :	39 (9)	Beatified :	21 (4)	Total : 60 (13)
Priests	» :	34 (19)	» :	294 (10 to 15)	328 (about 30)
Total		73 (28)		315 (15 to 20)	388 (about 43)

The secular clergy can therefore rejoice at seeing more than 380 of its members accorded the honors of the Altar during the

those introduced into the Universal Calendar of the Church, those included at least in the Roman Martyrology and those which are purely local. We know that legends found their way into early hagiography and this is why we are content merely to give a few statistics taken from the Roman Martyrology which we offer only as a rough estimate and with a great deal of reservation.

For the first four centuries of the Christian era, the Roman Martyrology lists close to 350 bishops and about 200 priests and other clerics belonging to the clergy of the time, i.e., to a clergy living in the world like our present-day secular priests. In most cases they are martyrs. It is interesting to observe that of the almost 200 lesser clerics listed here, nearly 45 of them belonged to the Diocese of Rome or in some way were connected with it.

For the next few centuries (until 800), we can estimate that the secular clergy are represented in the Roman Martyrology by approximately 200 bishops and about 40 priests and deacons. The ninth century begins the period which we have examined systematically; but, as we have already mentioned, the Martyrology mentions about 25 bishops and 13 priests and deacons who have neither been beatified, canonized nor have had their cult recognized. A list of saints in the secular clergy which would include all these cults, along with those which Rome has approved by canonization, beatification or recognition of cult, would reach a total in excess of 1200! This is not including the anonymous groups of martyrs in the Roman Martyrology. How large would the number be if the local cults were also included? One need only glance over the volumes of the *Vies des Saints et des Bienheureux* (by the Benedictines of Paris) to realize that the number would indeed be quite large.

last twelve centuries. About 265 of them were neither bishops nor religious : 11 were canonized and 9 beatified as confessors while 5 were canonized and about 240 beatified as martyrs.

Appendix II is an attempt to compile a Sanctoral for the secular clergy and it indicates, when possible, the particular work performed by these saints and blessed. Thus we find about 12 vicars general, 75 pastors, 35 curates, about 30 teachers, approximately a dozen of whom taught in seminaries, etc. We should also point out that the large group of sixteenth and seventeenth century English martyrs is made up almost entirely of priests who returned to England as missionaries.

We can also add that the causes of many other secular priests are presently under investigation. In this area particularly, we do not pretend to have all the latest figures. Not counting 67 venerables who were victims of the English Reformation, approximately 200 priests martyred during the French Revolution and the countless victims of the Spanish Civil War, we have discovered that the causes of about 40 bishops and 120 priests are presently under study at Rome. Apparently, then, there are between 400 and 500 members of the secular clergy who someday, let us hope, will be accorded the honors of the Altar.

Is there any need to justify our including in the Sanctoral those bishops who came from the secular clergy? The regular clergy continue to consider those who have become bishops as their own. Why should not the seculars do the same? Was it not in the diocesan clergy that they were prepared, at times over a period of many years, for the reception of the fullness of the priesthood? As one such example of this, we can cite St. Anthony Gianelli who served as a parish priest in the Diocese of Genoa for twenty-six years before he was consecrated Bishop of Bobbio, where he died after serving only eight years as a bishop. The biographies of saintly bishops attest that even though their sanctity may have fully developed and have shown forth in all its brilliance during their episcopacy, it had nevertheless been previously acquired and exercised during the time that they engaged in their humble ministrations as members of the diocesan clergy.

* * *

Clearly then, diocesan priests can lay claim to many patrons who came from the ranks of the diocesan clergy. In no way do we mean by this to restrict the scope and attraction of their piety. Nor is it our intention to be exclusive. All the saints are the object of our veneration, since they offer us an ideal to strive for in our own quest for sanctity. There are certainly many canonized and beatified religious who also deserve to be invoked as our heavenly patrons.

Consider the great founders of the religious Orders who took great pains to study the conditions of secular life, particularly for the clergy, in order to extend to them the benefits of their own spirituality. We are thinking particularly of St. Francis of Assisi, whose Third Order has contributed in a very special way to the sanctification of countless priests. Mention should also be made of the Third Orders of St. Dominic and of St. Norbert, the Oblates of St. Benedict and the various Marian congregations.

Those religious men and women who have been canonized and who consecrated their religious life, in large measure, to assisting the clergy through their prayer and penance, should also be mentioned here. Two such saints who immediately come to mind are Teresa of Avila and Theresa of the Child Jesus.

Whatever their position and individual ministry may be, our priests will discover that there were many saintly religious who once worked in the same field as they. With reference to the parochial ministry, we can cite Blessed Stephen Bellesini, hermit of St. Augustine, pastor of Genazzano, beatified by Pius X in 1904; St. Anthony Mary Pucci, Servite, who was pastor of St. Andrew's in Viareggio for 45 years and who was canonized by John XXIII in 1962; finally, St. Peter Fourier, canon regular and pastor of Mattaincourt in Lorraine, who was canonized in 1897 by Leo XIII. He is called the Curé d'Ars of Lorraine and belonged to the Regular Chapter of Chaumousey which he tried to reform. Since he did not succeed in this, and since he was constantly ridiculed by his confreres, he decided to ask for a pastorate. It was in the parochial ministry that he achieved his full stature and became renowned for great holiness, and this, no doubt, resulted in his being able, later on, to reform his Order. [1] We have also included in our list the names of a number of priests who founded religious societies or who joined already existing communities. Concerning those in the latter category, we can say that many of them had already attained a high degree of sanctity as members of the secular clergy. Just one example of these is St. John of Sam-Facondo who lived during the fifteenth century. It has been said of him, " On the very day that he joined the Augustinians, he took the habit, since he was already widely known for his sanctity. " [2] St. Joseph Calasanctius is another example. It was he who founded the Congregation of Pious Schools after having lived a priestly life that was outstanding for its holiness and zeal. [3] More recently, when Francis da Cruz, a priest of Lisbon, joined the Society of Jesus at the age of 80, he was dispensed from making a novitiate and from living the common life. When he died, Cardinal Cerejeira wrote that he had attained a heroic degree of virtue while still a member of the secular clergy. [4]

Dom Rousseau writes : " Although the legislators of early monasticism often emphasize the similarity between the complete detachment of the monk and the early Christian practice of sharing one's possessions with the community, in no way can we

---

[1] H. DERRÉAL, *Cité de la Vierge, Cité de Pierre Fourier* (Paris 1958), p. 13.

[2] *Vies des Saints et des Bienheureux*, by the Benedictines of Paris, *op. cit.*, Vol. IV, p. 217.

[3] *Ibid.*, Vol. VIII, pp. 538-40.

[4] Card. E. M. CEREJEIRA, *Obras pastorais* (Lisbon 1954), Vol. IV, pp. 301-2. On the circumstances surrounding the entry of Francis da Cruz into the Society of Jesus, see : J. M. GOSSELIN, *Le Père Cruz, le Vincent de Paul du XXe siècle* (Toulouse 1953). He writes : " Let us admit frankly that it is a credit to the clergy of Lisbon that he entered religious life adorned with virtues already the pride of the Patriarchate. The Society welcomed with joy and respect this priest who was venerated as a saint by all Portugal and who had been formed outside of it, but not outside its ideals and traditions. " (p. 117).

consider these early disciples of the apostles, who were married and lived in the world, the predecessors of the monks. " [1]   The apostles lived a type of life which bears no relation whatsoever to that lived by religious.   What is true, however, is that the twelve apostles and their early disciples lived the priesthood even before the distinction between the secular and religious way of life existed.

Since our spirituality is a spirituality of the priesthood as such, and since we consider any special observances that are added to it as secondary and merely works of supererogation, it therefore follows that we should regard the apostles and their early disciples as our great exemplars of clerical life.   In doing this, we in no way wish to lay any exclusive claim to them.

We can also include among our patrons several saints of the Eastern Church who were, so to speak, midway between the monastic life and the active ministry.   St. Athanasius seems to us to be typical of those priests of long ago who went apart into the desert in order to fortify themselves for the great task of winning back their dioceses and exercising their priesthood once again in the world.   St. Basil, thirty years his junior, lived the life of a monk from 356 to 370, the year of his Episcopal Consecration.   Even prior to this he had engaged in the active ministry, and it is interesting to point out that when he, who was the Father of Monasticism, became a bishop, he reproached his younger brother, Gregory, for not having come to Caesarea to assist him.   John Chrysostom spent four years in solitude, but for some time previous to this he had functioned as a member of the clergy of Antioch.   These monks certainly had great concern and a high regard for the active ministry.

[1] O. ROUSSEAU, *Monachisme et Vie religieuse, op. cit.,* pp. 5-6.

Chapter 17

The Lessons of
Our Models

On the occasion of the centenary of St. John Vianney's death, a number of excellent books were published which give us a more intimate glimpse into the fascinating life of this great saint. [1] Why should we not also endeavor to publicize the lives of other secular priests who deserve to be regarded as the outstanding models of the diocesan clergy? Pope John XXIII asserts that " Divine Providence has decreed that there should always be such zealous pastors of souls within the Church. " [2] Why should we not publish a collection of priestly biographies or a synthesis of spirituality inspired directly by the lives of those priests who have already been accorded the honors of the Altar or whose causes for beatification are presently under study? [3] We must, however, be realistic; and, therefore, we will only illustrate by a few examples the abundance of this spiritual documentation.

---

[1] Besides the basic well-known works of Msgr. F. TROCHU, we have also cited here books by Msgrs. R. FOURREY, J. ALZIN, B. NODET and A. RAVIER. See also Jean DE LA VARENDE, *The Curé of Ars and His Cross* (New York : Desclée, 1959).

[2] Pope JOHN XXIII, Enc. *Sacerdotii nostri primordia, loc. cit.*, p. 550.

[3] An American priest, R. A. HUTCHINSON, has published a fine book entitled *Diocesan Priest Saints* (St. Louis, London 1957). It treats twenty secular priests who have been raised to the altar. Between them they illustrate all the types of spirituality open to the diocesan priest. In Spain, the Apostolic Union of the Diocese of Valencia has edited two volumes (out of print) entitled *Flores del Clero secular*. Nowadays the pamphlet format is more appealing. Already over 40 have appeared in the collection *Semblanzas Sacerdotales* [*Priest-Portraits*] edited by Msgr. Antonio-Maria Perez Ormazabal, Vicar General of Vitoria. They consider not only priests raised to the altar, but also many others who led truly exemplary lives. We should point out the concern of Msgr. K. Cruysberghs to publicize the models of priestly life among the Flemish clergy, especially in his two fine books : *De goede Herder* (Anvers 1950) and *Het priesterschap in lering en voorbeeld* (Louvain 1959).

The first edition of our work had already appeared when we were shown a remarkable book by a Brazilian priest who also attempts to list the saints among the secular clergy : P. A. RUBERT, *A santidade no clero secular* (Santa-Maria 1954). He also includes the martyrs of the Paris Foreign Mission Society. Under each name there is a biographical note

In no way do we pretend to have made the best choice in this regard. [1]

* * *

Some will immediately object that there are many martyrs in the Sanctoral of the secular clergy and that martyrdom does not always crown a life that was exceptionally virtuous. Certainly, there are a few martyrs who have, so to speak, stolen into heaven [2] by being converted at the eleventh hour. Andrew Wouters, a Dutch pastor who lived a life of sin for many years, is one case in point. He took his place among the Gorkum martyrs by offering to replace some who had weakened and apostatized. He was canonized by Pius IX. [3] Among the English martyrs of the sixteenth and seventeenth centuries, we find a few apostate priests who had become Protestant ministers and were later converted. Is this not a tremendous manifestation of the infinite mercy of God?

However, martyrdom very often crowned a life that was already outstanding for holiness. It has been said of Blessed Noël Pinot that, during the period when he exercised his ministry as pastor of Louroux-Béconnais in the Diocese of Angers, " he sacrificed his life little by little before making a total oblation of himself through martyrdom. " [4] One has only to read the documents relating to the beatification processes of the priests martyred during the French Revolution to realize how truly exemplary were the lives they led prior to their martyrdom. The priests of Besançon, for example, could be canonized either as martyrs or as confessors. The courageous attitude of martyrs in the face of death often reveals the great and noble qualities

---

[1] So as not to clutter this chapter, we have seen fit merely to give a few references where it seems appropriate for order.

[2] M. WINOWSKA, *Les voleurs de Dieu* (Paris 1958).

[3] J. MEERBERGHEN, *De H. Martelaars van Gorkum* (Tongerloo 1928).

[4] Card. G. GRENTE, " Panégyrique du B. Noël Pinot, *Œuvres oratoires et pastorales* Vol. V (1930), pp. 109-27.

of their souls. When the Bishop of Lérida, Salvius Huix Miralpeix, was martyred in 1936 by the Spanish Reds, he asked to die last so that he would be able to absolve his companions at the very moment that they fell. Certainly, he was the good shepherd who was more concerned for his sheep than for himself.

We realize full well that the story of these Servants of God, who were renowned for sanctity throughout their lives, could be better told by those who were closely associated with them.

* * *

Even though most of the saintly priests of the nineteenth and twentieth centuries have not as yet been accorded the honors of the Altar, they have great value for us since they are closer to us in time and since they lived in a milieu which is in many ways similar to our own. We will therefore mention a few of these at random. We want it clearly understood, however, that, in accordance with the decree of Urban VIII, we intend in no way to anticipate the Church's judgment when we consider the sanctity of those who have not yet been canonized or beatified.

One particularly noteworthy fact is the high regard that these saintly priests had for the religious clergy. We have already seen how many religious congregations were founded as a result of the zeal of secular priests. This is especially true for religious societies of women, but it is equally true of societies for men. The fact that they were founders of religious societies may well be the reason why about 60 secular priests of the nineteenth and twentieth centuries are presently up for canonization or beatification. Is it an exaggeration to say that the causes of many other priests would have been promoted had they also been founders of religious communities? We simply mention this to indicate how many human factors have a great part to play in this area. Of course we realize how carefully causes are examined by Rome, and therefore their success or failure certainly does not depend solely upon whether or not they were founders of religious communities. Some of the priests proposed for our veneration became religious either by being professed in the communities they founded or by joining other already existing societies. Some of them simply gave the religious life a try, while others never had the opportunity to realize their desire of entering religion. Many others, at one time or another, manifested an attraction for a particular form of the religious life. Certainly none of them would deny that the example of the cloisters is extremely beneficial for the clergy, since all priests are expected to live in the spirit, at least, of the evangelical counsels in order to attain the degree of sanctity demanded by the priestly state.

Most of our models, however, maintained their status as secular priests and reacted against everything which might possibly interfere with it. This explains the hesitation felt by a number of them when observances peculiar to religious life were proposed to them. They pointed to the examples and teachings of SS. Philip Neri and Francis de Sales, whose influence, along with that of St. Vincent de Paul, seems to have dominated clerical spirituality during the nineteenth century. Later on, the Curé of Ars and the Turinese group composed of Cottolengo, Cafasso and Don Bosco, served as popular models for priestly spirituality. Some of the recent biographies of St. Pius X, written before his canonization, reveal the tremendous attraction of this country pastor who was later to become Pope. With the sole exception of John Bosco, these men spent their priestly lives as members of the diocesan clergy and engaged, partially at least, in the humblest ministries.

*   *   *

Another noteworthy fact is the remarkable spiritual relationship existing between priests to such a degree that there are sometimes specific groups of saints belonging to the same city or diocese. The case of Turin is so interesting that we have written about it to Cardinal Fossati, the Archbishop of this city, and this is his reply :

> The Lord has abundantly blessed this Archdiocese by creating a veritable constellation of saintly priests, all of whom belonged to the Diocese of Turin. Besides the stars of first magnitude, SS. Joseph Benedict Cottolengo, John Bosco and Joseph Cafasso, all of whom were secular priests, we have the causes of other secular priests in progress : Don Frederick Albert, pastor of Lanzo-Torinese, founder of a community of sisters for the education of young women; Don Clement Marchisio, pastor of Rivalba, and founder of the Daughters of St. Joseph, who provide everything necessary for divine worship; Don Balbiano, who, until his death, was a curate at Avigliano; Abbé Frà di Bruno, founder of the Little Sisters of Suffrage; Canon Joseph Allamano, founder of the Consolata Foreign Mission Society; Don Leonard Murialdo, founder of the Giuseppini. The cause of Don Francis Paleari, for thirty years spiritual director at the major seminary and Vicar General of the diocese until his death in 1945, was recently before our diocesan Curia. Deo Gratias. [1]

If merely the number of causes introduced at Rome is considered, the prize would certainly have to be given to the Diocese of Naples. Although this diocese already numbers a great many saints and blessed, there are 56 causes presently listed in its name in the official list published by the Sacred Congregation of Rites in 1953. Five out of the ten secular priests listed here were pastors and one was an archbishop, Xystus Riario Sforza. So great was the latter's prestige that Leo XIII asserted that had he survived Pius IX, he certainly would have succeeded him. [2] In order to appreciate more clearly the great examples of sanctity produced in this area, we need only recall St. Alphonsus Liguori, Venerable Louis Casaurea, Venerable

---

[1] Apparently the influence of P. B. Lanteri, and his associations of *Amitié Sacerdotale* accounts to a large extent for the tremendous zeal and holiness of the Clergy of Turin. See above, pp. 33-34.

[2] E. FREDERICI, *Sisto Riario Sforza* (Rome 1945), p. 3.

Emmanual Ribera and a number of other saintly religious who lived there.

During the first half of the nineteenth century, Lyon was also a center of sanctity. Consider the three fellow seminarians who, in the order in which they attained the honors of the Altar, completely reversed the scholastic standing that they had in the seminary : the first to be canonized was John Vianney, the poor student; next was Marcellinus Champagnat, the average student, only recently beatified; and finally the most intelligent of the three, Venerable John Claude Colin, who is still awaiting beatification. Among their friends and relations are to be found such men as Matthias Loras, the first Bishop of Dubuque; Venerable Anthony Chevrier; Joseph Maria Chiron; Pauline Jaricot; St. Peter Julian Eymard. Did not the Curé of Ars state that in order to surrender himself entirely to the love of God he had only to imitate his pastor at Ecully, Monsieur Balley? It has often been said that " priestly filiation is a filiation through imitation. " [1] In early Christian times there were cases where entire families became saints. In our own day we can cite the parents of the Little Flower, since their cause is seriously being considered. Just as the home can produce sanctity, so also can priestly friendships. This is the reason why a number of these saintly priests were inspired to found such fraternal associations for priests as the Apostolic Union, the Society of Priests of St. Francis de Sales and other similar groups. Organizations, however, are at most only a means to an end.

It is particularly clear from the history of the clergy that it is only proper and fitting that among priests there should exist an attitude of mutual trust, respect and spiritual assistance as well as a real willingness to collaborate together in the service of Our Lord.

* * *

A third fact worth considering is that all these holy priests realized, to quote Pius XII, that " their most important duty is

---

[1] M. MELLET, " Le vrai journal d'un curé de campagne, " *La tradition sacerdotale, op. cit.*, p. 270.

to secure their own sanctification. " [1]   In line with this idea, Father Mondésert recently wrote : " There can be nothing more instructive and encouraging than to discover how our predecessors, in the midst of their apostolic labors, were able to heed the call to an almost boundless degree of sanctity. " [2]   Many other like statements could be mentioned, but we will merely present two more that were cited in Pope John XXIII's encyclical on the priesthood.   " For the promotion of the kingdom of Jesus Christ in the world, " St. Pius X stated, " nothing is more necessary than the holiness of ecclesiastics, that they may give leadership to the faithful by example, words and by teaching. "   St. John Vianney once told his bishop : " If you want the entire diocese to be converted, all parish priests must become saints. " [3]

Our forms of piety and the special devotions that we practice will certainly vary, but there is one thing which will always be essentially the same for all of us.   It is particularly important, therefore, that the love of Jesus, which is the way to the Father, should shine forth in all of us.

" How wonderful it is, " Venerable Andrew Soulas of Montpellier used to say, " when one lends an attentive ear, the ear of the heart, to the gentle and friendly voice of God, of Jesus, the good and adorable Master.... Pray for the poor priest who, today more than ever, is aware of the number and extent of his miseries and infidelities.   Indeed, there are many priests who are guilty of not loving as they are expected to love! "   Another priest from Montpellier, John Gailhac, stated : " To be worthy of your vocation it is necessary that you be one with Jesus Christ : one with Jesus Christ, the flower of virginity, one with Jesus Christ, humble and obedient, one with Jesus Christ, holy and perfect who offered Himself as a sacrifice for the glory of God and the salvation of souls. "   The contemporaries of the Curé of Ars report that when he would say " Our Lord, " he

---

[1] Pope Pius XII, *Exhortatio apostolica Menti nostrae, loc. cit.*, p. 677.

[2] M. Mondésert, Introduction to *La tradition sacerdotale, op. cit.*, p. 24.

[3] Pope John XXIII, Enc. *Sacerdotii nostri primordia, loc. cit.*, p. 576.

pronounced these words in such a way that one could not help being moved. When he spoke of the love of Jesus, he would become so enraptured that he could hardly speak and would usually weep.

Devotion to the Sacred Heart of Jesus was characteristic of the nineteenth century, although it had a number of ardent apostles among the clergy of the preceding centuries. Thus, in the seventeenth century in Milan, George Martinelli translated the revelations of St. Margaret Mary into Italian and propagated this devotion throughout Italy. Similarly, devotion to the Heart of Mary also developed. St. John Eudes, who died in 1680, was largely responsible for combining these two devotions. The program of consecrating the world to the Hearts of Jesus and Mary has succeeded in large measure because of the zeal of such dedicated promoters as Joachim Rossello Ferro who, in 1890, founded the Congregation of Priests of the Sacred Hearts of Jesus and Mary. In fact, a number of religious institutes and confraternities in honor of the Sacred Hearts of Jesus and Mary were founded during the nineteenth century. Very often the promoters of these groups, such as Peter Marie Coudrin and Leo Dehon, for example, came from the secular clergy.

*   *   *

The great devotion that our priestly models had to Mary has resulted in so many beautiful sentiments and attitudes that we would certainly have great difficulty in choosing one over another. All these saintly priests shared the opinion of the Curé of Ars : " The heart of Mary is so fond of us that if the hearts of all the mothers of the world were to be joined together, they would only be like a piece of ice in comparison with the heart of Mary. " Their teaching was summed up by St. Pius X : " We are called, in a spiritual and truly mystical sense, the sons of Mary; and she, for her part, is a mother to each and every one of us. "

During the last century there lived in Bayonne a humble priest by the name of Edward Cestac who, without any knowledge of *The Treatise on True Devotion to the Blessed Virgin*, rivaled St. Louis Marie Grignion de Montfort in his preaching on Mary. He said :

> Confidence in Divine Providence does not exist for us apart from confidence in the Most Blessed Virgin since it is always through her and by her mediation that this loving Providence chooses to shower His gifts upon us. She presides over, directs and regulates all things.

This Servant of God always attribued to Mary whatever good he performed, since

> We are at the service and under the direction of the Most Blessed Mother of God. We merely carry out her work. As for me, I am her unworthy servant desiring only to secure the good pleasure of my sovereign Mistress. I am her business representative; I travel about on her business seeking her profit and using her purse which is never empty.

Very often people would ask him if the Blessed Virgin had appeared to him. " No, " he would reply, " I do not see her, but I feel her presence in the same way as a horse senses the hand of the rider directing it. "

Although very few of our saintly models expressed their love of Mary in the same terms as Abbé Cestac, they all, nevertheless, followed " this way of confidence and total dependence on the Blessed Virgin, the dispenser of all the treasures of Providence. " [1]

The Hail Mary is the most cherished of all prayers to Our Lady. When James Cusmano of Palermo was asked for the secret of his extraordinary success in the active ministry, he replied : " I always say a Hail Mary to the Mother of God. " Blessed Moyé said that the rosary was the basis of his devotion

---

[1] G. Bernoville, *Édouard et Élise Cestac ou l'Émulation mystique* (Paris 1951), pp. 30, 90 ff.

and the means by which he obtained many favors from God. During the war of 1866, Paul Taroni, spiritual director of the diocesan seminary of Faenza, instituted the recitation of the perpetual rosary for those engaged in combat. He was particularly fond of recommending this devotion to soldiers, since the Madonna of the Rosary is the Queen of Victories. Frederick Albert, archpriest of Lanzo-Torinese, stated that he always prayed a few Hail Marys for the success of the missions that he preached. Much could be written about the Bishop of the Rosary, Joseph Torras y Bages, who died at Catalonia in 1916. In a book entitled *El Rosario*, he shows that there is to be found in this devotion a veritable *Summa Theologica* of Christian piety which has value for the scholarly and the uneducated alike. Through its use of prayer formulas taught by God and by the Church and repeated over and over again with a gentle and completely human persistence reminiscent of the Psalter, the rosary comes down to the level of all men.

In conclusion, we wish to cite a prayer that Bishop Rudigier used to say each day before offering Mass. " Oh, Mother of Our Lord Jesus Christ, accompany me to the altar and stand by me and perform in my place and for me everything that I must perform. Bring to the altar especially your great love of Our Lord since it is your inviolable right and dignity as a mother to possess, carry and handle the body of the Lord, even though this dignity is given to priests. You belong to priests since you belong to Jesus. Mary, help of priests, assist me. "

* * *

All these priests were well aware of the tremendous importance of prayer in their lives. Venerable Anthony Receveur of Besançon stated that :

> The essential condition for a priest desirous of sanctifying others is first to sanctify himself by the practice of prayer. If you are priests of meditation, you will be saved and you will save many other souls along with you by leading them to meditation. If you are not faithful to meditation, you

will cause many souls to become rooted in sin; they will
be damned and so will you.... When prayer goes well,
all goes well; when it does not, everything seems to fail.
To stop praying is the greatest of all spiritual disorders and
also the greatest of all misfortunes. One who knows how
to pray well can be certain that he will be saved.

" What prevents us from becoming saints, " the Curé of Ars
declared, " is lack of reflection. A person who does not reflect
upon himself is not aware of how he is doing. Reflection, prayer
and union to God are all necessary for us. " This sentiment was
shared by all our saintly models. As an expression of their
esteem and praise for any one of these holy priests, the faithful
would usually observe : He celebrates Mass with devotion, he
prays frequently, it is apparent that he believes in what he is
doing.

The interior life of these men of God was centered upon the
celebration of the Mass. Certainly they were creatures of their
time, and many present–day priests are disturbed by the fact
that during this period there did not always exist a type of piety
approximating that of the present liturgical movement. This
criticism, however, can be exaggerated. In his *Introduction to
the Devout Life*, St. Francis de Sales spoke of " the sun of all
spiritual exercises, the most holy, sacred, and most sovereign
sacrament and sacrifice of the Mass, the center of the Christian
religion, the heart of devotion and the soul of piety. " Moreover,
this was the period when the French School contemplated the
states of Jesus Christ and particularly His state as Priest. This
is also the period when St. Vincent de Paul desired to become
a holocaust acceptable to God each time that he offered up the
immaculate Host at Mass.

The mandate given at Ordination, *Imitamini quod tractatis*,
was observed by all of these saintly priests. For James Cusmano,
every priest must be " a victim of his own priesthood and a priest
of his own victimhood. " Thus the altar becomes a source of
relief after many difficult hours of apostolic activity. " At times
I feel as though I am completely crushed under the weight of my

tribulations, " Clement Marchisio of Turin declared, " but let me assure you that after only five minutes spent before the Blessed Sacrament, I feel so envigorated and rejuvenated that what at first had appeared insurmountable, now seems easy and effortless. "

The Curé of Ars believed that the loss of fervor in a priest's life could be accounted for by the fact that " sufficient attention was not being given to the celebration of Mass. "   He, whose " custom it was to offer himself as an expiation for sinners, " used to weep " when he thought of the unfortunate situation of priests who were not living according to their holy vocation. " [1]

More often than we realize, our predecessors evidenced many other features of our present–day spirituality.

Many of the writings of Blessed John of Avila would remind one of those of Dom Marmion! Cardinal Bérulle and his school considered the Trinity and the mysteries of the Savior.   The Curé of Ars based his own spirituality on the dogma of the Trinity, and Père Lacordaire attests that through this humble priest he had come to know the Holy Spirit.

* * *

All these priests were noted for their joy and peace of mind. This was, no doubt, inspired by their unshakable confidence in God. We all know that there are occasions when a smile can be a real act of heroism.   Although a number of them had experienced great trials, they were always known to be friendly, cheerful and happy. Consider Andrew Hubert Fournet or St. Philip Neri, for example. Msgr. Fourrey, in describing the temperament of the Curé of Ars, wrote that he possessed a a quick sense of humor and that he loved to laugh, smile and

[1] Texts from the Vatican Archives cited by JOHN XXIII, Enc. *Sacerdotii nostri primordia, loc. cit.*, p. 566.

joke. [1]   St. Pius X, as we know, was also fond of joking! Seeking to promote a healthy spirit of cheerfulness among his seminarians, Don Taroni would frequently ask them : " Is everybody happy? "

When everything is done for God, why shouldn't a person be happy? What does the lowliness of one's occupation matter, when such is the will of God? Don Balbiano was the happiest of men as a country curate for forty-six years. Seraphino Morazzone of Milan spent forty-nine years as the pastor of a small parish numbering only about 200 souls. " Souls, " he used to say, " are not measured in quantity but in quality. A priest who seeks to advance them in virtue has to work hard even though they are few in number. " This is how Don Paleari expressed it : " Truly fortunate is he, who at the end of his seminary days, and later on at the end of his life and priestly career, can say with Christ : *Consummatum est*, I have finished my course, I have accomplished my mission. " These martyred priests also died joyfully. Consider Blessed Noël Pinot who, having been clothed in his priestly vestments by his executioners, mounted the scaffold and beaming with joy, exclaimed : *Introibo ad altare Dei.*

The adorable and loving will of God, the source of all confidence, is the guiding principle of the priest. Consequently, this effects his devotion to the duties of his priestly and diocesan state of life. It is recounted that when the Curé of Ars and Blessed Champagnat arrived at the parishes to which they had been assigned by their bishop, they fell on their kness and prayed that they would be able to devote themselves wholeheartedly to their pastoral duties.

From humble curates on up to bishops, the watchword seems to have been that which Don Bonilli, priest of Spoleto, took as his motto : " The duties of the priestly state come first. " The periodic flights of St. John Vianney to the Trappists or Carthusians should not mislead us. They were real temptations

---

[1] Msgr. R. FOURREY, *Le Curé d'Ars* (Lyon 1958), pp. 14-16.

for him — he who was fully aware, and would be the first to admit, that his vocation was to be a priest and shepherd to poor sinners. [1] Since this is the underlying principle of the priestly state of life, the importance of obeying the bishop and his successors is readily understandable. Examples of this obedience abound. One of the most remarkable examples is that of Canon John Bazin. Treating of the promise of obedience made at Ordination, he used to tell his priests : " Never violate it, and always be ready to fulfill it, even at the expense of your inclinations, interests and comforts. You will never bear more fruit than in the place where God wishes you to be. You will only be certain of being where God wishes you by going wherever obedience sends you. " On an occasion when an assignment that he had received was extremely difficult to accept, he remarked to his bishop : " Your Excellency, I wish only to be like putty in your hands and take whatever form you deem suitable. You take the place of God and that is sufficient for me. " The type of obedience that he described was also joyful. He stated :

> Let us not be merely content with performing everything asked of us according to the letter. Let us strive to obey willingly. By showing that we are satisfied with what we have to do, we will add a new lustre to our obedience. This will prove that we are acting free of constraint and solely out of love. We will derive great pleasure from doing whatever is commanded of us if we regard the command as an order coming directly from God. It is much easier to do something willingly than to do it grudgingly and half-heartedly.

Sometimes, this is not as easy as it seems. Peter Monnereau, pastor in the Diocese of Luçon, was ordered by his bishop to leave his parish which also happened to be the Mother House of a religious society of women which he had founded. He tells us that for a few minutes he did not know whether he was alive

[1] A. Ravier, *Un prêtre parmi le peuple de Dieu, le Curé d'Ars* (Paris 1959), p. 13.

or dead, but he adds : " It only took me fifteen minutes to make my sacrifice. " His suffering and immediate submission, stemmed from the " tremendous respect that he had for the dignity and authority of the bishop. " The future Confessor of the Faith and Bishop of Veracruz, Guizar Valencia, was once suspended by his bishop. His innocence was well known. In the meantime, however, he exhibited a truly marvelous degree of patience; and like an ordinary member of the faithful, he would go to receive Communion in the Cathedral. Bishop Volpi of Arezzo, who had made the vow of St. Theresa (the vow to do the most perfect thing), and had offered himself to God as a victim during the First World War, became involved in a violent controversy. The Pope demanded his resignation which he tendered immediately. He then went to live at Rome where he was a source of edification for all. He has been called " the radiant pearl of the episcopacy. " Similarly, Msgr. Rota, called " another Athanasius, " when he failed to receive the *exequatur* of the government to confirm his nomination as Bishop of Mantua, was recalled to Rome by Leo XIII. To obey the bishop, and especially the Pope, is to obey God.

Don Taroni instilled the spirit of obedience into his young clerics at the seminary of Faenza. " Obedience, " he would say, " is my guiding light. " He would also consider the love that they should have for the diocese : " Just as soldiers respect their regimental colors and are imbued with an *esprit de corps*, so we who are priests must love our diocese and our superiors. " He delighted in recounting the lives of the saints of the Diocese of Faenza and the history of its parishes.

* * *

Our saintly models were also humble. If Don Balbiano remained a curate for nearly 50 years, it was only out of humility. He realized that it was his lot to obey and not to command and only desired to devote himself completely to souls. This is why someone has said that good curates go straight to heaven,

I viceparoci vanno diritti, diritti in Paradiso. [1]   Edward Cestac, another priest who remained in a humble post, used to say : " I am only what I am before God.   In a few years you and I and everyone else will only be a little bit of dust.   What does it matter to me if I am esteemed or held in disrepute, or if people speak well or ill of me, since God loves me. "   This was the attitude of many priests of humble rank.   They knew that God had chosen them and would never repent of the love that He had for them.   They fit the description of country pastors that was given by Cardinal Saliège :

> A country pastor preaches and endeavors to the best of his ability to nurture the faith of his flock.   He loves young people and seeks to foster vocations among them.   He loves the simple country folk and lives in their midst and thereby shares as they do in the great beauty of God's nature.   He is not always a scholar or a man of influence — rarely is he someone who has been decorated, and even more rarely is he a Canon!   But he does believe in eternal life. [2]

Edward Poppe, priest of Ghent, described these saintly and humble priests as men who were animated by faith and who performed their duties silently and unnoticed.   They were always at peace with themselves and constantly sought to sanctify themselves for and by their ministry.

* * *

One virtue which is common to all these men is the spirit of poverty.   Although many of them, such as Cardinal Riario Sforza of Naples, Cardinal Richard of Paris, Jean Marie Camille Costa de Beauregard of Chambery, Jean Marie de La Mennais of Vannes, etc., came from wealthy families, they all possessed the

---

[1] E. BECHIS, *Un vicecurato santo, Don Luigi Balbiano* (Alba 1945), p. 92.

[2] Card. J. G. SALIÈGE, *Les menus propos du Cardinal Saliège*, fascic. VI (1947), p. 60.

spirit of poverty. Consider Anthony Moreau, for example. He belonged to one of the most influential families of his diocese, and yet he begged his bishop to give him a small country parish. Consider also Pius IX, who simplified life at the Vatican, and who said : " Papal dignity does not oblige me to eat a greater quantity or a better quality of food. I am exactly what I was before, a poor priest of Christ. " Blessed Moyé recounts what his mother once told him : " A good priest should live and die poor, and should only possess at his death an earthenware pot which he can smash with his foot before he takes his last breath. " This is similar to the advice given by Marguerite Bosco to her son John : " I was born poor, I have lived poor and I wish to die poor. Make up your mind independently of me. I neither wish nor expect anything from you. Remember one thing : if it should ever be your misfortune to become rich, I will never darken your doorstep. Never forget that. " Extremely fortunate are priests who have such parents! At any rate, the thought of enriching one's relatives should be completely dismissed.

" From the first years of my priesthood, " the last will and testament of St. Anthony Mary Gianelli declares : " I resolved that I would die poor and leave my parents in the poor and humble situation in which we were born. " We know that St. Pius X did not wish his sisters to change their way of life after he had been elected Pope. He was so imbued with the spirit of poverty during his life that the following inscription was engraved on his tomb : *Pauper et dives*, poor in earthly goods, rich in the things of God.

For many, the spirit of poverty involved a formal commitment. Blessed Louis Maria Palazzolo of Bergamo affianced Lady Poverty. He wrote : " I considered this a good thing; and I felt at the time a very strong inclination to dispose of all my possessions by giving them to the Oratory, to the Sisters of St. Dorothy and to orphans. If I had been certain that this would have pleased Our Lord, I would have done it immediately. I decided to discuss it with my spiritual director. " The latter approved, and the Servant of God immediately disposed of all his possessions. On the Feast of St. Andrew in 1856, while Anthony Chevrier of Lyon was reading the words of the Last Gospel *Et Verbum caro factum est,* he felt a sudden compulsion to give away all his possessions; and he resolved then and there to devote himself entirely to the formation of poor priests. This was how the Society of Prado began. Abbé Andrew Hubert Fournet, at the beginning of his priesthood, lived a very worldly life, seeking his own ease and comfort and delighting in rich repasts. One day a beggar reproached him for his way of life. He was completely shaken by this and immediately gave away all his possessions and embarked upon a life of poverty and self-sacrifice which resulted in his being canonized by Pius XI in 1933. The spirit of poverty is necessary for one who wishes to follow Jesus and particularly for one who agrees to be His priest. A number of our priestly exemplars believed that much good could be done if they retained at least a part of their possessions. James Abbondo, pastor of Tranzano, said that by doing this he would be in a better position to provide bread for the poor. Peter Monnereau, priest of Luçon, had made a vow of poverty; but he asked to be dispensed from it when he was named pastor of Brouzèle, because he considered it incompatible with his pastoral mission. We have already seen how Philip Neri used the same reasoning to dissuade St. Charles Borromeo from imposing the vow of poverty on his Oblates. Vows are less important than the spirit and observance of them. "I know," Peter Bonhomme of Cahors declared, "that in the world you cannot practice poverty as in the religious state. You can, however, have the spirit of poverty and obtain merit by practicing it. You will share in the rewards promised to those who practice voluntary poverty." A person can likewise live poorly in the midst of great luxury, as is evident from the lives of Pius X and Cardinal Richard. The spirit of poverty is particularly well expressed by a concern for the poor and unfortunate. St. Yves, who has always been a very popular saint in Britanny, used his talents as a lawyer to help the poor. Many of these saintly priests devoted their time and resources to orphanages and charitable works of all types.

The memory of St. Vincent de Paul is still so alive today that the title " another Vincent de Paul " is used to describe a priest who is outstanding for his charity. The work of Cottolengo is also well known. Relying solely on public charity, he was able to secure enough funds to feed about 8,000 of the poorest of the poor in Turin. Other names could also be cited such as the " Father of the Poor " of Dijon, Venerable Benignus Joly, who certainly deserves to be better known. The spirit of poverty is accompanied by tremendous confidence in God. When Blessed Moyé would invest his religious with the little wooden crosses that were to serve as their *vade mecum*, he would usually ask them " if they had more confidence in Divine Providence than in a duly notarized contract guaranteeing them room and board. " Don Marchisio would often say : " Pray and trust in God and be at peace. A person travels well in the carriage (*nella carrozza*) of Providence. I have but one recommendation to make to you. As long as you do not render yourself unworthy by your sins, God will never cease to provide for you. " After observing Placid Bacher, a pastor in Naples, constantly doling out food and money to the poor, someone asked him how he would continue to do this. He calmly answered : " Let God worry about that. " This was exactly how St. Vincent de Paul felt when he stated : " Never encroach upon Divine Providence. " Louis Baudoin of Luçon used to say : " The more a priest gives, the more he receives. What he hands out at the door will return through the window. " It is important, however, to act prudently and to follow the advice of a good spiritual director. In doing this, we will in no way be prevented from remaining faithful to the spirit of the Gospels and from imitating the example of these saintly priests. At a time when there are many different kinds of savings plans and insurance policies, a priest who neglects to provide for his old age and possible future sickness and accident cannot expect his superiors to assume such costly obligations for him. Such precautions are nowadays part of our way of life. Yet priests should realize that the goods of this world can easilly become real obstacles to their ministry. " Gold, " Don Paleari used to say, " can open all doors except those of Paradise. " Returning to an indictment similar to the one that Louis of Grenada had addressed to the worldly bishops of the sixteenth century, Canon John Bazin told the priests of the Diocese of Séez : " People will never be able to be persuaded to bear the cross and give up all the illicit and dangerous pleasures of life simply by the sermons of priests if these same priests, who are obliged more than everyone else to follow Christ to Calvary, are constantly in search of their own ease and comfort and look upon their ministry, which should involve all sort of hardships, fatigue and hard work, as a source of repose, pleasure and freedom from cares. "

* * *

These reflections show the necessity of self-denial, mortification and penance. As important as these elements are in the life of the priest, they must nevertheless be properly understood and practiced with prudence and moderation. " In two cases deer run slowly, " St. Francis de Sales stated, " when they are either too fat or too lean. " We have many cases of saintly priests who practiced exceptional mortifications. A case in point is Don Balbiano who always carried a snuff-box filled with ashes which he used to season the food that was served him. Consider also Henry Osso y Cervello, a Spanish priest, whose life of mortification and contemplation was greatly admired by the Carmelites of Sagunto with whom he occasionally stayed. There is no need to consider at length the Curé of Ars. Fortunately he seems to have had a very balanced attitude toward mortification. His initial severity toward his body rapidly became more humane; and it is this balanced attitude, Abbé Nodet concludes, " which attracts us to him and does not make him appear as a frightfully austere character. " [1]

Very often the spirit of penance can be effectively practiced in the midst of one's pastoral duties and simply hidden under a

---

[1] B. NODET, *Jean-Marie Vianney, Curé d'Ars*, 3rd ed. (Le-Puy 1958), p. 43.

smile. This certainly was the case with St. John Vianney. How he must have smiled when he recalled the repeated visits of one "particularly obnoxious individual. " He believed that " one hour of patience is worth more than several days of fasting. " The most mortified are often the most joyful. This is particularly true of those who bear the heavy crosses of the pastoral ministry. On one occasion Don Frederick Albert, the beloved Dean of Lanzo, was told that he seemed to be extremely tired. He replied with a smile : " What a tremendous thing it is to be tired for the love of God. "

Besides those who wore themselves out for Christ, there were many others who died for Him. This was the point to which total self-renunciation led many of our confreres. Two-thirds of the priests martyred during the French Revolution who are presently upon the altars or whose beatification is being sought were secular priests. [1] More than half of the sixteenth and seventeenth century English martyrs, including the laity, were secular priests : about 165 out of 316. [2] The introduction of the causes of those who died in the Spanish Persecution of 1936-39 has recently begun. The official list of victims reveals that out of the 7,000 priests, seminarians and religious who were put to death, 4,500 of them were secular priests. [3] The diocesan clergy have certainly been a credit to the Church.

Besides the martyrs, there are those who are customarily referred to as confessors of the faith — those who have suffered persecution for Christ and the Church without undergoing actual martyrdom. Consider those who survived the French Revolution, such as Andrew Hubert Fournet, Anthony Receveur, Francis Gaschon, William Chaminade, John Bazin, Maurice Garrigou, Louis Baudoin; in Switzerland, Peter Blanchard, pastor of Soyères; in Italy, Bartholomew Ferri and Placid Bacher. During the period of the Risorgimento and the Masonic contro-

---

[1] See above, p. 242, footnote 1.

[2] C. A. NEWDIGATE, *Our Martyrs* (London 1935, 4th ed.).

[3] *Guia de la Iglesia en España, Año* I (1954), pp. 277-78. It gives these statistics : secular priests, 4,266; religious men, 2,498; religious women, 283; seminarians, 249.

versies, five saintly bishops felt the wrath of political intolerance :
Aloysius Sodo of Telesi, John Baptist Scalabrini of Placentia,
Riario Sforza of Naples, Peter Rota of Mantua, John Volpi of
Arezzo. We should also mention such men as Cardinal Richard
of Paris, during the period of the Church-State controversy in
France; Hyacinth Vera, Bishop of Montevideo and defender
of the rights of the Church in Uruguay; Franz Joseph Rudigier,
Bishop of Lintz who appeared in full pontificals before a court
which rebuked him for a pastoral that he had written denouncing
the liberalism of the Austrian government; Raphael Guizar
Valencia, Bishop of Veracruz who was expelled from Mexico
twice within a period of fifteen years; Joseph Torras y Bages,
Bishop of Catalonia, the special target of Spanish anarchists at
the turn of the century.

There are many others who did not experience violent
persecution but who bore up under many types of crosses. They
accepted the trials sent to them out of love for Christ and their
flocks. Once when Peter Monnereau received an extremely
crushing letter from the Chancery Office, he fell upon his knees
before a crucifix and exclaimed : " Oh my Jesus, the more You
do to me, the more will I love You. " The supreme lesson is
the lesson of love, and this is why we entitled this chapter *The
Lessons of Our Models*. Don Taroni observed : " Priests must
live as lovers do. The love of Jesus should shine forth in their
faces, in their eyes, in their words and actions. For lovers,
whatever does not concern their love is esteemed as nothing;
and whatever pertains to their love is of supreme importance.
The greatest things count for nothing without the love of Jesus.
With the love of Jesus the smallest things have great value. "
The saints were well aware that it was not the work of men that
redeemed the world, but the Cross of the Savior.

Charles de Foucauld reminded us of this fact through the
life that he led. He used to say that Jesus' love for men, reflected
in the Eucharist and in the Gospels, should prompt us to have
a share in His saving sacrifice. Such a spiritual outlook as this
is particularly valuable when the most delicate fibres of the soul,

those which actually vibrate with the love of Christ, are subjected to ridicule and calumny. We are thinking particularly of such men as St. Joseph Oriol and St. John Kenty who were both suspected of heresy and also St. Anthony Mary Gianelli and St. John Vianney who were subjected to the vilest type of calumniation with regard to their chastity. In fact, the rumors regarding the Curé were so persistent in the area around Ars, but not at Ars itself, that the bishop conducted a formal inquiry into the entire matter. The Curé stated sometime after this : " I believed that the time would come when I would be beaten with sticks and chased from Ars, and that I would be placed under interdict by my bishop and would have to spend the rest of my days in prison. " [1] It is hard to believe that this priest, who was enraptured by the beauty of chastity, would have had to suffer so much for it. He would frequently say : " There is nothing so beautiful as a pure soul. Purity is like a rose in a bouquet; of all the flowers which compose it, the rose is the most beautiful and the most fragrant. " [2]

It is no surprise to find that many of our great priestly models attained a high degree of contemplation. SS. Philip Neri, Joseph Oriol, John Baptist de Rossi and John Vianney are just a few examples among those who have already been accorded the honors of the Altar. Although such men as Joseph Torras y Bages of Catalonia, Anthony Bermejo of Valladolid, Joachim Rosello Ferro of Majorca, Anthony Pennachi of Assisi, Peter Noailles of Bordeaux and Louis Baudoin of Luçon have not yet reached this stage, they too should be mentioned as having attained, during their lifetime, a high level of contemplation.

* * *

A priest in search of perfection should not forget the serious warnings given by St. Francis de Sales who attributed the success

[1] Msgr. R. FOURREY, *op. cit.*, pp. 33-34.
[2] B. NODET, *op. cit.*, p. 215.

of Protestantism to a lack of sufficient theological knowledge on the part of many priests. In fact, the Bishop of Geneva considered study an eighth sacrament. As we all know, the establishment of seminaries was the most important single factor in the Council of Trent's reform of the clergy. We have already seen the important part that John of Avila played in this great undertaking.

All the priests that we have considered in this section were strongly convinced of the necessity of study. Nicholas Mazza, a priest of Verona, would frequently tell priests : " Study hard, for an ignorant priest does more harm today than a bad layman. " Don Taroni frequently admonished his seminarians : " Do not set aside too much time for prayer. You have much to study; and he who studies, prays. Do not engage in too many pious practices. A person should only do as much as he can afford to do. Say ejaculations : this is a telegraph system which puts us in contact with heaven. " Some may object to this by citing the case of the Curé of Ars. It is true that his memory was somewhat rusty at the time that he began to study for the priesthood, but he did possess common sense and average intelligence. He was also fully aware of the obligation that he had to continue to read and study. Exclusive of books that were loaned and never returned, his library today contains over 400 volumes! This is not so bad for a period when there was not as much published as there is today. After examining 200 complex moral cases presented by the Curé of Ars, his bishop found that " his decisions were correct and his practice irreproachable. " [1]

Many of our saintly models spent their entire priestly lives in teaching. They taught in major and minor seminaries, in colleges, in vocational and professional schools and elementary schools. A few taught at institutions of higher learning. St. John of Kenty was a professor of theology at the University of Cracow;

---

[1] B. NODET, *op. cit.*, p. 18; M. MELLET, " Le vrai journal d'un curé de campagne, " *loc. cit.*, p. 279. See also J. ALZIN, " Saint curé d'Ars, Catéchismes, " *Les Écrits des Saints* (Namur 1958), pp. 12-13.

Nicholas Stenon, the Father of Geology, was a professor of geology at the University of Copenhagen and Francis Frà di Bruno taught mathematics at the University of Turin. We should not fail to mention John Henry Newman, the first Rector of the University of Dublin. This " illustrious and untiring seeker of truth " is recognized today as one of the greatest expositors of Christian philosophy and theology. [1]

There have always been outstanding theologians among the diocesan clergy. We need only mention such Doctors of the Church as St. Hilary, St. Athanasius, St. Leo, St. Isidore of Seville and St. Francis de Sales. We should also add St. Alphonsus Liguori, since he was formed in the clergy of Naples. The Sanctoral contains a number of others who someday may be proclaimed Doctors of the Church. St. Pius X, for example, was the guiding force behind the Eucharistic and Liturgical Revival. It was he who detected and condemned the errors of Modernism. The *Obras Completas* of Blessed John of Avila establish this Spanish priest among the most outstanding theological writers of all times. As for Italy, St. Gregory Barbarigo was considered one of the most eminent churchmen of the eighteenth century. It is quite possible, therefore, that both of these men will someday be declared Doctors of the Church. At any rate, the diocesan clergy can lay claim to quite a few bishops and priests who admirably combined great wisdom with great holiness. Besides listing in this category such well known figures as St. Yves Helory, St. Charles Borromeo, St. Joseph Cottolengo, St. Joseph Cafasso and John Henry Newman, we must not fail to mention a number of others who are equally deserving of recognition. Such men as Franz Josef Rudigier, Joseph Allamano, Paul Taroni, Louis Baudoin, Edward Cestac were all well known spiritual writers, and the remarkable Bishop of Catalonia, Joseph Torras y Bages, was known under several titles : the Philosopher of the Christian Social Order, the Bishop of the Bible and the Bishop of the Rosary.

---

[1] Pope Pius XII, *Apostolic Letter on the Occasion of the 16th Centenary of the Birth of St. Augustine* (July 25, 1954), *AAS*, Vol. XLVI (1954), p. 516. See A. PIOLANTI, " Newman, " *Enciclopedia cattolica*, Vol. VIII, col. 1805.

John of Avila, one of the earliest promoters of Christian Humanism in the sixteenth century, worked very hard at organizing schools and colleges in Spain. This work was later taken up by the Jesuits and soon spread throughout the world. [1] St. Francis de Sales next appeared on the scene. He proved to be extremely well aware of the problems of his own day. We know that he intended his *Introduction to the Devout Life* to be used by men of every rank and station. Later when he wrote the *Treatise on the Love of God*, he admitted that much had already been written on this subject, but he asserted : " I considered the state of souls at this time and felt that I had to write this treatise. It is always very important to consider the period for which one is writing. " [2] The writings of the Bishop of Geneva, because of their healthy balance and easy adaptability, are still of great value even today. Not only is St. Francis de Sales the Doctor of the Spiritual Life, as Pius XI referred to him on the occasion of the third centenary of his death, [3] but he is also, in the view of Pius XII, a model and guide for the modern apostolate. The late Pontiff declared :

> What a magnificent example for all — for the pastor of souls as well as for the militant layman involved in Catholic Action — at a time when the demands of the apostolate are confronting our generation with many problems similar to those which have confronted every true missionary of the Gospel throughout the course of history. From the Bishop of Geneva we can learn how to achieve a remarkable degree of balance in the exercise of the apostolic virtues.

After presenting a number of incidents from the life of the saint to illustrate this perfect sense of balance, the Pope continued : " The secret of this great harmony is to be found in the peace and happiness enjoyed by a soul which lived in the contemplation

---

[1] L. SALA BALUST, *Obras Completas del Beato Maestro Juan de Avila* (Madrid 1952), pp. 93-140; L. CASTAN, " El Padre Maestro Avila y su epoca, " *El Beato Maestro Juan de Avila, conferencias pronunciadas en la Semana nacional avilistica en Madrid, loc. cit.*, pp. 73-92.

[2] St. FRANCIS DE SALES, *Treatise on the Love of God*, " Preface. "

[3] Pope PIUS XI, Enc. *Rerum omnium* (Jan. 26, 1923), in *AAS*, Vol. XV (1923), p. 51.

and love of the divine will. " [1]   It is easy to understand why the influence of this scholarly and kindly bishop has always been so great.

* * *

We cannot fail to mention the important role played by our saintly models in organizing associations of Catholic Action and engaging in social and charitable activities. St. Vincent Pallotti and Pio Brunone Lanteri were early pioneers in these movements.   Edward Poppe of Ghent was one of the founders and early promoters of the Eucharistic Crusade.   Youth organizations were started by such outstanding men as John Joseph Allemand, the famous " Priest of Youth, " who founded a number of youth clubs at Marseille, and Peter Rota, the future Bishop of Mantua, who founded similar clubs in Italy.   The *Opera Cardinale Ferrari* at Milan is named in honor of Cardinal Andrew James Ferrari who promoted a number of social and charitable activities.   Among the early promoters of strictly social service organizations, there are a number of priests who may someday be beatified, such as Adolph Kolping of Cologne, Alphonsus Ariens of Roermond, Louis Brisson of Troyes and Leo Dehon of Soissons, who founded the Congregation of Priests of the Sacred Heart.   We must also mention Frederick Albert, Dean of Lanzo-Torinese, John Piamarta of Brescia and Leonard Murialdo.   These priests, who understood the plight of the rural classes, were particularly concerned with alleviating the grave social problems that had arisen as a result of the large–scale exodus from the country to the city.

There were many priests who engaged in works of charity. There are many names connected with this, and their activities ranged from running orphanages, hospitals and houses of hospitality, to caring for the poor, the sick, the lepers, visiting

---

[1] Pope PIUS XII, " Letter on the Occasion of the 350th Anniversary of the Consecration of St. Francis de Sales " (Sept. 12, 1952), *L'Osservatore Romano* (same date).

those in prison and ransoming captives, etc. We should not fail to mention all of the organizations that were set up to help the missions at home and abroad. Interestingly enough, the Oblates of Mary Immaculate, founded by Charles de Mazenod, and the Augustinians of the Assumption, founded by Emmanuel d'Alzon, are just two examples of religious societies that grew out of such organizations that were set up to help the missions.

St. Vincent de Paul, whom Leo XIII in 1883 proclaimed the *Heavenly Patron of All Societies of Charity*, is deserving of special mention. Even before his providential call to engage solely in charitable works, during the time that he served as pastor of Clichy-la-Garenne and Châtillon-des-Dombes, this great diocesan priest was a model of all that a good priest should be. He engaged in a number of varied activities — helping the poor in all sorts of ways, preaching missions, founding an institute of women to minister to the poor and the sick, reforming the clergy through retreats and conferences and through the establishment of diocesan seminaries. When we consider the tremendous influence that this man had upon all levels of society and upon the most influential men of his day, we can only agree with the following conclusion of Daniel Rops : " St. Vincent de Paul, dead some three hundred years, remains present among us. The Church of the centuries that followed him and the Church of our own day would not be as we know it if the former shepherd boy of Landes had not lived, thought and acted. " [1]

The work of St. Vincent de Paul was not mere activism. Bremond declares : " It was not charity which made him a saint, but it was his saintliness which made him truly charitable. The greatest of our men of action was given us by mysticism. " [2] It is very difficult to describe the friendship that existed between Vincent de Paul and Francis de Sales. It is quite certain, however, that Vincent was strongly influenced by the Bishop of Geneva during the time of his *conversion* and his decision to devote

[1] Henri Daniel Rops, *Monsieur Vincent*, Eng. trans. Julie Kernan (New York : Hawthorn 1961), p. 95.

[2] Quotation from Daniel Rops, *op. cit.*, pp. 39-45.

himself entirely to works of charity.   Although Francis de Sales did not have the time to write a *Treatise on the Love of Neighbor* as he had planned to do, he did much better than that. He fashioned the soul of one who was to become the hero and the modern paragon of Christian charity.   We can even say that both saints, by their words and deeds, have given the Church a living treatise on the love of God and neighbor—the type of spirituality necessary for the truly pious and apostolic way of life.

* * *

During the last few centuries of the Church's history the diocesan clergy has been like a fertile garden in which many new plants have grown up to adorn the kingdom of God and to increase its work in the world.   Consequently, the diocesan clergy will always play an important and necessary part in the Church's work for souls.

Chapter 18

The Patrons of Our Pastors and Curates

The voice of the faithful quickly proclaimed the sanctity of John Vianney, who died August 4, 1859, after 44 years as a priest and 41 years as pastor of the little village of Ars. Pius IX formally opened his cause in 1866 and declared this humble French priest Venerable in 1872. On January 8, 1905, Pius X beatified him and named him the patron of all French pastors. On May 31, 1925, Pius XI canonized him; and on April 23, 1929, this same Pope declared him to be the " Heavenly Patron of All Parish Priests. " [1] In 1959, on the occasion of the centenary of his death, Pope John XXIII declared : " The Catholic Church, which has raised to the honors of canonization this priest remarkable for his pastoral zeal and for his continuous ardor for prayer and penance, today, one hundred years after his death, with maternal joy proposes him to be imitated by all the clergy as a most outstanding example of the priestly ascetical life of piety, and especially of Eucharistic piety, and finally of pastoral zeal. " [2]

Although the Sanctoral already contained many outstanding pastors worthy of imitation, it was chiefly because of the tremendous example set by the Curé of Ars that greater efforts were made to consider the entire question of the status and sanctification of the parochial clergy. Recent popes have been particularly concerned with this as is evident from their writings.

---

[1] Pope PIUS XI, *Littera Apostolica Anno Jubilari* (April 23, 1929), *AAS*, Vol. XXI (1929), p. 312.

[2] Pope JOHN XXIII, Enc. *Sacerdotii Nostri Primordia, loc. cit.*, p. 549. Just before the publication of this encyclical, on June 6, 1959, the Sacred Congregation of Seminaries and Universities urged bishops to offer to seminarians the " striking example " of the Curé d'Ars. The text of this letter to the bishops, August 16, 1959, is reproduced in *La Documentation catholique*, Vol. LVI (1950), cols. 1051-60.

The election of Cardinal Sarto to the papacy only served to bolster these efforts. When it was announced that the Patriarch of Venice had been elected Pope, a number of people somewhat scornfully remarked : " But he is only a country pastor. " Pius X, however, was not displeased when he heard of the designation that had been applied to him; instead, he considered it a title of honor. He had been Pope for only a short time when he stated : " We declare quite openly that our preference will always be for the priest who, without neglecting sacred or profane learning, devotes himself especially to the care of souls by performing various duties of the ministry which are particularly fitting for the priest, who is animated by zeal for the glory of God. " [1] This great Pontiff also expressed a desire to see many parish priests accorded the honors of the Altar. It was he who beatified John Vianney and made him the patron of the pastors of France. He recognized the cults of St. Gamelbert, pastor of Michaelsbuch in Baveria and Blessed Bartholomew Buonpedoni, pastor in the Diocese of Volterra in Tuscany. He beatified Stephen Bellesini, an Augustinian, who was the pastor of Genazzano, a small town near Palestrina. This courageous priest died in 1840 as a result of his heroic action in ministering to the victims of a cholera epidemic. In 1909 he canonized Joseph Oriol, the apostle of Barcelona, who died in 1702.

Apparently, then, these canonizations and beatifications were completely in line with the aforementioned desire of the saintly Pontiff. In fact, he personally urged a number of dioceses to introduce the causes of several members of their clergy. It was chiefly because of his insistence that the cause of Anthony Pennachi, chaplain of St. Andrew's Oratory at Assisi, was introduced. [2] The same also can be said for the cause of Francis Gaschon, whom St. Pius X wished to name the patron of diocesan missionaries in the same way as he had named the Curé

---

[1] Pope Pius X, Enc. *E Supremi Apostolatus cathedra* (Oct. 4, 1903), *AAS*, Vol. XXXVI (1903-4), p. 136.

[2] Letter of Rev. Giuseppe-Placido Nicolini, O.S.B. (Jan. 9, 1956). On Antonio Pennachi see F. Rauco, *Una gemma del Clero di Assisi* (Foligno 1932).

of Ars the patron of parish priests. [1] Finally, he encouraged the cause of Andrew Hubert Fournet, priest of Poitiers, whom we will consider next.

* * *

Benedict XV occupied the Chair of Peter when, on the 10th of July, 1921, the heroic virtue of the pastor of Maille, Andrew Hubert Fournet, was solemnly proclaimed. The Pope delivered a truly memorable discourse on this occasion in which he said :

> We know that there is one particular group of individuals who will be especially pleased by today's decree. The pastors of souls have a greater right than any other group of ecclesiastics to say : Andrew Hubert Fournet was one of us. But why, it may be asked, are we particularly interested in pointing out the special reference that this decree has for pastors? It is not only because we wish to affirm that it was in the parochial ministry or, more precisely, directly through the parochial ministry that Venerable Fournet attained the heights of Christian perfection to which the Church today declares that he has arrived; it is principally because we believe that in the loving plan of Divine Providence the glorification accorded today to Andrew Hubert Fournet will serve to focus attention upon the tremendous importance of the parochial ministry — both for those who are engaged in exercising it and for those who reap the fruits of its exercise. This divine plan was particularly evident in the case of two pastors, Stephen Bellesini and John Vianney, both of whom were beatified, one shortly after the other, by our predecessor of happy memory. But now, less than twenty years after these beatifications, the Church reveals the progress made by another pastor's cause for beatification. The great number of these beatification causes undoubtedly serve to convince us of the important part played by the parochial ministry in effecting the long – awaited restoration of Christian society.

[1] H. POURRAT, *L'Exorciste, Vie de Jean-François Gaschon* (Paris 1954), p. 258.

Beloved Sons, let us endeavor to realize this fact and consider how profitable it will be to priests and laymen both now and in the future. [1]

The biography of Andrew Hubert Fournet observes :

> This discourse was widely hailed. The semi-official organ of the Vatican, *L'Osservatore Romano*, printed the complete text of the discourse in a special edition which was sent free of charge to all the pastors of Italy.... The first response to the discourse came from the pastors of Rome who assembled immediately to convey their thanks to the Vicar of Jesus Christ and to assure him that his appeal had been heard and that it would be heeded. [2]

It is indeed regrettable that this magnificent discourse of Benedict XV — which sums up so clearly and authoritatively the underlying thesis of this volume — only enjoyed an extremely limited audience. In line with the thought of Benedict XV, we already mentioned that the Sanctoral has, for a long time, contained over one hundred pastors and curates. [3]

Besides those who functioned throughout their priestly lives as pastors and curates, there are also a number of others, who, at some point during their priestly careers, engaged in the parochial ministry. This is particularly true in the case of bishops, such as, for example, St. Anthony Mary Gianelli, St. Anthony Mary Claret and the " country pastor " who later became Pope Pius X.

There are under consideration at Rome an impressive number of causes which are of interest to those engaged in the parochial ministry. Without counting the causes of priest martyrs, there are presently between twenty and twenty-five pastors and curates who are officially candidates for beatification or canonization. We must also add that there are between thirty

---

[1] Discourse of Pope Benedict XV reported by J. Saubat, *André Hubert Fournet*, Vol. II (Tarbes 1924), pp. 558 ff.

[2] J. Saubat, *ibid.*, pp. 563-64.

[3] See above, p. 249.

and forty causes of bishops and priests who spent at least a part of their priestly lives in the parochial ministry. As significant as this is, it is even more significant that practically all of these saintly priests were natives of either Italy, France or Spain. Imagine how large this number would be if other Christian countries had taken care to preserve the memory of their priests who died in the odor of sanctity. Naturally, the causes of the Servants of God can be helped along by Divine Providence; but, as we have already seen, men must still take an active part in promoting them.

* * *

At any rate, the great patron of the parochial clergy is the Curé of Ars who, by the grace of God, splendidly realized the great ideal of the priest among the people. The French School has described the priest as another Christ, who becomes one with Christ and continues His saving work among men. The Curé of Ars perfectly exemplified this ideal, and he is today regarded as a pastor who sanctified himself for and through his ministry. Father Ravier recently published a biography of the Curé of Ars in which he shows that the priestly ideal of this saint was entirely realistic and independent of any formal method of spirituality. He was simply a priest of Jesus Christ and a pastor of souls, and it was because of this that he reached such great heights of sanctity. By way of conclusion we can do nothing better than to quote Father Ravier's own conclusion :

> This *humble priest* was a pure transparency of Jesus Christ, the unique and sovereign Priest. In order for him to be conformed to his Model, he certainly must have received very exceptional graces. He is numbered among the greatest Christian mystics of all times. But what is particularly remarkable is that the Holy Spirit utilized means common to every priest to inspire him to achieve sanctity. He simply had to live his priesthood to the fullest. In order to be a true pastor of souls he sanctified himself,

and it was because he was a true pastor of souls that he became a saint.   There is no spiritual doctrine of the Curé of Ars; there is only the Credo of Baptism which he faithfully taught and according to which he generously lived.   Neither the great depth of his teaching nor the brilliant success of his apostolic endeavors have made him the Patron of parish priests—this was due rather to the zeal with which he taught and practiced what every pastor is expected to teach and practice.   He described the saints as having: " the love of God glued on their lips like little pieces of glittering gold. "   His parishioners said of him that: " When he pronounced the name of Jesus, his heart seemed to shine forth on his lips. " [1]

Whether a priest has many or only a few parishioners, whether he occupies an important post in the diocese or lives in relative obscurity is inconsequential.   The really important thing is that he is a priest and is serving where Divine Providence has destined him to serve.   Therefore, like our heavenly patrons, and particularly like the Curé of Ars, we should endeavor to live our priesthood *with pastoral zeal and a great fervor for prayer and penance.* [2]   If this is not sufficient to constitute a state of perfection, it is, unquestionably, a highly endowed *means* of achieving personal sanctification.

---

[1] A. Ravier, *Un Prêtre parmi le peuple de Dieu, le Curé d'Ars, op. cit.,* pp. 77-78.

[2] Collect from the Mass of St. John Vianney.

Conclusions

At the conclusion of this study, we believe that we can say that there is a spirituality proper to the diocesan clergy. In no way is this spirituality restricted, exclusive or opposed to any other type of spirituality. Rather, it is one that will benefit both priests and the Church.

Bishop Guerry wrote :

It has never occured to anyone to construct, a priori, an original spirituality for the use of parish priests which would isolate them from the mainstream of the Church and which would make them into *sacristy priests*; and, as we well know, parish priests have no particular affection for this type of life. We can only speak of a spirituality of the diocesan clergy from the perspective of the unity of the Church. This spirituality must therefore tie in with that of the Church. What, therefore, is the problem? First of all it is necessary to know whether there exist special means by which the diocesan clergy can participate in the entire mystery of the Church. It is also necessary to bring out clearly the aspects of our common patrimony which are particularly suited to the diocesan clergy. Far from intending to construct an artificial theory a priori, we ask instead that cognizance be taken of an existing reality. We ask that the positive originality of the condition of the diocesan clergy be grasped by priests in order that they may build, on the very nature of their special vocation in the Church, a means of promoting their own sanctification and of enabling them to fulfill more effectively the mission which has been especially entrusted to them in the vast life of the Church. [1]

[1] Msgr. E. Guerry, " Communication sur la spiritualité du clergé diocésain," *La Maison-Dieu*, 3 (1945), pp. 80-81.

We can therefore say that the spirituality of the diocesan clergy is the spirituality of the duties of the priestly and diocesan state of life. The following seem to be the principal characteristics of this state of life :

1. Certainly the chief exemplar of every priesthood is Christ. But in the order of participation, the priesthood of Christ [1] is only fully realized in the bishop. [2] The episcopal state is also particularly instructive for the diocesan priest since his collaboration with the bishop must be complete. In fact, this collaboration fully expresses the very notion of the Church's ministry. It is therefore quite important that the theology of the episcopacy be adequately explained. In this way the diocesan clergy will be able to draw from it the necessary inspiration and motivation for their priestly lives. It is also very important to show how the Church profits from the diocesan priest's union to the bishop and collaboration in his pastoral ministry. It is also necessary to show how this collaboration in the common mission of the bishop contains very valuable means for sanctification.

2. Closely united to their bishop, who by divine right is a member of the Hierarchy and as such is expected to join with the Pope in assuming the responsibilities of the entire Church, the diocesan clergy should avoid any narrow particularism. Instead, they should be attentive to the problems facing the Church throughout the world and should profess complete filial submission to the Sovereign Pontiff. In order to do this they must have a proper understanding and appreciation of their vocation.

3. Like their bishop, the diocesan clergy have committed themselves to work for the good of the local church, the diocese. It is in the diocese that they are firmly rooted, and it is here that they achieve their stability (*stabilitas in loco*). Committed by

---

[1] St. THOMAS, *Summa Theol.*, III, q. 63, a. 3.

[2] Father Monsabré remarks that " St. Thomas says that it is an overflow from the priesthood of Jesus Christ : *Christus est fons totius sacerdotii*. But this overflow does not come from the soul of the Eternal Priest directly into the souls of those who are to share in His power and His dignity; it comes through the hands of a man who is at the highest level of the Hierarchy. " " Le générateur du sacerdoce, " *Les Conférences de Notre-Dame, op. cit.*, p. 174.

their vocation to serve the diocese, they must always be ready to take the good with the bad. Since they venerate the bishop as their father in God, they should realize that they all constitute the presbyterium of the bishop. They should also have fraternal regard for one another and realize the necessity of coordinating their apostolic labors. Only in this way will team work and even community life be possible. Community life, however, is only secondary; and it is only possible when the particular circumstances of the parochial ministry do not rule it out.

4. Since the exercise of the parochial ministry is the most important function of the diocesan clergy, the most representative type of the diocesan priest is the pastor. It is he who has received, by title, the responsibility for running a parish and caring for souls. Thus, in the name of the bishop, the pastor acts as the teacher, shepherd and father of the faithful entrusted to his care. It should also be observed that although the duties of the diocesan clergy are extremely diverse, they are, nevertheless, all performed for the same purpose : the direction of the diocesan flock, the bishop's flock. All the activities of the diocesan clergy are concentrated and centered in the pastoral duties of the bishop; and, therefore, every diocesan priest should be like a pastor in the concern and feeling that he manifests for the parochial ministry.

5. We must also stress that if the exercise of the pastoral charge is to be effective, it is not merely sufficient for the pastor to live in the midst of his flock. His presence among them must be active and vigilant, and he must be ready to provide whatever will contribute to the life of his flock. His most important duty is to celebrate Mass, since it is through this action that he ministerially engages in the great vivifying and redemptive work of Our Lord. Therefore it is around this, the most important ministerial activity of every priesthood, that the parish priest should organize his pastoral activity. His primary concern must therefore be to gather his parishioners around the altar, so that they can participate actively and personally in the mysteries taking place there. Thus, the great importance of preaching, catechizing

and conducting a parish school is immediately evident. It is also important to meet frequently with one's parishioners. Even more important is the administration of the sacraments and particularly the sacrament of penance. A pastor who is worthy of the name will never abandon the practice of hearing confessions even though the pressures resulting from the present–day apostolate may be exceedingly heavy. A priest could devote practically all of his time to just one phase of the modern apostolate. Yet, he realizes full well that he must be concerned with all the demands of his ministry.

6. Diocesan priests willingly choose to share the same type of life as their flocks. They become easily attached to their people, and it is thrilling to observe how well they know and love them and how very often they are loved by them in return. This is usually not apparent in the hustle and bustle of everyday life, but parishioners express it in a particularly striking way when their pastor dies or is transferred. The parochial ministry, provided it is wholeheartedly exercised, sustains and inspires the faithful much more than some seem to realize. This is precisely what Cardinal Richaud meant when he said : " Secular priests should always be conscious of the great treasure that they carry within themselves. " [1]

7. This is true enough. However, diocesan priests have still another great advantage which the spiritual writers of the sixteenth and seventeenth centuries clearly revealed. The spirituality of the diocesan priest is the simplest and least complicated of all spiritualities. It emphasizes what is essential in the priesthood and in no way obliges a priest to follow a particular school of spirituality; yet, his spirituality may be strongly influenced by any one of these schools.

The diocesan priest, therefore, has the entire field of Christian spirituality from which to pick and choose and still preserve his freedom and flexibility. The organization, traditions

---

[1] Card. P. M. RICHAUD, *Y a-t-il une spiritualité du clergé diocésain?, op. cit.*, p. 18. See also the fine article of Msgr. G. GARRONE, " Le prêtre, qui est-ce, pour lui-même? " *Prêtres diocésains* (1958), pp. 102-05.

and very spirit of the secular clergy all allow for the freedom of movement and adaptibility which is often the envy of other groups. Naturally, there are restrictions and limits placed upon this because of the necessity of collaborating with the bishop. But, after all, collaboration is part of the very nature of every priestly vocation. When we examine the question of adaptation, we readily see that the secular clergy adapt most easily to the conditions of their flocks. As in any field, it may also occasionally happen in the priesthood that a number of real abuses exist and that certain activities are done solely out of routine. But as long as the heart of the bishop and the hearts of his priests are receptive to the inspirations of the Holy Spirit, the clergy will always be assured of tremendous spiritual resources and powers to exercise their ministry effectively. Did not many of the founders of religious orders throughout the centuries come from the ranks of the secular clergy? Were not many of the souls who have illuminated the history of the Church and the annals of sanctity fashioned, at least during their youth, by parish priests?

* * *

In an address to the members of the Apostolic Union of the Clergy, His Holiness Pope John XXIII summed up the way of life of a zealous priest in these words : " Accept His sweet yoke and His light burden, practicing the virtues which are proper to every consecrated life : dedication to God and to the care of souls, tireless work for the Church, practice of the fourteen works of mercy, prompt and wholehearted obedience to your bishop and a respect filled with manly tenderness for all things sacred. " [1]

If the entire program of the pastoral ministry is to be truly effective, holiness of life is certainly demanded. Sanctification forms an integral part of the duties of the priestly state. Pope Pius XII declared :

[1] Pope JOHN XXIII, *Exhortation to the Apostolic Union of the Clergy* (March 14, 1959), *L'Osservatore Romano* (March 14, 1959).

The necessity for a Christian renewal, which all men of
good will appreciate, urges us to turn our thoughts and
affections in a special way to the priests of the whole world
because we know that their humble, vigilant and painstaking
work among the people, whose difficulties, sufferings and
bodily as well as spiritual needs they realize, is capable
of restoring morals through the practice of the precepts
of the Gospel and of establishing firmly on earth the
Kingdom of Jesus Christ. But the priesthood cannot
in any way procure the full effects which are demanded
by present–day needs unless priests shine forth among
the people with the marks of sanctity, as worthy ministers
of Christ, faithful dispensers of the mysteries of God, God's
helpers, and ready for every noble work. Without holiness
the minist y confided to their care will never be fruitful. [1]

Pope John was just as definite in his encyclical on the
Curé of Ars. [2] The spirituality of the priest, therefore, cannot
simply be a spirituality of action, since apostolic activity must
be accompanied by prayer and a sincere attempt to achieve one's
own sanctification.

The Mass, as we have said, is the prayer par excellence, the
very essence of sacerdotal devotion. A few days before his death
Cardinal Mercier wrote a final letter to his priests in which he
urged them : " Always celebrate Mass as though you were at
Calvary, and bring to it all the fervor of faith and devotion of
which you are capable. " He added further : " The celebration
of Mass is the most important thing that you do each day, and
therefore it must be the central act of each day.... In order to
live out your priesthood properly, you must above all celebrate
Mass and administer the Sacraments devoutly. " [3] This is the
very essence of priestly spirituality.

* * *

[1] Pope Pius XII, *Exhortatio apostolica Menti Nostrae, loc. cit.*, p. 658.

[2] Pope John XXIII, Enc. *Sacerdotii Nostri Primordia, loc. cit.*, pp. 560-61, 565-66, 576.

[3] Card. D. J. Mercier, " Lettre à son Clergé " (Jan. 18, 1926), *Œuvres pastorales*,
Vol. VII (Louvain 1929), pp. 641-42.

Diocesan authorities should strongly encourage those priestly associations whose purpose it is to help secular priests persevere and advance in virtue. His Holiness Pope John XXIII, stated that he was extremely pleased by the success of these associations. [1] However, discretion is called for since great care must always be taken neither to impair the flexibility of the clerical structure nor to reduce the clergy to a regimented way of life that would run contrary to their best traditions. The following quotation is taken from a book written by Cardinal Richaud. It expresses quite clearly our own view on this question.

> When we envision the future of the Church's apostolate, must we picture the parochial clergy as having to live like religious? Is there any reason why secular priests should be compelled to join Third Orders or associate themselves with a particular society or institute, which, although it does not demand the taking of religious vows, nevertheless offers all the safeguards proper to a religious society? This will depend, in large measure, upon the temperament of each person and upon the circumstances of time and place. The personal attractions of one individual will differ from those of another. Some things considered necessary at one time may not be considered so now. Certain things may be possible in some countries and altogether impossible in other countries. This is why any attempts to regiment the diocesan clergy would most probably be extremely dangerous. We should also remember that the holiness expected of the secular priest should be viewed differently from the holiness expected of the religious. We should not be confused by categories, and we should be careful not to impose on certain souls burdens that they may not be able to support. We should especially endeavor not to destroy the effectiveness of certain vocations by depriving them of the simplicity which constitutes their most important quality. The sacrifice is one, and it should unite as closely as possible those who perpetuate it. Every priest who offers the Sacrifice of the Mass must mention the Pope and his own

---

[1] Pope JOHN XXIII, *Exhortation to the Apostolic Union of the Clergy, loc. cit.*

bishop. Right now, in the middle of the twentieth century, the apostolate for souls must be better organized, more carefully planned and more diligently carried out than ever before. For this reason, let us not transform simple means into principles. Let us endeavor to preserve our originality which transcends many differences. Family unity is not achieved by obliging each of its members to have the same opinion on all questions and to work at the same trade. Rather, this unity is achieved when differences of opinion among the members of the family are tolerated and when the particular vocation of each one is fully respected. Might not the attempts that are now being made to effect a greater regimentation and uniformity in the life of the diocesan clergy result in a weakening and lessening of what the Angelic Doctor refers to as their greater interior holiness? There are many situations in which a diocesan priest would not completely benefit from the advantages of a regular life, and thus he would be only partly living this life. What would be gained in regularity, would be lost in personality, adaptation and extension. [1]

There is no doubt that a person can effectively strive for perfection by living according to the spirit, at least, of the evangelical counsels. However, if in order to persevere and advance in this life, he feels that he should join a particular association, or if he is even considering taking vows, he should make up his mind independently of any human consideration, trusting completely in the Holy Spirit.

It is our view that, when the time comes to make a choice, it is important to choose those solutions which will more effectively guarantee the fulfillment of the duties of the pastoral state of life — the ability to be completely at the disposal of the bishop and to collaborate fraternally with all the priests of the diocese.

We have many outstanding heavenly patrons who came from the ranks of the diocesan clergy. By reading their lives or simply by glancing through the Sanctoral which lists a large

---

[1] Card. P. M. RICHAUD, *Y a-t-il une spiritualité du clergé diocésain?*, *op. cit.*, pp. 24-27.

number of them, it is easy to see that the ways of God are many and varied. Besides those officially honored by the Church, there is another group of saintly priests who are in heaven. This heavenly throng, the *Almus Sacerdotum Chorus* mentioned in the Lauds hymn for the feast of All Saints, is composed of priests from every nation and century, young and old, rich and poor. It is essential that diocesan priests cooperate with the grace of their priestly consecration by dedicating themselves entirely to the service of God and by fulfilling, wherever they are sent, the duties of their priestly and diocesan state of life. This should be done, as the first Pope prescribed, " willingly, according to God; not for the sake of base gain, but eagerly; nor yet as lording it over your charges, but becoming from the heart a pattern to the flock. " [1]

Could there be any better way of concluding this book than by quoting the words of Pope John XXIII? Inviting all priests to allow themselves to be led by St. John Vianney to the heights of priestly holiness, the Pontiff declared :

> We know very well the cares and worries of these priests of our own time. We know the difficulties which today stand in the way of their apostolic activity. Although we are saddened by the fact that the souls of some of them are being tossed about by the waves of this world and are being overcome with weariness, still we know from experience that the faith of a far greater number is firm amidst adversities; and we are aware of the ardent zeal of soul with which many generously strive for the highest things. But it was to both groups that, at the time of their priestly ordination, Christ the Lord directed these words which are filled with consolation : " Now I shall not call you servants, but friends. " May this encyclical letter of ours help all the clergy to nourish and to increase this divine friendship, since the joy and all the fruit of the sacerdotal ministry depend upon this friendship. [2]

[1] 1 Pt 5, 2-3.

[2] Pope JOHN XXIII, Enc. *Sacerdotii nostri primordia, loc. cit.*, p. 548.

May this humble publication of ours, with the help of Christ and the mediation of Mary, achieve the same effect for our esteemed colleagues in the priesthood. [1]

Haec locutus sum vobis ut ... gaudium vestrum impleatur (Jn 15, 11).

---

[1] There are numerous books on priestly spirituality. These are just a few standard works : Card. H. E. MANNING, *The Eternal Priesthood* (London 1883); J. GIBBONS, *The Ambassador of Christ* (Baltimore 1897); Card. D. J. MERCIER, *A mes séminaristes* (Brussels 1908), *Retraite pastorale* (Brussels 1910), *La Vie intérieure, Appel aux âmes sacerdotales* (Brussels 1918); H. MAHIEU, *Vitae Sanctitate Excellatis Oportet* (Bruges 1937); C. MARMION, *Le Christ, idéal du prêtre* (Maredsous 1951); F. TINELLO, *Quaderni sul sacerdozio* (Rome 1955 ff.); Msgr. K. CRUYS-BERGHS, *Priesterlijke Vroomheid* (Louvain 1956); Msgr. J. C. HEENAN, *The People's Priest.* Many other works could be cited — meditation books, retreat books, commentaries on the Ordination Rite, etc.

Of special interest to bishops is the valuable book published by the Vatican Library : J. BORGONOVO, *Memoriale Vitae et Sanctimoniae Episcopalis, Regole di perfezione, di vita, di governo* (Vatican City 1950).

Note from the Holy See on the Perfection of the Diocesan Clergy

By a letter of July 13, 1952 the Sacred Congregation of Extraordinary Ecclesiastical Affairs transmitted to us and to other bishops a detailed note from His Holiness Pope Pius XII in reply to requests for clarification which had been submitted, from various quarters, to the Holy See.

1. When it is said that a priest who wishes to strive for perfection must become a religious or at least become a member of a secular institute; and if a young man who is undecided between the secular priesthood and religious life is given the answer that it is a question of generosity; when it is asserted that one who decides for the secular clergy proves that he has not enough generosity to give himself entirely to the service of God; if it is thought that a young man who is hesitating in this way cannot be advised to enter a seminary rather than a religious Order; if some go so far as to assert that the Church " tolerates " the secular clergy as second-best, but that the ideal would be that all priests would be religious—all this is a false interpretation and an erroneous application of the Holy Father's allocution of December 8, 1950 (*AAS*, 1951, XLIII, 26-36). The bishops are within their rights if they oppose a form of propaganda for recruitment on the part of religious societies which has theoretical foundations that are inexact and liable to lead into error and which, in practice, is at least lacking in loyalty; bishops are also within their rights if they place proper and definite limits to such propaganda by an administrative decision.

2. The above-mentioned allocution of the Holy Father had as its primary purpose the clarification and definition of three points;

(a) What is the position of the regular clergy *(clerus religiosus)* in relation to the secular clergy *(clerus saecularis)* in the constitution given by Christ to His Church (pp. 27-29)? The answer was : ..." if one considers the order established by Christ, neither of the two particular forms of the twofold clergy enjoys a prerogative of divine law, because that law does not give preference to one rather than the other, nor does it exclude either of them " (p. 28).

(b)   What is the relation of the " cleric " and the " religious " in regard
to the " state of perfection " considered as the state of the evangelical
counsels (p. 29)?   This was the answer : " The cleric is not bound by the
divine law to practice the evangelical counsels of poverty, chastity and
obedience; and especially he is not bound in the same way and for the
same reason as one for whom this obligation arises from a public vow
made when entering the religious state.   That, however, does not prevent
the cleric from assuming these obligations privately and on his own
initiative. . . .   The reason why the religious cleric makes profession
of the condition and state of perfection is not because he is a cleric, but
because he is a religious. "   Furthermore, it was expressly stated that
even *secular institutes* realize the essence of the " state of perfection, "
" because the members are in some way bound to the observance of the
evangelical counsels " (p. 29).

If " clerics " join together in such a *secular institute*, " then they also
are in the state of acquiring perfection, not because they are clerics, but
because they are members of a secular institute " (p. 30).

(c)   What are the objective reasons for adopting the religious state?
What is said in the papal allocution about the religious state, considered
in itself, as a state of perfection, should not be identified, as has been done
by certain religious societies in the manner of recruitment about which
complaints have been made, with the vocation of the individual to personal
perfection, whether within the " state of perfection " or outside it.   The
three points thus clarified are not immediately concerned with the individual
person, but with the " state, " its *de jure* status and its essential nature.
They do not, therefore, touch upon the vocation of the individual to
a particular state in the Church; nor do they touch on the vocation of the
individual to personal perfection in the state which he has chosen; nor
do they touch on the perfection actually attained by the individual in his
state or vocation.

The point under discussion, therefore, is not the personal perfection
of the individual.   That perfection is measured by the degree of love,
the degree of " theological charity, " which is actually realized in the
individual.   The criterion of the intensity and purity of charity is, in the
words of the Master, the fulfillment of the will of God.   The individual
is thus personally more perfect before God according as he carries out
more perfectly the will of God.   In this respect, the state in which he lives
is of little importance, whether he be a layman or an ecclesiastic, or, if he
is a priest, whether he be a secular or a religious.

It follows that it would not be correct to say that the secular priest,
in regard to his own personal sanctification, is any less called to perfection
than the religious priest; or to say that the decision of a young man to

follow the vocation of a secular priest is a determination to a lower personal perfection than if he had chosen the priesthood in the religious state. It is possible that it might be so; it is equally possible that one person's choice of a state other than the state of perfection may spring from a greater love of God and a greater spirit of sacrifice than another person's choice of the religious state.

Thus, as far as the priest is concerned, and this applies also to the candidate for the priesthood, it is not difficult to perceive that, by reason of the dignity and the duty of the priestly office, he too is called in a special way to personal perfection. That holds true even in the case where the individual who is clothed with the perfection of the priesthood is living lawfully in the " state of marriage, " as is the case in the Oriental Rites.

By way of conclusion, therefore, it must be stated that the call of the individual to sanctity or personal perfection, and the adoption and permanent practice of personal perfection, cannot be identified with the question of the " state of perfection " in the juridical sense of the term. The state of perfection is so called and is such inasmuch as, through the means of the three evangelical counsels, it removes the principal obstacles which impede the effort to obtain personal sanctity; or, to speak more exactly, it is by its nature suited to the removal of these obstacles. But the mere fact of embracing the state of perfection does not mean that it necessarily realizes its potentialities in the life of the individual religious, that it actually leads to sanctity; that depends upon the effort of the individual, upon the measure in which, in cooperation with the grace of God, he applies the evangelical counsels in his life.

An Attempt at a Sanctoral of the Diocesan Clergy

As we stated on page 249, this sanctoral only includes those secular priests who died after the year 800 and whose cults have received official approbation by Rome through canonization, beatification or the recognition of cult. We shall also occasionally include a few names that are found in the Roman Martyrology. It should also be recalled that the names in italics designate diocesan priests who later entered the religious life. Biographical and bibliographical notices for the majority of names cited here may be found in the 13 volumes of the *Vies des Saints et des Bienheureux* compiled by the Benedictines of Paris.

    A.   The capitalized letters between parentheses indicate the following references :

C   Martyrs of China : see " Martyrs béatifiés parmi le clergé autochtone d'Extrême-Orient, " *Bulletin de l'Union missionnaire du clergé*, April, 1960, No. 138, pp. 71-72.

E   English martyrs of the sixteenth and seventeenth centuries : see C. A. NEWDIGATE, *Our Martyrs* (London 1935).

I   Martyrs of Indochina — see above.

L   Martyrs of Laval : see Msgr. E. CESBRON, *Les Martyrs de Laval* (Rome, 1955).

M   *Martyrologium Romanum.*

S   September martyrs : see *Vies des Saints et des Bienheureux, op. cit.*, Vol. IX (1950), pp. 57-70.

The numbers between parentheses refer to the pages of this volume.

    B.   Abbreviations :

adm.   Priest who was engaged in diocesan administration (secretary, member of the Curia, procurator, etc.).

c.   Confessor non-Pontiff.

c.p.   Confessor Pontiff.

chap.   Priest who functioned as a chaplain, particularly in convents.

char.   Priest engaged in works of charity.

d.   Doctor of the Church.

cler. form.   Priest engaged in educating the clergy (rector or seminary professor, spiritual director, etc.).

m.	Martyr non-Pontiff.
m.p.	Martyr Pontiff.
miss.	Missionary.
p.	Pontiff : see *c.p.* and *m.p.*
sem.	Seminarian.
teacher	Priest involved in teaching in schools other than seminaries.
univ.	University Professor.
v.g.	Vicar General or, in mission countries, Vicar Delegate.

N.B. — It is not always easy to be exact in this area. However, we have indicated the principal work in which these priests engaged. We have already stated that the majority of the English martyrs returned as missionaries to England in order to win it back to the Faith. The feast day given for many of the martyrs is the feast day of the group of martyrs to which they belonged. When they have their own particular feast day, it is usually the anniversary of their death.

St. Abond, *m.* (M)	July 11
St. Adalbert of Prague, m.p. (232)	April 23
St. Adrian III, *c.p.* (232), *pope*	July 8
St. Albert of Louvain, *m.p.* (M)	November 27
Bl. Alexander Briant, m. (E)	December 1
Bl. Alexander Rawlins, *m.* (E)	April 7
St. Alphonsus Liguori, c.p., d. (240)	August 2
St. Amator, *m.* (M)	April 30
St. Anastasius, *m.* (M)	June 14
Bl. Andrew Abel Alricy, *m.* (S)	September 2
Bl. Andrew Angar, *m.* (S), *curate*	September 2
St. Andrew Avellino, c. (239)	November 10
Bl. Andrew Duliou, *m.* (L), *pastor*	January 21
Bl. Andrew Dung or Lac, *m.* (I), *pastor*	November 21
St. Andrew Hubert Fournet, *c.* (243), *pastor*	May 13
Bl. Andrew Grasset, *m.* (S), *canon*	September 2
Bl. Andrew Kim, *m.* (243)	February 5
St. Andrew Wouters, *m.* (239), *pastor*	July 9
St. Anno, *c.p.* (232)	December 4
St. Anthony Mary Claret, c.p. (242), *pastor*	October 24
Bl. Anthony Francis de Ravinel, *c.* (S), *sem., deacon*	September 2
Bl. Anthony Charles du Bouezt, *m.* (S), *v.g.*	September 2
St. Anthony Mary Gianelli, *c.p.* (242), *pastor*	June 7
Bl. Anthony Grassi, *c.* (239)	December 13
Bl. Anthony Middleton, *m.* (E)	May 6
Bl. Anthony Matthew Nogier, *m.* (S), *chap.*	September 2
St. Anthony Mary Zaccharia, c. (239)	July 5
St. Ariald, *m.* (234), *de acon*	June 27

Bl. Armand de Rastignac, *m.* (S)	September 2
Bl. Armand Foucaud de Pontbriand, *m.* (S), *v.g.*	September 2
Bl. Augustus Chapdeleine, m. (243)	February 28
Bl. Augustine Poulain Delaunay, *m.* (S)	September 2
Bl. Augustine Robert de Lézardières, *m.* (S), *sem.*, *deacon*	September 2
Bl. Augustine Philippot, *m.* (L), *pastor*	January 21
Bl. Augustine Tchao, *m.* (C), *pastor*	November 24

Bl. Bartholomew Buenpedoni, *c.* (234), *pastor*	December 12
St. Bellinus, *m.p.* (M)	November 26
St. Benno, *c.p.* (232)	June 16
Bl. Bernard Due, *m.* (I)	November 24
St. Bernwald of Hildesheim, *c.p.* (232)	November 20
St. Bertrand of Angoulême, *m.p.* (233)	June 6
St. Bertrand of Comminges, *c.p.* (233)	October 16
Bl. Bertrand Anthony de Copenne, *m.* (S), *curate*	September 2
St. Bienvenuto Scotivoli, c.p. (232)	March 22
St. Bogomil, c.p. (233)	June 10
St. Bruno the Great, c. (233)	October 6
St. Bruno of Segni, c.p. (232)	July 18
St. Bruno of Wurtzburg, *c.p.* (232)	May 27

St. Cajetan of Thien, c. (239)	August 7
Bl. Ceslaus, c. (234)	July 17
Bl. Cécard de Luni, *m.* (232)	June 16
St. Charles Borromeo, *c.p.* (238)	November 4
Bl. Charles Carnus, *m.* (S), *teacher*	September 2
Bl. Charles Victor Véret, *m.* (S), *deacon*	September 2
Bl. Christopher Bayles, *m.* (E)	March 4
Bl. Christopher Buxton, *m.* (E)	October 1
Bl. Claude Chaudot, *m.* (S)	September 2
Bl. Claude Colin, *m.* (S), *char.*	September 2
Bl. Claude Fontaine, *m.* (S), *curate*	September 2
Bl. Claude Louis Marmoutant de Savigny, *m.* (S), *curate*	September 2
Bl. Claude de Bizefrano, *m.* (S)	September 2
St. Conrad of Constance, *c.p.* (232)	November 26
Bl. Cuthbert Mayne, *m.* (A), *teacher*	November 29

Bl. Daniel des Pommerayes, *m.* (S), *pastor*	September 2
Bl. Denis Claude Duval, *m.* (S)	September 2
St. Domicius, *c.* (M), *canon*	October 23
Bl. Dominic Cam, *m.* (I)	July 20

Bl. Edmund Arrowsmith, m. (E)	August 28

Bl. Edmund Genings, *m.* (E)	December 10
St. Edmund Rich, *c.p.* (232)	November 16
Bl. Edward Campion, *m.* (E)	October 1
Bl. Edward Catherick, *m.* (E)	April 13
Bl. Edward James, *m.* (E)	May 6
Bl. Edward Jones, *m.* (E)	May 6
Bl. Edward Stransham, *m.* (E)	January 21
Bl. Edward Powell, *m.* (E), *curate*	July 30
Bl. Edward Waterson, *m.* (E)	January 7
St. Elias, *m.* (M)	April 17
St. Emil, *m.* (M), *deacon*	September 15
Bl. Emmanuel Trière or Trieu, *m.* (I) (241)	September 17
St. Eulogus, *m.* (M)	March 11
Bl. Eustace White, *m.* (A)	December 10
Bl. Everard Hanse, *m.* (E)	July 30
Bl. Francis Dardan, *m.* (S), *teacher*	September 2
Bl. Francis Joseph de La Rochefoucauld-Maumont, *m.p.* (S) (240)	September 2
St. Francis de Sales, *c.p.*, *d.* (238)	January 29
Bl. Francis Dickenson, *m.* (E)	April 13
Bl. Francis Duchesne, *m.* (L), *teacher*	January 21
Bl. Francis Dumasrambaud de Calandelle, *m.* (S), *adm.*	September 2
Bl. Francis Caesar Londiveau, *m.* (S), *curate*	September 2
Bl. Francis Louis Méallet de Fargues, *m.* (S), *v.g.*	September 2
Bl. Francis Migorte, *m.* (S), *pastor and teacher*	January 21
Bl. Francis Joseph Monnier, *m.* (S), *curate*	September 2
Bl. Francis Joseph Peg, *m.* (S), *curate*	September 2
Bl. Francis Urban Salins de Niart, *m.* (S), *canon*	September 2
Bl. Gabriel Desprez de Roche, *m.* (S), *v.g.*	September 2
St. Galdinus, *c.p.* (232)	April 18
St. Gamelbert or Amalbert, *c.* (233), *pastor*	January 17
St. Gaspar del Buffalo, c. (243), *miss.*	December 28
Bl. Gaspar Claude Maignien, *m.* (S), *pastor*	September 2
St. George, *m.* (M), *deacon*	July 27
Bl. George Jerome Girauld, *m.* (S), *pastor*	September 2
Bl. George Napper, *m.* (E)	November 9
St. Gerard of Potenza, *c.p.* (232)	October 30
St. Gerard of Toul, *c.p.* (232)	March 24
St. Gilbert of Simpringham, c. (233), *pastor*	February 4
Bl. Gilbert John Fatrel, *m.* (S), *chap.*	September 2
Bl. Gilles Louis Lanchon, *m.* (S), *chap.*	September 2
Bl. Godfrey Van Duynen, *m.* (239), *pastor*	July 9

Bl. Gomidas Keumrudjian, *m.* (241), *pastor*	November 5
Bl. Gregory X, *p.c.* (232), *pope*	January 10
St. Gregory Barbarigo, *c.p.* (238)	June 18
St. Grimoald, *c.* (M), *archpriest*	September 29
St. Gumesendus, *m.* (M), *pastor*	January 13
St. Guy of Acqui, *c.p.* (232)	June 2
Bl. Henry Hippolytus Ermès, *m.* (S), *pastor*	September 2
Bl. Henry John Milet, *m.* (S), *curate*	September 2
St. Hugh of Grenoble, c.p. (233)	April 1
Bl. Hugh Green, *m.* (E)	August 19
St. Hyacinth Odravaz, c. (233)	August 17
Bl. Innocent XI, *c.p.* (238), *pope*	August 12
Bl. Innocent da Berzo, c (243),	March 3
St. Ismido of Die, *c.p.* (233)	October 3
Bl. James André, *m.* (L), *pastor and rural dean*	January 21
Bl. James Bell, *m.* (E)	April 20
Bl. James Burin, *m.* (L), *pastor*	October 17
Bl. James Chastan, m. (E)	September 26
Bl. James Claxton, *m.* (E)	April 28
Bl. James Francis de Luberzac, *m.* (S), *chap.*	September 2
Bl. James Dufour, *m.* (S), *curate*	September 2
Bl. James Fenn, *m.* (E)	February 12
Bl. James Joseph Lejardinier des Landes, *m.* (S), *pastor*	September 2
Bl. James John Lemounier, *m.* (S), *v.g.*	September 2
Bl. James Alexander Menuret, *m.* (S), *pastor*	September 2
Bl. James Nam, *m.* (I)	November 24
Bl. James Leonard Rabé, *m.* (S), *chap.*	September 2
Bl. James Louis Schmid, *m.* (S), *pastor*	September 2
Bl. James Thompson, *m.* (E)	November 28
St. Jerome Emilian, c. (239), *char.*	July 20
Bl. Jerome de Torres, *m.* (239)	September 12
Bl. John Almond, *m.* (E)	December 5
Bl. John Amias, *m.* (E)	March 16
Bl. John Juvenal Ancina, *c.p.* (238)	August 30
Bl. John Baptist Aubert, *m.* (S), *pastor*	September 2
Bl. John Peter Bangue, *m.* (S), *chap.*	September 2
St. John Bosco, c. (243), *teacher*	January 31
Bl. John Boste, *m.* (E)	July 24
Bl. John Baptist Bottex, *m.* (S), *pastor*	September 2
Bl. John Anthony Boucharenc, *m.* (S), *v.g.*	September 2
Bl. John Francis Bousquet, *m.* (S), *member of a diocesan Curia*	September 2

Bl. John Andrew Capeau, *m.* (S), *curate*	September 2
Bl. John Charles Caron, *m.* (S), *pastor*	September 2
Bl. John Cornelius, m. (E)	July 4
Bl. John Dat, *m.* (I) (241)	October 28
Bl. John of Avila, *c.* (239), *diocesan miss., teacher*	May 10
Bl. John Baptist Delalande, *m.* (S), *pastor*	September 2
St. John of Kenty, *c.* (233), *univ., pastor*	October 20
St. John Baptist de La Salle, c. (240), *canon, teacher*	May 15
Bl. John Joseph de La Vèze-Bellay, *m.* (S), *chap.*	September 2
Bl. John de Ribera, *c.p.* (238)	January 6
St. John Baptist de Rossi, *c.* (241), *canon, teacher, char.*	May 23
St. John of San-Facondo, c. (233)	June 12
Bl. John Duckett, *m.* (E)	September 7
Bl. John Mary du Lau d'Alleman, *c.p.* (S-240)	September 2
St. John Fischer, *m.p.* (E) (238)	June 22
Bl. John Gallot, *m.* (L), *pastor*	January 21
Bl. John Goizet, *m.* (S), *pastor*	September 2
Bl. John Francis Gros, *m.* (S), *pastor*	September 2
Bl. John Anthony Guilleminet, *m.* (S), *curate*	September 2
Bl. John Louis Guyard of Saint-Clair, *m.* (S), *canon*	September 2
Bl. John Haile, *m.* (E), *curate*	May 4
Bl. John Hewett, *m.* (E)	October 5
Bl. John Hoan, *m.* (I), *pastor*	February 18
Bl. John Ingram, *m.* (E)	July 24
Bl. John Ireland, *m.* (E), *chap.*	March 7
Bl. John Baptist Jannin, *m.* (S), *chap.*	September 2
Bl. John Kemble, *m.* (E)	August 22
Bl. John Lacan, *m.* (S), *chap.*	September 2
Bl. John Larke, *m.* (E), *pastor*	March 7
Bl. John Charles Legrand, *m.* (S), *teacher*	September 2
Bl. John Peter Le Laisant, *m.* (S), *curate*	September 2
Bl. John Peter Lemaître, *m.* (S)	September 2
St. John Leonardi, c. (239)	October 9
Bl. John Thomas Leroy, *m.* (S), *pastor*	September 2
Bl. John Lloyd, *m.* (E)	July 22
Bl. John Lockwood, *m.* (E)	April 13
Bl. John Philip Marchand, *m.* (S), *curate*	September 2
Bl. John Martin Moyé, c. (241), *miss., pastor*	May 4
Bl. John Munden, *m.* (E)	February 12
Bl. John Baptist Nativelle, *m.* (S), *curate*	September 2
Bl. John Nelson, m. (E)	February 3
St. John Nepomucene, *m.* (233), *pastor, canon*	May 16
Bl. John Nutter, *m.* (E)	February 12
Bl. John Payne, *m.* (E)	April 2

Bl. John Michael Phelippot, *m.* (S), *teacher*	September 2
Bl. John Pibush, *m.* (E)	February 18
Bl. John Plesington, *m.* (E)	July 19
Bl. John Robert Quéneau, *m.* (S), *pastor*	September 2
Bl. John Joseph Rateau, *m.* (S)	September 2
Bl. John Robinson, *m.* (E)	October 1
Bl. John Ruysbroeck, c. (234)	December 2
Bl. John Henry Samson, *m.* (S), *curate*	September 2
Bl. John Sarkander, *m.* (239), *pastor*	March 17
Bl. John Anthony Seguin, *m.* (S), *curate*	September 2
Bl. John Shert, *m.* (E)	May 28
Bl. John Peter Simon, *m.* (S)	September 2
Bl. John Southworth, *m.* (E)	June 28
Bl. John Tchan of Nan-see, *m.* (C), *major sem.*	July 9
Bl. John Tchan of Tae-kuo, *m.* (C), *minor sem.*	July 9
Bl. John Baptist Turpin, *m.* (L), *pastor*	January 21
St. John Vianney, *c.* (243), *pastor*	August 9
Bl. John Wang, *m.* (C), *sem.*	July 9
Bl. Joseph Bécavin, *m.* (S)	September 2
St. Joseph Cafasso, *c.* (243), *cler. form.*	June 23
St. Joseph Calasanctius, c. (239), *teacher*	August 27
St. Joseph Benedict Cottolengo, *c.* (243), *char., cler. form.*	April 30
Bl. Joseph Falcoz, *m.* (S), *chap.*	September 2
Bl. Joseph Nghi, *m.* (I), *pastor*	November 8
Bl. Joseph Nien or Vien, *m.* (I)	November 24
Bl. Joseph Louis Ovievfe, *m.* (S)	September 2
Bl. Joseph Thomas Pazery de Thorame, *m.* (S), *canon*	September 2
Bl. Joseph Tchang, *m.* (C), *sem.*	February 18
St. Joseph Oriol, *c.* (240), *pastor*	March 23
Bl. Joseph Pellé, *m.* (L)	January 21
Bl. Joseph Yuen, *m.* (C), *pastor*	November 24
Bl. Jules Honoré Pazery de Thorame, *m.* (S), *v.g.*	September 2
St. Julian of Cuença, *c.* (M)	January 28
Bl. Julian Francis Hédouin, *m.* (S)	September 2
Bl. Julian Le Laisant, *m.* (S)	September 2
Bl. Julian Morin de la Gérardière, *m.* (L)	January 21
Bl. Julian Moulé, *m.* (L), *pastor*	January 21
Bl. Lawrence (family name unknown), *m.* (S)	September 2
Bl. Lawrence Nguyen, *m.* (I), *pastor*	February 18
Bl. Lawrence Richardson, *m.* (E)	July 27
St. Leo IX, *c.p.* (232), *pope*	April 19
Bl. Leo of Satzuma, *m.* (239), *minor sem.*	September 10
St. Leonard Vechel, *m.* (239), *pastor*	July 9

St. Lié, *c.* (M)	November 5
Bl. Louis Aleman, *c.p.* (M)	September 16
Bl. Louis Francis Barret, *m.* (S), *curate*	September 2
Bl. Louis René Benoist, *m.* (S), *curate*	September 2
Bl. Louis René Nicholas Benoist, *m.* (S), *curate* (brother of the preceding)	September 2
Bl. Louis Gastineau, *m.* (L), *curate*	January 21
St. Louis Marie Grignion de Montfort, c. (240)	April 28
Bl. Louis Lawrence Gaultier, *m.* (S), *chap.*	September 2
Bl. Louis John Lanier, *m.* (S), *cler. form.*	September 2
Bl. Louis Le Danois, *m.* (S), *curate*	September 2
Bl. Louis Longuet, *m.* (S), *canon*	September 2
Bl. Louis Marie Palazzolo, *c.* (243) *char.*	
Bl. Louis Mauduit, *m.* (S), *pastor*	September 2
Bl. Luke Kirby, *m.* (E)	May 29
Bl. Luke Loan, *m.* (I), *pastor*	November 24
Bl. Mark Crisin or Crespin, *m.* (239), *canon, cler. form.*	September 7
Bl. Mark Louis Royer, *m.* (S), *pastor*	September 2
Bl. Marcellin Champagnat, c. (243), *teacher, pastor*	June 6
Bl. Marie Francis de La Gardette, *m.* (S), *curate*	September 2
Bl. Marie François Moufflé, *m.* (S), *curate*	September 2
Bl. Martin Francis Loublier, *m.* (S), *pastor*	September 2
Bl. Martin Thin, *m.* (I), *pastor*	November 8
Bl. Mathurin Victor Deruelle, *m.* (S), *chap.*	September 2
Bl. Michael-Andrew Binard, *m.* (S), *univ.*	September 2
St. Michael Garricoïts, c. (243), *curate*	May 14
Bl. Michael Leber, *m.* (S), *pastor*	September 2
Bl. Myles Gérard, *m.* (E)	April 30
Bl. Nézel, *m.* (S), *sem.*	September 2
Bl. Nicholas Bizé, *m.* (S), *cler. form.*	September 2
Bl. Nicholas Cléret, *m.* (S), *chap.*	September 2
Bl. Nicholas Gaudreau, *m.* (S), *pastor*	September 2
St. Nicholas Janssen, *m.* (239), *curate*	July 9
Bl. Nicholas Claude Roussel, *m.* (S)	September 2
Bl. Noël Pinot, *m.* (241), *pastor*	February 21
St. Norbert, c.p. (232)	June 6
Bl. Oddin Barolli, *c.* (234), *pastor*	July 21
Bl. Oliver Lefèvre, *m.* (S), *chap.*	September 2
Bl. Oliver Plunkett, *m.p.* (238)	July 11
St. Osmund, *c.p.* (232)	December 4
St. Otto of Bamberg, *c.p.* (232)	July 2

Bl. Peter Tuy, *m.* (I), *pastor*	October 11
Bl. Peter Louis Verrier, *m.* (S)	September 2
Bl. Peter James Vitalis, *m.* (S), *curate*	September 2
St. Patrick Tun, *m.* (C), *sem.*	July 9
St. Paul, *m.* (M), *deacon*	November 24
Bl. Paul Khoan, *m.* (I), *pastor*	November 24
Bl. Paul Le Bac Tinh, *m.* (I), *pastor*	February 18
Bl. Paul Lieou, *m.* (C), *pastor*	November 24
Bl. Paul Loc, *m.* (I), *cler. form.*	February 18
Bl. Paul Ngan, *m.* (I), *curate*	November 8
Bl. Paul Tchen, *m.* (C), *sem.*	February 18
Bl. Paul Tinh, *m.* (I), *cler. form.*	February 18
St. Perfectus, *m.* (M)	April 18
Bl. Philibert Fougère, *m.* (S), *pastor*	September 2
Bl. Philip Minh, *m.* (I), *v.g.*	November 24
St. Philip Neri, *c.* (239)	May 26
Bl. Philip Tchan, *m.* (C), *sem.*	July 9
St. Pius X, *c.p.* (246), *pope, pastor, cler. form., adm.*	September 3
Bl. Peter Paul Balzac, *m.* (S)	September 2
Bl. Peter Bonzé, *m.* (S), *pastor*	September 2
Bl. Peter Briquet, *m.* (S), *univ.*	September 2
Bl. Peter Brisse, *m.* (S), *canon*	September 2
St. Peter Marie Chanel, m. (243), *miss., pastor*	April 28
Bl. Peter Louis de La Rochefoucauld-Bayer, *m.p.* (S) (240)	September 2
St. Peter of Trevi, *c.* (232), *deacon*	August 30
Bl. Peter de Turménie, *m.* (S), *univ., curate*	September 2
St. Peter Julian Eymard, c. (243)	August 3
Bl. Peter-John Garrigues, *m.* (S)	September 2
Bl. Peter Louis Gervais, *m.* (S), *chap.*	September 2
Bl. Peter Francis Hénocq, *m.* (S), *teacher*	September 2
Bl. Peter Louis Joret, *m.* (S)	September 2
Bl. Peter Khanh, *m.* (I), *pastor*	February 18
Bl. Peter Khoa, *m.* (I), *curate*	November 24
Bl. Peter Landry, *m.* (S), *curate*	September 2
Bl. Peter Florent Leclercq, *m.* (S), *cler. form.*	September 2
Bl. Peter Luu, *m.* (I), *pastor*	February 18
Bl. Peter Maubant, m. (243)	September 26
St. Peter Paschasius, *m.p.* (233)	December 6
Bl. Peter Francis Pazery de Torame, *m.* (S), *v.g.*	September 2
Bl. Peter Ploquin, *m.* (S), *curate*	September 2
Bl. Peter Qui, *m.* (I), *pastor*	February 18
Bl. Peter Robert Regnet, *m.* (S)	September 2
Bl. Peter René Rogue, m. (240)	March 3
Bl. Peter Saint-James, *m.* (S), *chap.*	September 2

Bl. Peter Thi, *m.* (I), *pastor*	December 21
Bl. Peter Thomas, *m.* (L), *pastor*	January 21
Bl. Peter Tuan, *m.* (I)	November 24
Bl. Polydorus Plasden, *m.* (E)	December 10
Bl. Ralph Crockett, *m.* (E)	October 1
Bl. Ralph Sherwin, *m.* (E)	December 1
St. Raymond Peñafort, c. (233)	January 23
St. Raynaud of Ravenna, *c.p.* (233)	August 18
Bl. René Ambroise, *m.* (L)	January 21
Bl. René Nativelle, *m.* (S), *curate*	September 2
Bl. René Nicholas Poret, *m.* (S), *pastor*	September 2
Bl. René Joseph Urvoy, *m.* (S), *cler. form.*	September 2
St. Richard of Chichester, *c.p.* (232)	April 3
Bl. Richard Featherston, *m.* (E), *chap., teacher*	July 30
Bl. Richard Kirkman, *m.* (E)	August 22
Bl. Richard Leigh, *m.* (E)	August 30
Bl. Richard Newport, *m.* (E)	May 30
Bl. Richard Thirkeld, *m.* (E)	May 29
Bl. Robert Anderton, *m.* (E)	April 25
Bl. Robert Dalby, *m.* (E)	March 16
Bl. Robert Johnson, *m.* (E)	May 28
Bl. Robert Le Bis, *m.* (S), *pastor*	September 2
Bl. Robert Morton, *m.* (E)	August 28
Bl. Robert Watkinson, *m.* (E)	April 20
Bl. Robert Wilcox, *m.* (E)	October 1
St. Roderick, *m.* (M)	March 13
Bl. Roger Dickenson, *m.* (E)	July 7
St. Rudesindus, c.p. (232)	March 1
Bl. Saintin Huré, *m.* (S)	September 2
Bl. Sebastian Valfré, *c.* (241)	January 30
St. Sisenard, *m.* (M), *deacon*	July 16
St. Stanislaus of Cracow, *m.p.* (232)	May 7
Bl. Stephen Michael Gillet, *m.* (S), *cler. form.*	September 2
Bl. Stephen Pondinelli, *m.p.* (233)	August 14
St. Sylvester Guzzolini, c. (233)	Novembre 26
Bl. Thaddeus Lieou, *m.* (C), *pastor*	November 24
St. Thebout of Vienna, *c.p.*	May 21
Bl. Thomas Abel, *m.* (E), *chap., teacher*	July 30
Bl. Thomas Alfield, *m.* (E)	July 6
St. Thomas à Becket, *m.p.*	December 29
St. Thomas of Canteloup, *c.p.* (232)	August 25

Bl. Thomas René Dubuisson, *m.* (S), *pastor*	September 2
Bl. Thomas Ford, *m.* (E)	May 28
Bl. Thomas Garnet, m. (E)	June 23
Bl. Thomas Hemerford, *m.* (E)	February 12
Bl. Thomas Hélye, *c.* (233), *chap.*	October 19
Bl. Thomas Holford, *m.* (E)	August 28
Bl. Thomas Kwang, *m.* (I)	July 20
Bl. Thomas Maxfield, *m.* (E)	July 1
Bl. Thomas Monsaint, *m.* (S), *curate*	September 2
Bl. Thomas Plumtree, *m.* (E), *teacher*	January 4
Bl. Thomas Reynolds, *m.* (E)	January 21
Bl. Thomas Somers, *m.* (E)	December 10
Bl. Thomas Thien, *m.* (I), *sem.*	November 24
Bl. Thomas Tunstal, m. (E)	July 18
Bl. Thomas Twing, *m.* (E)	October 23
Bl. Thomas Woodhouse, m. (E)	June 19
St. Turibius, *c.p.* (238)	March 23
St. Ubald of Gubbio, *c.p.* (232)	May 16
St. Ulric of Augsburg, *c.p.* (232)	July 4
Bl. Urban II, c.p. (232), *pope*	July 29
St. Veremundus, *c.p.* (232)	March 23
Bl. Vincent Abraham, *m.* (S), *pastor*	September 2
St. Vincent de Paul, *c.* (239), *pastor*	July 19
Bl. Vincent Diem, *m.* (I)	November 24
St. Vincent Kalubka, c.p. (233)	March 8
St. Vincent Pallotti, *c.* (243), *char.*	January 22
St. Vincent Mary Strambi, c. p. (242)	January 1
Bl. William Andleby, *m.* (E)	July 4
Bl. William Dean, *m.* (E)	August 25
Bl. William Filby, *m.* (E)	May 30
Bl. William Freeman, *m.* (E)	August 13
Bl. William Gunter, *m.* (E)	August 28
Bl. William Harrington, *m.* (E)	February 18
Bl. William Hart, *m.* (E)	March 15
Bl. William Hartley, *m.* (E)	October 5
Bl. William Lacey, *m.* (E)	August 22
Bl. William Marsden, *m* (E)	April 25
St. William of Bourges, c p. (232)	January 10
St. William of Saint-Brieux or Pinchon, *c.p.* (232)	June 29
St. William of York, *c.p.* (232)	June 8
Bl. William Paterson, *m.* (E)	January 22

Bl. William Richardson, *m.* (E)   February 17
Bl. William Ward, *m.* (E)   July 26
Bl. William Way, *m.* (E)   September 23

Bl. Yves Andrew Guillon, *m.* (S), *univ.*   September 2
St. Yves Hélory, *c.* (233), *adm., pastor*   May 19
Bl. Yves John Peter Rey de Kervigie, *m.* (S), *curate* September 2

Index of Names

The first part of this Index refers only to the last seven Popes and the *Acta Sanctae Sedis* published during their pontificates.

The second part lists the other names cited in this book.

This index does not include those references already embodied in the Sanctoral, *Appendix II*.

I

Leo XIII :

Encyclical *Satis Cognitum*, June 29, 1896 : 61, 70.

Apostolic Constitution *Conditae a Christo Ecclesiae*, December 8, 1900 : 127.

Decree *De Tuto* on the occasion of the beatification of John of Avila : 14.

Other references : 14, 32, 52, 247, 251, 259, 269.

Pius X :

Encyclicals *E Supremi Apostolatus*, August 4, 1903 : 286.
        Acerbo Nimis, April 13, 1906 : 157.

Exhortation to the Clergy *Haerent Animo*, August 4, 1908 : 52.

Other references : 40, 52, 54, 55, 80, 94, 139, 149, 155, 251, 258, 261, 262, 266, 267, 271, 279, 285, 286, 288.

Benedict XV :

Discourse on the Heroic Virtue of A. H. Fournet, July 10, 1921 : 288.

Other references : 52, 287-89.

Pius XI :

Encyclicals *Rerum Omnium Perturbationem*, January 26, 1923 : 116, 280.
        Rerum Ecclesiae, February 28, 1926 : 77, 79, 200.
        Casti Connubii, December 31, 1930 : 114, 116.
        Ad Catholici Sacerdotii Fastigium, December 20, 1935 : 52.

Apostolic Letter *Anno Jubilari*, April 23, 1929 : 285.

Discourse on the occasion of the approval of two miracles for the canonization of A. H. Fournet and Marie de Sainte Euphrasie Pelletier, January 8, 1933 : 115-16.
Other references : 22, 52, 55, 132, 280.

Pius XII :

Encyclicals *Mystici Corporis*, June 29, 1943 : 60, 69, 70, 99.
    Evangelii Praecones, June 11, 1951 : 50, 68.
    Sacra Virginitas, March 25, 1954 : 179-80.
    Fidei Donum, April 21, 1957 : 61, 66, 78-79, 96, 97, 133, 157.
    Ad Sinarum Gentem, October 7, 1957 : 69.
    Ad Apostolorum Principis, June 29, 1958 : 63.
Apostolic Constitutions : *Provida Mater*, February 11, 1947 : 120, 121, 132.
  Sacramentum Ordinis, November 30, 1947 : 93, 97.
  Munificentissimus Deus, November 1, 1950 : 75.
  Quemadmodum ad nos, May 25, 1953 : 65.
  Dum Alterna Vicissitudine, January 1, 1955 : 65.
  Sedes Sapientiae, May 31, 1958 : 186.

Apostolic Letter on the occasion of the 16th centenary of the birth of St. Augustine, July 25, 1954 : 279.

Motu Proprio *Primo Feliciter*, March 12, 1948 : 120.

Apostolic Exhortation *Menti Nostrae*, December 20, 1950 : 53, 178, 181, 295-96.

Letters : to Bishop J. Cesbron, Bishop of Annecy, on the occasion of the 350th anniversary of the Episcopal Consecration of St. Francis de Sales, September 12, 1952 : 281.
  to Cardinal V. Valeri for the Madrid Congress on Religious and Priestly Perfection, September 20, 1956 : 123, 181.
  to Cardinal M. Feltin for the centenary of the death of Venerable Olier, March 25, 1957 : 181, 183.

Homelies, Allocutions and Discourses :
  to the Pastors of Rome, March 16, 1946 : 188.
  to the Pastors of Rome, March 23, 1949 : 190-91.
  for the canonization of St. Vincent Strombi, June 11, 1950 : 121, 142, 176.
  to the First Congress of Religious : December 8, 1950 : 116, 152, 179, 181, 182, 194, 202, 204.
  to the Directors of Catholic Action and the Members of Marian Congregations, May 3, 1951 : 181, 188.

Paul VI :

> Quotation from St. Augustine, cited in his first public address as Supreme Pontiff (see front).

II

Printed in Belgium by Desclée & Cie, Éditeurs, S. A., Tournai. — 10.671